Shimmering Sword

Samurai, Western, and
Star Wars
Sword Fighting

Nick Jamilla

Shimmering Sword

Samurai, Western, and
Star Wars
Sword Fighting

Nick Jamilla

NBK Publishing
Montgomery Village, Maryland

NBK Publishing
Montgomery Village, MD
www.ShimmeringSword.com

This book was formatted entirely on WordPerfect.

Library of Congress Control Number: 2002103485
ISBN 0-9718796-0-5

Printed by Morris Publishing
3212 E. Hwy 30
Kearney, NE 68847

for your constant support

brian willis

for your education

tom howson
saotome sensei
kubo sensei
endo sensei
masuda sensei
george meyer

for your insights into *star wars*

karl austin
robert brown
shane ward

for your universe

george lucas

contents

Preface

Three years ago, in anticipation of the premiere of *Star Wars: The Phantom Menace* in 1999, I wrote three articles on Jedi sword fighting for www.EchoStation.com. These articles were so well received that I decided to pursue a more public avenue of sharing what I soon realized was a background that paralleled Jedi training. Buoyed by so many gracious e-mails, I composed several query letters and soon had invitations to do bookstore talks/demonstrations and an offer to give a sword fight demonstration for the Washington, D.C. *Episode I* charity premiere which took place several days before the general release of the movie. The enthusiasm of my audience was so positive that I decided I might continue the dialog by writing a book that answers in part or in whole many of the questions that were asked of me during my public appearances. Thus, the idea for *Shimmering Sword* was born.

Central to the thesis of this exploration of Jedi swordsmanship is the assumption that had we lived in a world in which the lightsaber and the laser beam existed in the manner as they do on Lucas' movies, lightsaber fighting *would have* and *could have* existed. In this sense, despite George Lucas' premise that *Star Wars* takes place "A long time ago in a galaxy far, far away...", the Jedi universe is very much of the science fiction genre, which has traditionally explored the human condition and his and her relationship with technology. *Star Wars*, therefore, has less to do with myth (the archetype of Man versus the gods) or fairy tales and fables (Man versus Nature) than it has to do with a spiritual awakening of the inner spirit when confronted with utter and complete self-annihilation. The Death Star is representative of the folly of nuclear weapons, and not God's punishment by cataclysmic inundation.

Star Wars is not a philosophical allegory nor a religious parable. Rather, it takes an episodic look at the human condition in its polar extremes of goodness and evil. Most see this dichotomy of light and dark as two exclusive opposites, but Lucas' movies are profound examples of the gray area that is the balance of the outer fringes. Instead of a carefully delineated *yin* and *yang*, the two twisting orbs are more a confusion of light and its fading absence. While the Jedi may seem good and the Sith bad on a superficial level, there is, and always has been, a subtle subtext to *Star Wars* that we, as humans, live mostly, if not completely in the gray.

Despite the popular consensus, encourage by Lucas and his philosophical mentor Joseph Campbell, *Star Wars* is not a myth, but an epic in the ancient tradition, telling the tales of men and women as masters of their own destiny. Even in the most dire of tragedies, Man overcomes the Fates by accepting a self-destructive end instead of cowering to omnipotent beings such as the gods or the mightiest of goddesses Mother Nature. Interventions by the gods become incidental when compared to the emboldening spirit of evolving writers, who began to assert the inner strength of humans — fortitude, independence, free will, indomitability — rather than humanity's supplication and submission to "greater beings."

Instead of the admission of spells and magic (powers borne of ignorant sentimentality), the New Human strikes a balance among the instinct to believe the inexplicable (magic being the emotions of the heart), the fruit of his intellect (technology reflecting the growth and development of the mind), and the determinism of his actions (ethics which represent the actions of the hand). Combining these three aspects, the New Human finds his most extreme, and often necessary, role; that of swordsman, the individual who must combine his instinctual feelings for survival and self-preservation, the sword of his own creation, and a code of moral conduct which dispenses life and death at an instant's notice. These New Human characteristics find their expressions in the father and son characters of Anakin/Darth Vader and Luke Skywalker. One is the New Human who finds fulfillment in the evil and nefarious ends of selfishness, while the other is he who finds fulfillment in the pursuit of justice and peace. Lucas' ultimate message is that good eventually trumps evil, Luke redeeming his father by bringing him back to the side of goodness. Lucas' vision of humanity is an optimistic one without being utopian or overly romantic.

It is against this background that I explore the world of the Jedi Knight which finds its basis in the reality of human history. *Shimmering Sword* discusses swordsmanship as a way to better understand the Jedi Knights, which is an artistic expression of our own real-world existence. As such, I have attempted to write a book for the general reader with an interest in better understanding the sword fight in *Star Wars*. It focuses on the human activity surrounding the traditional weapon of the sword which forces men to confront each other head to head. It is an exploration of the cultural conditions of men and women who find that there may sometimes be no choice other than the resort to the use of force. The premise of this book is not "Could it happen?" but "How did it happen?" and can this help the reader better understand his world by understanding that of the Jedi.

While *Star Wars* may seem a blatant juvenile form of artifice unworthy of serious discussion, it is no different from any other fiction which asks the audience to suspend reality for a time. Whether that suspension of reality makes an impact on us or not is often a function of how transferable that fiction is to the real world. The more real it seems, the more enjoyable and profound the experience. It is, therefore, incumbent upon me to examine the historical precedents that have informed the development of the lightsaber in the *Star Wars* universe so that we might better understand ourselves.

Much of *Shimmering Sword* refers to historical examples as the basis of *Star Wars* lightsaber fencing. So too does my own history affect the views and perspectives of swordsmanship which do not, by any significant measure, reflect the general experience of fencers of the Western tradition. Students of Japanese martial arts will probably share many of my interpretations of the sword art and fighting, though modern arts have the tendency to become more competitive than life transforming. It will, however, help the reader evaluate the text by knowing some of my experiences which serve as the lense through which I look at swordsmanship.

I began my twenty years in the martial arts at the age of fifteen when I heard about a local fencing club in Ft. Myers, Florida on the radio. An avid player of *Dungeons & Dragons*, I was drawn to fencing because I wanted to know what it must have been like to wield a sword. I had already seen *Star Wars* earlier but was not that impressed with lightsaber fights until much later. With the help of my instructor Tom Howson, I learned the basics quickly and was soon participating in local tournaments around the state and in national tournaments around the country.

Though I tried to find a university which had a competitive fencing team, I opted instead to go to Georgetown University for its program in International Relations. My hope was that a city of Washington's size probably offered fencing somewhere in its locality. I did find a club, but while I got to fence, I practiced without a regular coach and fenced a rather erratic schedule.

Because of my studies in international affairs, I discovered that I was legally a Filipino citizen until the age of twenty-one. I only had one chance, so I contacted the national fencing organization in Manila and asked if they were sending fencers to the World Fencing Championships in Lausanne, Switzerland that year. The head of the national federation said there was already one person scheduled to go, but because each country was allowed three representatives, I was welcome to participate as long as I paid all of my expenses getting there. In addition, they also invited me to participate at the World University Games in Zagreb, Yugoslavia.

I was overjoyed at the prospect of competing at the world level, but I performed miserably. I had no teammates to practice with, I was fatigued from my travels, and I had little stability having to move from one hostel to another in the weeks and days preceding the competitions. While I did not rank in last place at either the World Championships or the World University Games, I was out of my league. My only consolation is the fact that I was probably one the best fencers to have ever represented the Philippines in fencing. In addition, I had my first and only diplomatic experiences as the Head of Delegation at both competitions.

The experience affected my perspective on Western fencing profoundly. While my performance was lackluster, I did have a unique opportunity to observe the best fencers in action. What I found repulsed me. Instead of meeting dignified and respectful swordsmen, world-class fencers were aloof, self-centered, and arrogant. The highest thing on their mind was winning, which created an atmosphere of unrivaled one-upmanship. This was, of course, competition, and winning medals depended on that state of mind, but something in my heart told me that if these were the people I was supposed to emulate as a fencer, I wanted nothing to do with it.

To this day I view the Olympics with a strong dose of cynicism. Despite the façade of peaceful competition, the Olympics is tainted by a nationalistic pride, nepotism, outright corruption, and the overvalued worship of a technician who can accumulate the best statistics. Originally, the Olympics were a celebration of the Greekness of a collection of city-states, but it was also an exclusive club which served as a propaganda tool to demonstrate the Greeks' martial prowess. It was a fillip to the face of barbarians (i.e., non-Greeks) who were not worthy of participating alongside the Hellenes. Today, TV portrays the Olympics as a community of peaceful competition between nations, but underneath its picturesque veneer is a cut throat network of self-centered egos. While I do not disparage the effort of athletes striving for self-perfection, there is an unhealthy focus on a search for fame and wealth.

The one redeeming aspect of my world-class fencing experience was the reception of the Philippine delegation at the opening ceremonies of the World University Games. I was one of three representatives of the Philippines to walk behind the flag of the nation of my parents' birth. Such small delegations usually receive but token applause from a crowd which awaits the largest delegations from the most powerful countries of Great Britain, the United States, China, and, at the time, the Soviet Union. But just one year earlier, the Philippines had dominated world headlines as Filipinos in a patriotic fervor of "people power" deposed their dictator Ferdinand Marcos. Croatians knew the yoke of oppression and they expressed their nationalistic desire for more freedom by cheering the Philippine delegation loudly as we walked around the track. Many stood up from their seats in our honor, while others waved the pointer finger and thumb, making an "L" sign which was the symbol of the political party of Cory Aquino who became president after Marcos fled the country. The loud chorus of cheers that followed us through the stadium was equal to that of the cheers for the United States. Their open welcoming of the Americans contrasted with the Croatian silence and cold stares as the delegation of the Soviet Union walked along the avenue of nations. It was obvious that the Yugoslavs still remembered the threatened invasion of the Soviet army in 1956. I will never forget the friends I made in Croatia and the welcome the city of Zagreb gave me during their opening ceremonies.

Once I returned Stateside, I virtually gave up fencing. When I met Martha Matthews, who was a clerk for Justice Blackmun at the U.S. Supreme Court, she introduced me to a curious martial art called *aikido*, which had at the heart and spirit of its practice a love for the enemies who might attack. You learned how to defend yourself, but you also learned how to fight without doing permanent physical damage to your assailant. Suspicious at first, I finally joined the *dojo* after seeing classes in Japanese sword in which students used wooden practice swords called *bokken*. Aikido, which is predominantly an empty-handed fighting art, is basically the set of skills a samurai would use if he had lost his sword in battle.

Training under Shihan Mitsugi Saotome, I had the instruction of a world-renowned teacher who had trained directly under the founder of aikido, Morihei Ueshiba, who himself had derived his art from the martial techniques of an aiki-jujitsu style of fighting from Hokkaido. Saotome impressed me not only with his technical ability which stresses martial competence, but also by his philosophical interpretations of aikido. It was his influence which opened my mind up to the fact that it was possible to pursue combative arts without the need to participate in competition.

After two years of aikido in Saotome's headquarters dojo in Washington, D.C. as well as training under the supervision of George Meyer who teaches aikido at the U.S. Naval Academy, I decided to go to Tokyo where I would train at the Aikikai Hombu Dojo, a kind of Mecca for aikido students the world over. For four years, I went to daily practice and quickly became a devoted follower of two generous instructors, Masuda Sensei and Endo Sensei, who taught me both the vigor and kindness of daily practice.

In Tokyo, I also decided to pursue my interest in *kendo* (the Japanese equivalent of Western fencing), which uses bamboo swords called *shinai* instead of foils, epees, and sabres. Here too, my instruction was deeply influenced by the kind and disciplined instruction of Kubo Sensei, headmaster of the Kyumeikan Kendo Dojo on the outskirts of Tokyo. Not only did his ability to speak fluent English help me learn kendo (he lived the U.S. for a year in his youth), but also his gentle but tough spirit encouraged me to persevere in the most difficult of practices. Under his training, I also began my studies of *iaido* (the art of sword drawing), *jodo* (the art of short staff), and *naginatado* (the art of Japanese halberd).

When I wasn't doing martial arts or writing novels, I made a full time living as a teacher. Starting first as a French conversation teacher in my senior year, I continued for four years teaching English as a second language in Japan. Upon my return to the States, I began teaching middle school English, French, math,

and social studies. In addition, for the last five years I have been
teaching fencing to ten to fifteen-year-olds, and now college students. When I'm not teaching fencing at Georgetown University,
I still find time to occasionally train on Saturdays with the U.S.
Naval Academy Aikido Club in Annapolis, Maryland.

Before moving to the body of this work, there are some
points of clarification, as well as basic expectations on the part of
the reader which I must address. It will be assumed that the
reader is familiar with the plots of the four finished, and soon to
be five films. If there is any basic question about major *Star Wars*
characters, information can be most easily obtained by visiting
the official Lucasfilm website at www.StarWars.com.

For the sake of brevity, I often substitute the episode number
of the five *Star Wars* films interchangeably with the titles of the
movies.

Episode I	*The Phantom Menace*
Episode II	*Attack of the Clones*
Episode III	untitled
Episode IV	*A New Hope*
Episode V	*The Empire Strikes Back*
Episode VI	*Return of the Jedi*

I will also refer to *Episodes IV-VI* collectively as the Original
Trilogy, and *Episodes I-III* as the Prequel Trilogy. Because of the
plethora of *Star Wars* materials, I *only* consider the original
movies, their screenplays, and novelizations, which are considered, for the sake of argument, canon sources of information.
Generally referred to as the Expanded Universe (EU), Del Rey,
Bantam Books, Dark Horse Comics, West End Games, and Wi-
zards of the Coast have come up with so vast a collection of writings in novels, comic books, and graphic novels, that it is now
necessary to consult a detailed timeline to know where within
the *Star Wars* universe a story takes place. Because plots are
fleshed out by individual authors based on the needs of a parti-

cular time frame determined by editors at a publishing company licensed with Lucasfilm Ltd., it is easier for me to stick to the original films which are both accessible to the general public and the direct work of George Lucas, the creator of the franchise.

Clarification is also necessary for the overlapping definitions of the martial arts discussed in this book. By "martial arts," I refer to all combative arts whether their professed purpose is battle or friendly competition. Competitive fencing, kendo, and aikido (the three arts I have practiced for twenty years) fall into this general category. "Sword arts," or more simply "swordsmanship," refer to combat with the intention of using a sword specifically for attack or defense in a battle or duel situation. If the focus of sword fighting is on the competition or the "way" of an art, I will specifically mention the art by name.

It should also be noted that in most instances I will use the terminology of the competitive arts (kendo and fencing) to express concepts, ideas, and movements in sword fighting used specifically for battle. It is my assertion that while the modern, competitive forms of the older "killing" sword play are often exercises and games of tag which do not reflect real battlefield fighting, the essence of true swordsmanship used for that purpose can be learned and discovered if one's intention is to learn the "killing" aspect of the art. It follows then that the basics of classical *kenjutsu* (traditional Japanese sword fighting) can be learned by adapting modern kendo techniques. This is not to say, however, that a modern kendo fencer can pick up a live-bladed *katana* (Japanese curved sword) and automatically become an expert in its use, nor the Western fencer with a small sword. Practice specifically with a real weapon is still necessary for proficiency and eventual mastery.

When referring to the Jedi and their lightsabers, I have consciously and purposely refrained from using the self-created terms of "lightsaberist" and "lightsaber art." The Jedi, for the sake of linguistic style, will be referred to as "swordsmen" or the more cumbersome name of "lightsaber fighter." Jedi will be use to represent both its singular and plural usage, while kendo and aikido practitioners will be referred to by their Japanese names which add the suffix -ka. Ergo, *kendoka* and *aikidoka*.

Japanese teachers take the title Sensei (as in Saotome Sensei) which refers to the time honored position of teacher. Within context, I may refer to Sensei with an uppercase "s" when its antecedent has already been stated. Sensei with a lowercase "s" is the general term for teacher, which is not to be confused in Japanese with the word for instructor (which does not rank as high as teacher) nor with the title Shihan, which refers to an officially recognized master teacher within a Japanese martial art. It is generally assumed that a 4th degree (*dan*) blackbelt can be addressed by the title Sensei.

For the sake of cultural differentiation, I will refer to European sword arts (broad sword, rapier, two-handed sword, et al) as "Western swordplay" or more generally as "Western fencing." "Eastern" martial arts will include any and all Asian fighting arts, while I may occasionally refer to the Japanese martial arts collectively as "samurai arts."

This book is meant for the general reader. For this reason, the use of academic footnotes has been eschewed in favor of easier readability. Unfamiliar terms will be offset by italics and will be explained within the text. An asterisk will refer the reader to a footnote at the bottom of the page. For those with a deeper, more academic interest, a bibliography is given at the end with the understanding that no bibliography is conclusive.

The use of italics follows standard usage when naming a specific book, film, ship, et al. In the case of Japanese words which have in effect become indigenous English words when used within the context of a specific martial art, the word will be italicized in its first instance in a chapter and then in regular type thereafter. Most italicized words can be found in the glossary.

Probably the greatest deficiency of this edition is the lack of pictures to illustrate the many shapes into which a sword can be fashioned. I have made up for this by including pictures at the www.ShimeringSword.com website. From its homepage, links to my *Star Wars* and non-*Star Wars* related writings can be found.

It is hoped that with the success of this edition, a revised edition can be completed in anticipation of *Episode V*.

It will be quickly noted that my references to *Star Wars* lightsaber fighting are compared to Japanese martial arts exclusively. For reasons that will be explained later in the book, let it suffice at this point to say that lightsaber sword fighting is directly influenced by Japanese sword fighting arts specifically, and more recently by the Chinese art of Long Fist wu shu. While I may be criticized for limiting the scope of my comparisons to samurai arts, I would rather be accused of cultural myopia than being a charlatan expert in Chinese martial arts with which I only have cursory familiarity and incidental training. Perhaps this book will invite a fellow martial artist of the Chinese tradition to write a book similar to this one.

I am a creature of my own experience and personal preferences, and from the many comments people have given me from my talks, there is a general acceptance for my particular perspective, which is undoubtedly biased toward Japanese martial arts. This prejudice cannot be stricken from my perspective, and it rests with the reader to consciously take my background into account when they judge this work according to their own intellect. I invite the reader to do so, and relish an informed discussion.

Many of the examples given in this book are anecdotal, exposing me to criticism for this lack of academic discipline. I counter that the discussion of any sword fighting technique will inevitably require anecdotal evidence. If the swordsman is to be trusted, then his assertions should be taken as a confession of an honorable person bereft of the intention of subterfuge. While this does not exclude the refutation of my assertions or the questioning of my conclusions, I have gone to great lengths to express a consistent perspective on the subject of swordsmanship. Certainly a martial artist who believes the sword should only be used in the utilitarian purpose of killing will undoubtedly reject my thesis, as will the idealistic pacifist who looks as the sword as an antique symbol of power. There is plenty of room in between, and

I place myself somewhere therein.

To experienced martial artists, much of this book would have the ring of simple common sense. Much is gleaned from the experiences and conclusions that have occurred to me over the past twenty years I have been doing and reflecting on the martial arts. Certainly many of my seniors will recognize this enterprise as perhaps premature, but my intent is to make connections not for the experts in their own personal martial art, but to collect thoughts for those who would like to understand the sword fighting aspect of the *Star Wars* universe in comparison to the historical fencing tradition of two different and unique styles.

In respect to the reader's intelligence, I will not dumb down the text by using vague or general terminology where precise, and perhaps, uncommon words best fit. Depending on a person's experience both within a martial art, and even in life, this book can be understood on many different levels. It is a different book to the housewife and the war veteran, as much as it reads in a particular way for those with an academic background or none at all. This potential rereading must be acknowledged by any who attempt to understand the many ideas and concepts presented within these pages.

For librarians and parents, a quick warning about the contents of this book, which is recommended for high school students and older. The topic of sword fighting is a subject which, at its very heart, acknowledges the life and death of those that participated in the sword's use. No longer does the pursuit of the art of the sword as generally practiced in public have the goal of inflicting or advocating the infliction of harm to another person. Rather, its goal, if one can be given in the name of sword practitioners all over the world, is the improvement or entertainment of the person through an ancient art. Learning swordsmanship no more promotes the killing of another person than does the capture of a pawn by a queen in chess infer the torture or execution of the piece. There are certain descriptions that do give specific detail in the uses of a sword, which could often become an instrument of butchery though the sword is more often used representatively as a symbol of peace through strength.

Lastly, it is imperative that all training in sword work should be done under the auspices of proper teachers. Those interested in learning the art of swordsmanship should inform and educate themselves before participating in a critical dialog with any potential instructor, especially those bearing the title Master. One must know the goals and purposes of learning any martial art. Care must be exercised in the education of skills that confer the power to coerce.

With this, I beg the reader for his and her forgiveness in an extended introduction, and that you may continue on to the present subject at hand.

Sic Anima Tecum
Nick Jamilla

Mentors have a way of seeing more of our faults than we would like. It's the only way we grow.

— Padmé

1

Jedi Universe

When *Star Wars* made its debut in 1977, George Lucas created an epic which did something that no film or book had successfully done. By turning the most fundamental technological change in history on its head — the superiority of the firearm over the sword — Lucas blended the speculative world of science-fiction with the most ancient and classic tales of mythology. Lucas created the universe of the Jedi, and without them there could be no *Star Wars*.

It is easy to be mesmerized by the shimmering effect of the lightsaber, but the importance of the sword is secondary to the function and purpose of the person who wielded it. The lightsaber, like the sword was for humans on Earth, is but a tool to help an individual accomplish a goal by threatening to use the sword as a weapon. It is tool of coercion and deterrence which requires in the best of circumstances that the sword never be drawn at all.

This is a difficult concept for the youthful and immature spirits of young men and women who desire to wave their shiny blade through the air to make it sing. It is obviously a male phallic symbol, but women too, no less drawn to the power to control, affect change, and influence the world around them can be equally drawn to the enchantment of wielding the sword. The sword has achieved a cult status and figuratively represents the means by which evil can be thwarted and destroyed. There is romance in drawing the sword which harkens back to classical times when warriors took arms to settle a quarrel, to protect one's nation, and defend one's honor. It was a tool for the adventurer as well who experienced the world full of treasures to be discovered and countless injustices to be righted. But when one seriously examines the uses of the sword, it was as much an instrument of revenge, conquest, and murder.

By examining the principles of the sword — swordsmanship — and the people who used the sword, it is hoped that a more fuller understanding of the Jedi Knights of *Star Wars* can be gleaned. A Jedi did not become Jedi simply because he carried a lightsaber, but by carrying one and knowing how to use it effectively, the Jedi became inured to a manner of existing which differed from modern soldiers who rely on the safety of distance to carry out their task.

The very nature of the sword as a weapon personalized battles and created a mind-set which views the opponent not as a target to be struck down, but as an individual. While it is true that ranged weapons have always existed alongside the sword (they probably predated it), the goal of any swordsman who understood the destructive nature of the weapon was to avoid the conflict altogether. Sun Tzu and Clausewitz (notable military strategists) understood the explicit rule that it is better to avoid a confrontation if particular ends can be obtained through negotiation or threat. Recourse to the sword was a means of last resort, either by its offensive or defensive use.

Lucas, when he began creating his fantastic universe, borrowed elements of culture, science, and narrative from every corner of the world. Like Tolkien who created Middle Earth to breathe life into the Elvish language he devised, Lucas too created an alternate world in which to place his Jedi. Lucas' inventiveness was not simply an exercise in entertainment. He had a message to tell which was best told through the unfolding visual medium of film. The Jedi were not puppets simply for our amusement, they were individuals who, through their story, told us something about ourselves. We, the audience, are the Jedi, and if we could see the Jedi Knights on screen as believable characters, the audience might hopefully learn the message that ultimately our choices have a direct impact on who or what we become. In order to make us believe, Lucas had to make the world of the Jedi as real as our own.

Doug Chiang, design director for *The Phantom Menace*, emphasized this point in a *Cinefex* interview when he lamented the typical George Lucas ritual of quickly tossing aside elaborate designs and drawings on which Chiang had spend hours rendering in his Skywalker Ranch office. Sifting through sketches, drawings, and even paintings, Lucas had a vision of what he wanted for his movies, and key in his decision making process was that the movie-goer had to instantly recognize any new hardware, whether it was a weapon, space ship, robot, costume, or any other prop that would appear on film. Even for characters like Qui-Gon Jinn, Darth Maul, and Jar Jar Binks, the audience would have to know them instantly.

The opening scene in *A New Hope* best exemplifies the *in res media* concept. Staring at the endless void of space, the shocking power of the rebel blockade runner fading into the distance pursued by a massive bristling space fortress, the audience has no idea what is about happen. Their senses, both visual and auditory, however, are overpowered by the intensity of that moment. For many, including myself, those opening moments would change our lives forever. Lucas says in many interviews that he was fascinated by the samurai movies of Akira Kurosawa which he saw as a child. He didn't know anything about Japanese history or culture, but he was fascinated by the fact that you did not need to know much about their culture in order to understand the story. Kurosawa's samurai movies were stories about people, and on a planetary level, the humanity of one human was, on its most basic levels, something that people shared wherever and whenever they lived. Lucas needed only to preface the audience with a scrolling exposition. From an artistic point of view, those words were a simple, but necessary convention to bring the audience into a shared state of expectation. With John William's overture and sudden hush of the instruments, the audience sat waiting with bated breath as if at the very top of the first peak in a roller coaster just before plummeting into the ride's opening dive. Lucas did not let his audience down.

It is in those opening scenes that we are introduced to the saga's first, and most important character — Darth Vader, a fallen Jedi Knight, now a Sith Lord, who is the servant of an evil emperor. We did not know he started out as an innocent young boy, but seeing Vader's massive frame, his black robes, and his terrifying mask, our first instinct is that this guy *is* evil. And at that moment, that is all we need know.

As a student of art, anthropology, and history, Lucas created a plausible world that has immediacy and substance. Down to the smallest detail, Lucas has conceived in his head a consistent rational that makes his alternate universe seem not only plausible, but as real as our own.

The sword, kimono, and samurai helmets served as inspiration for Vader, Mongolian hairstyles as models for Queen Amidala's Senate costume, and the Theed Palace on Naboo was based on the famed Hagia Sophia mosque in Istanbul. Even colors are used to psychological ends: Darth Vader's red lightsaber reflects the Western association of aggressiveness, the blacks, whites, and grays of the Death Star represent an aseptic world devoid of color, while the white robes of Princess Leia represent the purity of heart, soul, and spirit represented in classical tales.

Quite often the world Lucas has created is extremely comprehensive. The culture of the Gungans, the race of which Jar Jar Binks is a member, derives its power from organic energy mined from the depths of the ocean. It powers everything from the lights in the city of Otoh Gunga, the energy staffs carried by soldiers, their submarine bongo, as well as the energy ball and shields used to fight against the battle droid army at the end of *The Phantom Menace*. The capital of the Republic Coruscant has become a city planet over thousands of years. It has developed until there is no natural earth left to build upon. It is a society in which water from polar caps is piped to its equator, food is flown in from other planets, and raw materials are bought, exchanged, and traded in a complicated intergalactic commercial system. Spacecraft travel along invisible highways in the skies, while hovering taxis and levitating transports take people across the city and planet in the same way millions travel in busses, subways, and jets in cities all over Earth today.

In a universe where the Jedi walks along a corridor in the same way a warrior traversed the battlefield or the monk crossed the nave of a church, we can believe that *Star Wars* may have happened. The journey of stories does not simply take an audience to another world just for the sake of it. Stories are meant to change the listener as much as the protagonist is changed by the end of his story. Stories, especially fairy tales, are commentary on the inner psychology of us as human beings. The story of *Star Wars* would have been as cogent (and perhaps as seductive) to the Babylonians, the Romans, and the ancient Chinese.

Lucas did not create the human condition, he merely imitates it. Core to his memorable narrative is an eclectic borrowing from world myths, which makes his epic more august and grander in scope and intensity. These fantastic elements are the basic fare of the fairy tale, stories told to children as a subtle education in the guise of the bedtime story. The lessons of such chronicles have a profound and lasting effect on children, who, in adulthood, often see good and evil, love and marriage, and life and death as mere projections of their distant memories. By drawing on them, *Star Wars* is a world that is both palpable and fantastic.

Mythic elements serve as a link between the ancient and the modern, often telling in rather black and white terms how the world once was, and through its example, how the world ought to be. It is a teaching tool, a kind of cultural syllabus meant to teach truth rather than history. Having its own vocabulary, the modern becomes reacquainted with the historical path through the retelling of a largely fictional tale. So-called Truth, however, is not a hard substance, but a fleeting and subjective instruction. And where its simplicity seems juvenile, serious interpretation of the epic story often turns out to be more problematic than instructive.

The blanket generality of many lessons taught in myth

admits many gray areas in which men and women find themselves. The *Star Wars* universe borrows from them for greater effect. The prescription of "do good" faces myriad tests when following a rule may have the unintended consequence of doing a greater harm. Within the *Star Wars* universe, of paramount question is how does one rectify the Jedi's role as peace maker with his trained ability to resort to force? Myths may seem to paint the world in black and white, but the real truth is that Lucas' epic universe is a vibrant pallet of colors and hues.

Lucas transcends both space and time by speaking to a commonality of human emotions and experiences. Whether it is the competition between Luke and Han for the affections of a Princess in *A New Hope* or the need of a deposed Queen Amidala to liberate her planet from the control of greedy, self-serving Neimoidians, the characters, the motivations, the sentiment are those encountered by every person as they go through life. The desire for love, the value of liberty, the necessity of peace and order are concepts to which everyone can relate. It is this that surely makes the *Star Wars* saga popular around the world.

But an important element of Lucas' drama is an expression of very American experiences, especially in its similarity to the Western. Cultures around the world have had their own brand of frontiersman, but the ordeal of the Old West pioneer righting justice in singular vigilantism is a pervasive theme which dominates almost all American action/adventure films. This cowboy experience of taming the land and establishing a homestead is Act I. Bandits then come to town and force the frontiersman to rid the land of the scourge — Act II. And finally, through growth and experience, he succeeds in reestablishing law, order, and justice — Act III. While Americans are not the only people to have frontiersmen, their can-do spirit, their unrelenting optimism, and constant (if not often naive) idealism remains very dissimilar to his Russian counterpart who was always conscious of his Imperial heritage, the ghazi, a Muslim frontier soldier, who was always committed to his duty as a fighter for Islam, and the Canadian frontiersman who was always a minuscule subject buffeted by the violent elements of Mother Nature.

Transcending this hopelessly romantic picture of the frontier hero, however, is a sobering realism of the swordsman. While Luke Skywalker begins as a lonely boy yearning for life, he is propelled into a larger world by the circumstances of his birth and the death of his Aunt Beru and Uncle Owen. Luke will not simply avenge the death of his family, he will enter the world of the Jedi which draws its greatest inspiration from the medieval traditions of warrior knights. Not only was Luke imbued with virtues of self-sufficiency and devotion of kinship, but he is then propelled into a society in which loyalty, justice, and honor are ideals by which a Jedi must live his or her life.

While Luke's inexperience leaves him open-eyed and won-drous of the world, he is quickly reigned in by the duties and ob-ligations to which all swordsmen find themselves subject. As a Jedi Knight, Luke does not undergo Jedi training to become an anonymous Lone Ranger or masked Zorro. Lucas' universe, like Earth, is very much about the polis and the fact that each person is a political being who not only must find his way through the uncertainties of the whole universe, but he must become an important player in it.

In order to become a Jedi Knight, Luke must prove himself worthy and capable of wearing the lightsaber, which, to use Kenobi's words, "was an elegant weapon, in a more civilized day." No longer was Luke in the gangster world of Tatooine. He would have to fulfill the first quest of destroying the Death Star and then continue on through two duels to once again save the universe. And now, with the recent installments of *The Phantom Menace* and *Attack of the Clones*, we learn more of the respon-sibilities of the Jedi Knights who are the actual guardians of the Republic, a galactic union in which interstellar trade, commerce, and cultural exchange have continued peaceably for a thousand generations.

Lucas brings us deeper into his universe by further

enunciating the role of the individual vis-à-vis an unfolding conspiracy which threatens the very foundations of civilization itself. At stake is the Galactic Senate which has remained a forum for discussion and negotiation, promoter of the free exchange of ideas and the liberty of individuals and particular alien species to find a cosmic role in the universe and participate in the play of life. When that balance is threatened, the Jedi Order, guardians of peace and liberty, must find a role that combats the corruption and decadence of the Republic. While no civilization admits its own fall, history endlessly recounts the ebbs and flows of greatness to insignificance and back again.

While the Jedi Knights play the part of guardian of civility, there is a threat which originates from the very Jedi Order itself. With the Jedi Temple as a monument to stability on Coruscant, chaos and disorder springs out of the very discipline which has made the Jedi Order powerful protectors of order and certainty. From a distance, the Jedi Order plays roles within the galactic government as diplomats, envoys, and peace makers, but deep in its history sprang individuals who rejected the Jedi — the Sith, fallen Jedi who would foment dissension and cessation.

From even the earliest scripts, the concept of rival orders of knighthood has been consistently present. One good, the other evil, the Jedi and Sith stand for compassion on one side, and greed and selfishness on the other. It is an old vocabulary. One of good and evil, "the simplest part of a complex cosmic construction," Lucas admits.

The Jedi are servants of the Supreme Chancellor, the equivalent of the U.N. Secretary General. Some ten thousand in number of differing alien species, Lucas calls them "intergalactic therapists" with a chuckle. Identified before the age of one, Jedi aspirants are taught meditation, self-contemplation, and service to the galaxy. Their abilities and skills distinguish them from mere commoners, their training being a rigorous mix of academics, fighting, and paranormal skills. Whether it is history, philosophy, economics, political science, or the art of negotiating, Jedi strive to be versed in the professional training of the university. In training halls, Jedi learn swordsmanship with the light-saber, military skills, as well as a full regime of physical training and acrobatic skills. They also have the esoteric studies of "sixth senses" that stem from the Force which include the development and refinement of telekinesis, mind control, the control of raw energy such as that used by the Emperor. Through these arcane, but effective arts, a Jedi might even be able to see, perhaps predict the future, though "Always in motion is the future," warns Master Yoda.

In the beginning there were no Sith Lords, but there was dissention. Some of the Jedi, as they explored the Force and its nature, realized a greater potential harnessing the Force for more powerful ends. These Jedi came to disagree with the Order's creed of humility and compassion. It was weak and effete. The world changed with the exercise of power, and with the Dark Side of the Force came the ability not to simply push events in one direction or another, but to completely change the course of history.

The Dark Side was strength. It had a vitality. It gave control to its user. "So what if selfishness and greed would result?" its practitioners argued. These were all natural aspects of nature. Why not use them to further your own ends? If harnessed correctly, the Dark Side of the Force would give a Jedi unimaginable power. A thousand years earlier, one Jedi left the order, then another. Together they would call themselves the Sith, a competing order that gave the Republic a vastly more powerful alternative to the Jedi. The bow had been unstrung.

With each new defection from the Jedi there was a new member of the Sith. They took the title Darth to distinguish themselves from the Jedi. Their lust for power became greater and greater, and their anger and hate of the Jedi increased. With their growing numbers, their contempt for the Jedi seethed and desired some action against their former taskmasters. The desire to crush the Jedi came to command their judgment, but as is the case with all human institutions, the strength, resolve, and determination of each Sith was not equal. Some were stronger in the Dark Side than others. Some desired immediate action against the Jedi, others a more deliberate approach. The Sith began to bicker among themselves. Squabbles turned into open disagreement; disagreement to open fighting; and eventually intrigue and betrayal. Factions developed and the burning hate for the Jedi turned into hate for each other. Soon there the numbers of the Sith dwindled until there were only two.

Blood flowed in a miasma of death. Clever and powerful enough to be the only Sith left standing, the last Sith, Darth Bane, kept new counsel. One that would allow the Sith Order to survive given its propensity toward self-destruction. He vowed to limit the number of Sith to two — himself and an apprentice — and their methods would become clandestine, furtive, and secret. They vowed to destroy the Jedi, whom they still saw as their antithesis and threat to their own existence. Training and cultivating the dark powers of the Sith arts, the Sith Lords prepared for the moment when they would have revenge against the Jedi. Apprentice succeeded the master, and his apprentice succeeded him in turn. The predatory and cancerous ritual of apprentice replacing his predecessor continued for hundreds of years, their burning anger waiting patiently for a time when the Jedi would be vulnerable. That time would arrive, their nefarious order being the phantom menace of *Episode I*.

With the advent of Darth Sidious, the Sith Order would finally establish the road that would elevate their order to greatness. Through assassination and rigged elections, Sidious, under a false name, would establish himself as Supreme Chancellor. Through subterfuge and treachery, he fomented crisis and disorder in the galaxy so that the people would cry out for a strong leader. The Jedi would discern Sidious's attempt to take over the galaxy, but by then it would be too late. The Jedi would be accused of treachery, and some would allow themselves to be publically tried, sealing their fate in the eyes of the public. They would be executed and the rest hunted down with the help of a powerful Jedi — Darth Vader — who would hunt down his former comrades. Sidious would declare himself emperor and then lock himself away in the safety and security of his palace of the renamed capital of Imperial City. The galaxy's fate would be sealed for a time until Vader's children would bring their father back from the threshold of doom, thus saving his soul and the galaxy itself.

In Jedi lore there is a prophecy of a Chosen One — "one who will bring balance to the Force," according to Mace Windu, member of the Jedi High Council. Anakin is the Chosen One, but how does this prophecy affect the inevitability and destiny of the Jedi's life? Does one control one's destiny? Can one influence it? Is everyone predestined to a particular role in the universe? Anakin, as he grows into adulthood must discover answers to these questions. Though tragic at first, the mechanism for his fall to the Dark Side are those that affect every person on the planet. For the Jedi, who are masters of their own destiny because they have the weapon that can change the universe, their most critical decisions will affect the thousands of worlds which are part of the Galactic Republic.

Assisting the Jedi is a mystic belief in an all powerful energy field. "It surrounds us and penetrates us. It binds the galaxy together," Ben Kenobi tells Luke. The Force creates a spirituality in the *Star Wars* universe which helps guide the Jedi in their quest for justice. Though Lucas is neither a theologian, nor an allegorist, he borrows freely from many religions.

The Force contains many elements of Christianity, Taoism (Daoism), Zen Buddhism, as well as other pagan or mystical practices. Without creating his own religion, Lucas included the Force as a way to awaken a questioning spirit so that a person might ask him or herself whether there was a God, or not. Lucas believes in a God. He cannot define what or who God is, but seeing that there are truths to all religions as "containers of faith," the Force serves as a vital and central spiritual focus for the Jedi. While Lucas' creative borrowing from various religions prevent anything but an ambiguous mysticism, there are real precedents for this type of warrior-monk, which will be discussed in Chapter Five.

Religion has in many ways been about whose "magic" is stronger than another. Luke, in *Return of the Jedi*, uses his power of telekinesis as a way to win the submission of the Ewoks. Later, after telling the tale of the Rebellion, the Ewoks would commit themselves to the Rebel cause. Religion, like all of human endeavors, evolved from mere inklings and ideas to sophisticated philosophical and spiritual concepts. Many outward religions have ornate rituals and practices, while others have simple principles to guide its believers. Animistic cultures see spirits in all living things. Others, like Egypt and Imperial Rome, saw divinity anthropomorphized in the form of the nation's leader. The Jewish, Muslim, and Christian religions believe in a God that revealed his message through a divine messenger. Hindus believe in a cyclical transmigration of the souls in which perfection develops step by step as one improves his soul through a good life. Still others, like Taoists and Zen Buddhists admit a spirituality of balance in the cosmos, while an organizational set of rules like Confucianism establishes a divine order of existence that reflects the perfection of the universe.

The closest *Star Wars* comes to the complete philosophical development of established religions is his concept of midi-chlorians, which is the source of the Jedi's "magic" powers. The more midi-chlorians a Jedi has, the more powerful in the Force he is. Because of the Force's loss of complete spirituality, there has been great debate among *Star Wars* fans all over the world about the universality of midi-chlorians, which parallel the role of mitochondria vital to sustaining life in all living organisms. The polemic represents the audience's perception that only a chosen few, not everyone including themselves, could become a mighty Jedi. Fans, as if they lived in *Star Wars* felt cheated and disenfranchised by this revelation, many of them preferring an ambiguous spirituality of the Force to its scientific quantification.

The theme of technology versus spirit has been present in *Star Wars* from the first film. Will technology save the human race and perpetuate it? Or is there a spiritual aspect of humanity that will carry her forward? It touched an emotional chord following a cultural questioning of all American organizations in the 1970's, including the U.S. government and organized religions. Spiritualists will reject the notion that the ineffable can be reduced to a series of ones and zeros, yet science admits a growing mastery of the genetic makeup of the human race. It is of impeccable timing that Lucas' *Attack of the Clones* is released at a watershed in the developing of cloning technology in the medical and scientific community. Ultimately, the problem is whether humans are parasitic, living off of but in relation to the rest of nature, or whether our free will creates within us something unique in the universe.

Lucas has always had a material concept of the Force. It is clearly expressed in the earliest drafts of *A New Hope*. The strength of a Jedi came from a control of the flow of the Force. It could be drained from a person, leaving them worn and deprived of physical energy. Lucas also saw a messianic role for particular individuals. Not everyone could be the Chosen One. Not anyone with the simple desire or will could be a Jedi, which is actually true of many elite military groups like the SAS, the SEALS, the Green Berets.

Lucas saw the Jedi Knights and Sith Lords as masters of the Force, but different in their choice of using the Force, whether for positive or negative ends. The knights of goodness were called the Jedi Bendu and the Dai Noga Warriors, while the knights of evil were the Legions of Lettow. They were of one faith — faith in the Force — but of rival goals. One vied to use the Force for good, called the Ashla, the other for evil, called the Bogan. These terms were stricken from Lucas' screenplays when he realized he didn't have to formally name good and evil which could as easily be referred to as the Light and Dark Side of the Force. Lawrence Kasdan, who co-wrote the screenplay for *The Empire Strikes Back*, described the Force as a "combined vibration of all living things," an elegant notion as Lucas' Kenobi and Yoda.

Lucas' simple purpose was to make a simple dichotomy of human nature. He is not talking about separate religions or faiths, but of choices. Does one choose to do good or evil in life?

In good Christological fashion, Lucas asserts that goodness is superior to evil. The vices of anger, fear, and aggression therefore lead to a corruption of perfection. Perfection was once Man's right, until, interestingly enough, Adam decided to exercise his mind. The first man did not fall from grace until he took a bite from the tree of knowledge. All at once Man's naiveté and ignorance was replaced by learning and understanding. As punishment, Adam and all of his descendants would have to work and toil for a living. He would have to exercise his brain, and if, at the end of time, Man had behaved correctly, properly, and justly, he would once again be admitted into union with God.

Another concept from earlier scripts included the existence of the Kiber Crystal (spelled Kyber Crystal in Alan Dean Foster's novel *Splinter of the Mind's Eye*), a gem that enhanced the strength of the Force in the user who possessed it. It was a cruder concept of the Force; it was a talisman to be carried and fought over in the narrative like a holy grail that had to be guarded and kept from the hands of evil lest they use it to maniacal ends. In the end, much like the Ashla and Bogan, Lucas realized he didn't need to have a thing to possess the Force. It could be found within a person.

Throughout the present episodes of *Star Wars*, the Jedi have always been admonished to listen to one's instincts, to one's heart. It is a very sentimental and romantic notion posited on the belief that something somewhere inside of you will guide you properly. A direct bow to Joseph Campbell's idea to "follow one's bliss." Follow your heart's desire and do not fall into the expectations of the world at the price of your own selfhood. It requires a personal journey, whether in physical travel or in a personal questioning of the self. It is a metaphor for self-fulfillment. Be a writer. Be a dancer. Be a teacher. Be an lawyer. Be whatever your inner spirit tells you.

The Jedi/Sith dichotomy of evil as a corruption of good also gives force to another important theme: the redemption of Vader. Redemption implies that a fall from grace can be expunged by a conversion of the soul — a sinner can repent. Christianity admits the frailty of human character, but it also allows for the absolution of past evil deeds. It is a theological question of whether redemption can be achieved by a conversion of the heart or by an act of atonement. In *Return of the Jedi*, both must be fulfilled. Vader realizes in his heart that the evil he has done was wrong. But he also makes up for his sins through the outward penance of destroying the Emperor.

While not implying that this theme is a Christian allegory, it cannot be denied that a Christian influence is present. Redemption, for example, does not agree with Taoist philosophy that there be a balance of good and evil. Christianity does not give a status to evil except as a corruption of good. Humans sin because they are imperfect. Therefore, it follows that when one is in union with God, one will achieve perfection.

It may then be said that Lucas has succeeded in getting some people to explore the idea of God by his vague introduction of the Force into his *Star Wars* films. In this sense, the theme of the Force is analogous to the paintings, frescoes, and statues of a medieval cathedral, which were designed not only to elevate sacred persons who imitated Christ, but to help ordinary people understand their faith. The Force does not substitute for the theological debate, but it gets the faithful to contemplate the meaning of belief, if they ever had one at all. Albeit, it is still a rudimentary understanding of faith, but the engagement of questioning is the beginning of all of the most profoundest debates. That the Jedi are a spiritual organization is a statement in itself about the diminished role material goods and a materialistic life should play in a fulfilling life.

Related to the mystical nature of the Jedi, much has been made of the idea that *Star Wars* is myth. Lucas, himself, says that it was his intention of creating "a myth for modern times." But the story of *Star Wars* is not myth simply because it contains mythical elements. And from a theological perspective, *Star Wars* has too simplistic a view of the world: that of good and evil. But myth sounds more serious and believable, more profoundly adult, when in fact his story is epic not mythological. This, how-ever, does not diminish the richness of ideas that can be gleaned by examining the mythical elements of *Star Wars*.

Lucas admits he was heavily influenced by such books as *Hero With a Thousand Faces* and *Mask of God*, both written by Joseph Campbell, with whom Lucas later became friends. Raised a Catholic, Campbell began to distance himself from Christian theology after his studies at the Universities of Dartmouth, Columbia, and Paris in favor of a more universal approach. He examined how myths shared universal ideas about how we should live. Myths, he says, are not simply entertainment, but "allegoric instruction," giving listeners a construct and model for behavior.

Myths typically explain some of the fundamental questions peoples have about their reality — the nature of the universe, its creation, and how we should act in the world. Through exegesis we learn of our origins. The past tells us something of how the world is, and how it will be. Myths transmit ways of acting by defining virtue and vice, and it usually has some religious component and imparts an existence in relationship to the world, Mother Nature, the gods. Through our relationship with those outside forces, human beings find an affirmation of their exis-tence or a reason why they were created.

But the story of the Jedi as Lucas tells it is not about our relationship with the universe but with its inhabitants. This is not to say that the Jedi are not spiritual, but that their story is about the Jedi's relationship with other human beings and how the creations of his own hand have the potential to be the means to his own undoing. *Star Wars* is about human relationships. It is about our strengths, our frailties, our desires, our compassion. That too is the story of the swordsman who does not fight against the gods and their capricious whims, but against mem-bers of his own race. Like the sword, the Death Star is an in-trinsically destructive tool created for the destruction of not only planets, but the people that live on them. In this sense, *Star Wars* addresses human concerns and becomes an epic story of individuals who have the power to control the universe.

Were we to find ourselves in the situations of the Chosen One (Anakin) and the New Hope (Luke), what choices would we make? The lightsaber of the Jedi is the weapon of a swordsman. The lightsaber gives the Jedi the choice to use his weapon to vanquish evil and champion justice, or he can use it for the most selfish and basest of ends. The sword is both the symbol of power and means for achieving it. How the Jedi use their lightsabers is analogous to how we use our talents and abilities.

The Skywalkers' tale has captured an emotional vibration in the world. Abandoning the hard core scientific elements of the Sci-Fi genre but placing the Jedi within it, Lucas creates more of an emotional saga rather than intellectual one. The lightsaber is well suited to this romantic expression for it is a swordsman's adventure that Lucas has developed. And how Jedi swordsmen use their lightsaber is an example of how we ought to live our lives. Do we use the sword as a tool to amass power and wealth, or do we employ it to fight for justice? Luke's answer — Lucas' answer — is not unexpected.

Sword Culture

No phrase goes to the heart of swordsmanship so succinctly as Yoda's instruction to Anakin in *The Phantom Menace* when he said that "Fear leads to anger; anger lead to hate; hate leads to suffering." Were it not for fear, there would be no need for the elaborate codes of conduct that rule a person's behavior both in a civilized society as well as that on a battlefield. In the name of self-protection and self-preservation, swordsmen throughout history and across continents have always hidden their uncertainty and covered their trembling hearts behind the mask of bravado and a face-saving masculinity. It is this fear of embarrassment or failure, of lost of life or face which make warriors draw their swords, those crude but sharp instruments which make for a poor, but often effective substitute for a dull mind.

The swordsman, however, like the Jedi, are not errant warriors with kind intentions. They are part of a culture which has established rules based on human fear and experience of combat. While training to become the best swordsmen of the universe, the Jedi, like accomplished diplomats, the greatest leaders, and the most creative individuals, do not need the brute force of strength. Instead, they become masters of wisdom and intelligence which has the skills of the sword at his disposal should words fail them.

Battlefield Experience

The fear of death is ultimately the most basic emotional urge a person can ever confront. It becomes even more prevalent in the minds of swordsmen. The basic drive for self-preservation during a surprise situation is instinctual and has evolved over thousands of years: for men it more often instructs the body to stand and fight, for women the opposite. Life on the battlefield becomes a testing ground for the best able to survive.

The battlefield, on the other hand, allows more time for the brain to calculate the odds as opposing armies face up in lines against each other. As individuals, there is the commanding thought that one person against an army of others can hardly make a difference. It is, therefore, in numbers and in close proximity to other men in the same situation which make the individual desire to become part of the whole. The individual stands a better chance of survival in the group.

Rituals reassured individuals by shaping the psychology of the men so that they may better prepare for the final moments of their lives. The gathering of warriors into lines and ranks puts order into a situation that seems wild and chaotic. It gives the feeling that organization will be key to victory. Religious rites assure men that their cause is just in the eyes of God and sends the message that God is awaiting them if this be a person's last battle. The imbibing of wine, mead, or beer served as a final drink with one's comrades. It also had the intoxicating effects of dulling physical pain and reducing a person's natural inhibition to walk directly into the danger of combat. The presence of older, more experienced men behind the younger, served as reassurance to green troops that others among them knew what to expect and what to do. Experienced soldiers also served as a deterrence to the coward who might flee the front line. Without preparations like this, the cohesion and resolve of the army would be seriously reduced.

Once lines had been formed, men would be ordered forward and when lines met on the middle, the victorious army would be the one which pushed the enemy back without losing its own cohesion. Once a break in the enemy's line was created, men could push into the ranks, attacking the flanks of opponents who expected and desired to fight by pushing their own way through the enemy. Survival now becomes a question of ability, numbers, intensity, and tactics, all the while being thwarted by poor visibility, unfavorable ground, and the elements. Tactics are high in the mind of the swordsman slashing at his enemies, while a planned overall strategy will make use of an army's strengths while limiting its weaknesses.

In the front lines, a sense of a successful attack depends on the continued momentum of a push forward and a feeling that fewer casualties are being taken than are being given out. As men move forward, instincts take over, men automatically looking for opponents to engage until there are none left. Victory is assured when the whole company pushes forward as individuals at the outer periphery engage in one-on-one exchanges. When the men on one side begins to fall and the approach of enemies force soldiers backward, the will to fight falters and eventually the warrior must either take a stand (and hope to come out victorious) or to begin a retreat to save his own life. His withdrawal may be organized and coordinated with his company who also see the inevitability of defeat, or, more often, it becomes a self-interested every-man-for-himself mentality in which flight takes the quickest and most direct route out of the battlefield.

When the enemy begins to surrender or to flee, the moment of individual victory is at hand. But battles often take hours to fight, the complete victory being dependent on a series of successes, not that of a single company. When soldiers look around and see their side pushing the enemy back, he is emboldened to continue the fight. When his compatriots lay sprawled on the ground dead or dying, he is cowered and seeks to retreat until he can find others of his side for solace and support.

The battlefield is a training ground for its survivors in which the education is the pragmatic exchange of attacks and defenses. In the midst of the front line, there are no rules. It is each man for himself, and the desire for fair play is non-existent when one's very survival is at stake. It is from this experience that the swordsman learns that survival is a brutal taskmaster.

Once an individual survives one battle, he becomes more convinced that he will be able to survive the next battle, being more prepared for the horrors that he is to experience. By virtue of his profession, the soldier becomes a pragmatist, understanding that the force of arms is the ultimate power in the universe. By defeating an enemy, the swordsman learns that victory only comes to those who have the superior command of fighting skills, battle tactics, and strategy. The battlefield is the proving ground to the swordsman that strength dominates and destroys all of the pleasantries, cultural refinement, and good intentions peaceful societies hold in esteem. This is the reality of the swordsman — power comes at the edge of his weapon.

Codes of Conduct

While survival is at the forefront of the soldier's thoughts during combat, it becomes evident after the clash that a favorable outcome is highly dependent on training and preparation. Raw courage and determination are important traits in the warrior, but skills and preparation guarantee that the human spirit is not unnecessarily hamstrung before the battle has even begun. The experienced soldier realizes that once the battlefield is left, there is another world in which he must live — that of civilized society.

In the heat of the battle or in the campaign of war, the most basic emotions of hate and anger come to dominate the swordsman's mind. The vilification of the enemy is easy propaganda which gives the troops a simple reason for combat as well as invectives to sling at their enemies. Swordsmen of the aristocracy, however, recognize that men of value and worth understand that there is a code of shared conduct which governs them and their opponents even in the chaos of battle.

While battle is a reluctant proving ground for civilized men, the reality of hand-to-hand warfare teaches that when sword edge can touch an opponent's flesh, men become one and the same, creatures of determination that kill in order to preserve their own life. When words fail and negotiation has reached its limits, the swordsman, more than any other type of soldier, understands and recognizes the destructive potential of a clash of arms. By staring into the brutish character of others forced into war, the swordsman is also reminded that his opponent is not simply some abstraction, but another being who bleeds, feels pain, and dies. Without this understanding, there can be no hope for peace and the State of War would continue. Without high-minded leaders and diplomats, many of whom know the harsh realities of war, there can be no less incentive to avoid war than by knowing first hand its destructiveness.

The repugnance of war does not only come from the hard experience of battle, however. Thoughtful martial artists too, because of the very nature of their discipline, can learn the lessons of war's horrors. The Jedi, too, who, at the time of *The Phantom Menace*, do not know of mass scale battles, must understand the nature of their sword arts if they are to become active participants in the vast universe of galactic diplomacy. The Jedi must understand human and political motivations as well as the strengths and weaknesses of the people and aliens with whom he is to negotiate. Without this knowledge, the Jedi cannot possibly understand his own position, nor that of his adversary. It is from his knowledge as a melee combatant that a Jedi understands that power plays are a pragmatic reality in the world of diplomacy. The training of the lightsaber makes the Jedi's outlook toward others highly personal.

Because combat began as confrontation between individuals, the combat between warriors at arm's length was seen as a heroic exploit which gave the individual, both commoners and elites, the opportunity to prove themselves in the most severe form of masculine competition — combat. Contrast this with the modern armies which, because of the technology of the firearm, fights ideally from a distance under the protection of camouflage and natural or man-made barriers. The nature of warfare has changed, but there still exists the need to make modern wars into the heroic combat of the past. This is good in that the soldier will see the human side of the struggle of war, but it also has the potential of romanticizing the waste and carnage of human life.

The sword itself holds a particular meaning for human societies because it was the first weapon intrinsically created to take another human life. It was not a tool, which implied some peaceful utility, nor was it a hunting weapon like the spear and the bow. And while the club was an easier man-to-man fighting instrument, the conscious invention of the sword demonstrated for the first time in societies that competition was no longer between bands of wandering humans, but of conflict between people who had less conflict with nature than they did with each other.

The sword finds its origins in the early knives, which were made of chipped flint. They were a flexible tool capable of cutting meat, stripping bone, puncturing hides, and could, in an emergency, be used for self-defense. As human skills evolved, the quality of the blade improved as well. Stone proved a poor substance out which to fashion blades, but with improvements in metallurgy, society was transformed by the sword as profoundly as it was by newer, more complicated forms of organization and farming techniques. Early swords were made out of copper, bronze (a combination of copper and tin), iron, and finally steel. It was a simple object to create and construct (essentially a long knife), allowing cultures around the world to develop the sword independently, though with minor variations in size, shape, and style. Its inherent form remains either the single-sided or double-sided blade. Techniques of the sword (the subject of Chapter Four) evolved over thousands of years, the sword remaining the principal weapon of many societies until the technological achievement and preponderance of the firearm.

Warfare, however, was not the desired or total experience of either civilians or warriors. Much more of the soldier's time was spent honing skills, preparing defenses, or on the road marching from one battle to the next. It was a difficult life which required discipline and a hardiness which civilians do not encounter with the same intensity. Barracks life has and always remains a disciplined and often difficult existence. Indeed it is the soldier's

very training which seems contradictory to life during peace
time. While being taught the art of war, the soldier was expected
to behave in a civilized society. It seems that this cultural paradox is a reality with which all civilizations have had to come to
grips. Even among the most cultivated and enlightened cultures,
the need to resort to acts of war were sometimes necessary and
even desirable.

Victor Davis Hanson's excellent monograph on infantry
battle *The Western Way of War* posits the credible theory that the
battlefield was an effective and efficient method of deciding
differences between rival city-states. Apart from wars of conquest and empire building, even the most democratic societies of
Greece came to the conscious conclusion that settling questions
of land rights and ownership were best settle by a single,
decisive battle, rather than a long, extended campaign which
citizens in neighboring city-states neither sought nor desired.

What soldiers learned from the battlefield would become a
source of enlightenment which would forever affect the way
armed men would interact. On the one hand, there was a simple
recognition that in war all of the basic rules of human interaction
are dispensed with. On the other, there was a general recognition
that the imposition of rules of engagement would be useful to
limit unbridled warfare.

Most civilizations have known periods in which no authority
or predominating power reigned over others. In such situations,
bands of soldiers lay waste to whatever land and possessions
they can take for their own appetites. Control of violence and the
men who could inflict violence became an issue of vital importance. Even the most savage commander must at some point
recognized that the free reign of armed militants could not be
allowed in either the military camp, nor the conquered town or
village. Restrictions, in some form, had to be imposed. Either the
spoils of war would be destroyed or the army would degenerate
into its own self-destruction. Out of this evolved the iron discipline of military life, which eventually developed into a series of
expected behavior most commonly referred to among swords-

men as a code of honor.

Off of the battlefield, the solder presented as much a threat
to the society as it did enemies it conquered. It was easy for the
swordsman to takes his experience on the battlefield and apply
it to experiences in the civilian world. Business, politics, and
even the arts could be seen as the mere expression of competing
interests which saw more value in their individual success than
a more tempered and caring mode of behavior. But religion and
civilian values have always placed a higher value in peace than
in the chaotic world of continual warfare. Societies, while often
benefitting from the great technological and cultural leaps
because of war (many countries achieved their very existence
through revolution), there is no question that the progress of
societies that nurture and care for their citizens through peaceful
regulation far surpasses the destructive changes brought about
through war.

While the need for a soldiery is deemed a reluctant necessity,
rules that limit the power of swordsmen in society have always
been seen as a necessary part of the swordsman's life, which is
divided into two basic spheres of action — self-regulation and
coercion.

Self-regulation corresponds to the public civility most reflected in the concept of Honor, which acts as a public code of conduct that governs individuals who are given the privilege of
carrying a sword.* Often this State of Civility & Honor is referred
to by swordsmen as Point of Honor. The other state of affairs is
that of the battlefield in which a State of War exists between individuals and between civilizations, cultures, and countries. Point
of Honor is an ethical standard of behavior that the swordsman
must follow in society, while the State of War is a coercive situation in which power and control are determined by the armed

---

*The concept of honor may seem to apply to those who carry
any weapon, but the regulation of present-day constabularies that carry guns stems from duties and obligations associated with the performance of their duties as a professional, not from being part of a
brotherhood of melee combatants.

struggle. It requires the swordsman to be an individual of two minds — one of peace and one of war. Where the two do not meet is often a source of post-traumatic battle syndrome, wherein a soldier can not mentally separate the experience of one state of being from the other.

Throughout history, the soldier has always had to examine his relationship to the state because he serves both as protector of it as well as its greatest threat. The swordsman was praised during times of war as the guarantor of freedom in his role as soldier, cavalryman, and knight, but reviled as dictator if he took control of the state for his own personal aggrandizement. Society, therefore, has a love-hate relationship with the military, for it must trust the swordsman in being a guardian not a usurper. Society can only trust the swordsman if he is trained properly.

Pragmatic Struggle

Ultimately, the proper swordsman must respect not only the Code of Honor, which rules their own life from within, but also the law of the land, which are the rules of every citizen, including the swordsman. While there is no reason why the swordsman might not take power for himself, there are principles inherent in the cult of honor which temper the swordsmen and encourage him to respect law of his own volition.

Honor as a public morality stems from the basic idea that a swordsman is part of an elite group which can impose restrictions on an individual who breaks the code of the group. Knowing that the collective desires not to discipline a member publically, the individual is encouraged to behave properly and according to the rules of the group. He has particular rights of challenging the group within the parameters of the rules, all the while being subject to verbal coercion and the threat of punitive measures. Since training in the sword is a long and difficult challenge, there is plenty of opportunity to create in the individual a pride in belonging to the group and a sense of obligation to it. Should these fail, men of honor can both discipline by fines or eventually through ostracism. Should those measures not prove sufficient in reigning in the recalcitrant member, force of arms (for all the members are swordsmen) was the last recourse.

Implicit in this relationship is the assumption that power, being the final arbiter in the real world, will achieve a desired end in a civil society. It reflects the real state of the world and permits regulation in what otherwise would be a permanent State of War. Because the proponents of this form of "peaceful coercion" were the Europeans of the great continental nations, this mode of operation became the basis for the international organizations that would develop during twentieth century. The concept of collective force disciplining a single, defiant nation was at the heart of the League of Nations. This collectivist spirit hoped to be a supra-national organization in which mere alliance and regionalism in a state of international anarchy (which led to the conflict of World War I) could be prevented. States, however, while bowing to the ideas of Woodrow Wilson's proposal of a peace program (the Fourteen Points), did not act out of a belief in a greater, pan-national organization. They were still acting as self-interested nations who accepted war as a proper and some-times necessary arm of national policy. Because of internal pressures and the rise of fascism, communism, and militarism, use of force was seen as a natural, if not inevitable, tool of the dema-gogue. Such ideologies attributed much of the inevitability of struggle — whether of ideas, class, or armaments — as deter-mined by the very state of human culture. Determinists — pro-ponents of the belief that cultures, society, and past history predetermine future events — believed that human civilization was at a crossroad in its historical development. But when the swordsman draws his sword, he becomes an actor within the world, who must, in order to survive, change the world around him. Or die trying. The swordsman cannot admit determinism without admitting the futility of his own profession.

The League of Nations ultimately failed because individual nations, including the United States which did not even join the League of Nations, pursued an individual policy that had little concern for the general state of the world if it meant one's own nation would suffer. In a world of political survival-of-the-fittest, there seemed to be a sense that the finite world of one country's gain meant another country's loss.

What the League of Nations lacked in its pragmatism, the United Nations made up in its commitment to idealism. While acting within a world of inevitable unilateralism, the spirit of nations after the carnage of World War II was a commitment to a higher authority than the mere punishment of rogue nations. An emphasis was placed on the creative use of international standards of law as exemplified by the Nuremberg Trials and the strengthening of international bodies like the World Court in which due process, fairness, and judgment according to high standards of conduct were respected. Law would not simply be the arbitrary will of the victor, exemplified by the Treaty of Versailles.

The swordsman's code of honor went through a similar evolution. Recognizing the pragmatism of resorting to power, Point of Honor became as corrupt as the League of Nations. What worked on a personal level as a self-regulating honor system with a mechanism for disciplining defiant members became a rogue body of elitist oligarches. Under the short-sited principle that courts of honor could rule in cases where civil and criminal law had no jurisdiction, the court of honor became an alternate justice system which, in the end, could not regulate itself because individuals through their ability to manipulate the sword succeeded in thwarting the actions of the group. The Point of Honor system had its own courts made up of aristocratic swordsmen who, in the name of honor, defied the law of the land in which they lived.

The court of honor simply gave individual swordsmen a framework of the honor system to justify their own vigilantism. The honor system and the duel was envisioned as a code of behavior which rested on the premise that in the forum of public opinion civilized people would refrain from the public staining of individual character because the recipient of such verbal abuse

could challenge his detractor to a duel. Instead of preventing un-
civilized exchanges such as the public embarrassment of calling
an individual a liar, a cheat, or a coward, the honor system was
used to bait weaker opponents into a situation that inevitably
resulted in the defeat of the weaker swordsman. The arms race
of developing better fencing skills was fueled as gentlemen of
distinction fell into the trap of thinking the State of War would
settle quarrels of perception and intellect.

Commoners aspiring to higher positions in society began to
recognize the blood thirsty futility of settling differences with the
duel. At first they became reluctant participants as commoners
entered the aristocratic world of knighthood, but as societies
developed more refined ideas of democratic liberalism, the
examination of the traditional Point of Honor system came to be
understood as a sophist veil of unlawful and defiant aristocratic
privilege. Not only did commoners lack the education of elite
rules of governance (a brotherhood of *noblesse oblige*), they lacked
the skills of swordsmanship which were considered an important part of an aristocrat's upbringing. Commoners used logic,
common sense, religion, and the developing tools of cannon and
guns to wrest the privilege of exclusive Point of Honor away
from the swordsmen. In effect, the Point of Honor system became a separate court of law that distinguished itself apart from
and superior to the laws of the nation.

The failure of Point of Honor lay in the arrogance of swordsmen who continued to act in civilian society as if they were still
on the battlefield. Instead of esteeming the laws of the nation,
they esteemed the laws of Point of Honor because it served their
interest. The true goal of Point of Honor was a self-regulating
system of conduct which was essentially based on trust of the
judgment of individuals who belonged to the class of swordsmen.

Ever since civilizations first organized their earliest laws,
there has always existed a concept that law was the best protector of people's interests. Replacing arbitrary whims, the codification of proper behavior became a way to equally protect and

guarantee rights and privilege of aristocrats and eventually the commoner as well. While not necessarily guaranteeing equality, it did allow for the peaceful intercourse with sovereigns (and its military) and important economic and privileged players in the country. Because laws had to apply universally, the basis of most law systems found its roots not in power struggles, but on the concept of justice. It did not pretend to uphold equality (though that concept is heavily linked to justice), justice did resolve to express standards of behavior which were considered correct, fair, and just.

Jurists, knowing that simple enunciation of idealistic behavior was useless unless there was some form of enforcement, enunciated the need for policemen to force individuals to conform. Usually this role fell to the executive branch of government (in most cases a sovereign king) who implicitly committed him or herself to abiding by the laws when the military was used to defend national laws. When the sovereign was influential enough to command the military, the role of the swordsman and the law were in proper harmony. The swordsman could therefore feel reassured that his lawful behavior served not only his self-interest but that of justice as well. The sword became the symbol of justice.

Adjunct to the need of law to be enforced through the use of coercion was the concept that swordsmen came to have their privilege of exerting power because the sword was placed in their hands by a recognized authority. While that authority often came to the swordsman from a sovereign (the king, a state bureaucracy, divine representatives), the swordsman not only owed allegiance to his lord, but also to greater societal goods — nationhood, freedom, independence. There came to exist an assumption that since law was reflective of proper behavior, the swordsman too was bound by those laws. When the swordsman chose to disobey a law by virtue of his physical ability to do so, he ceased playing the role of power broker, statesmen, soldier, and gentlemen. They became, instead, bullies, thugs, thieves, and murderers.

In the international area of post-World War II geopolitics, the attempt to place the military in the service of international law has been a change which has met with relative success. While the Cold War depended highly on the self-interest of primarily the United States and the Soviet Union, a greater dependence has been successful in applying universal principles of law at the heart of governmental action. Where Point of Honor was once an expression of modes of proper behavior for the swordsman, the international legal system has titularly become the mode of proper behavior for sovereign states. When countries, especially the most powerful, begin to act out of a greater sense of concern for the public good, the success of international justice has a greater chance of being achieved. More than at any other period of history, the present international community of self-interested national governments has recognized the interdependence of both economic and political interests. Of even greater import is the more prevalent appreciation for the fact that pragmatic action can be exercised with deference to the idealism of justice.

The honor code of swordsmen as applied to geopolitical state of the world (and in the case of the *Star Wars*, to universal state of the Galactic Republic) must resolve itself not in the idealistic vacuum of the court, but in the real world. A point of dispute often falls on the distinction of individual action and the need of the group. While some invoke the ancient maxim that "the needs of the many may outweigh the needs of the few," the actual state of human politics often revolves around the needs of the minority and the needs of the majority.

Especially in nations where democracy and liberal freedom are held as principal assumptions of political organization, the question of a majority's tyranny still arises. Even if it is assumed that the majority is wise enough to properly manage the affairs of the whole, there will always exist the potential to use the swordsman (the military) to suppress the minority simply because it disagrees with the majority. The minority, if it is not stamped out through suppressive means, has two recourses: it can convince the majority to come over to his position, or it can raise an army of swordsman to act on its behalf. Because the State of War will eventually judge the victor through the pure exercise of power, it is incumbent on those in positions to coerce to have a proper respect for the law.

Because law holds justice as a standard for its norms, the swordsman, to properly remain the swordsman, must respect the law. Without the swordsman's support, there can be no effective justice. There are therefore two kinds of swordsmen — one who derives his power from the sword (State of War) and one who derives his power from the exercise of the sword in the name of justice (State of Civility & Honor). One is honorable because he strives to achieve justice, while the other loses his status as a guardian of society and becomes a common thug or dictator.

The enlightened swordsman, if properly trained, will submit himself to regulation. He will bow to proper authority, which in principle is submission to idealistic behaviors. He will be considered dishonorable if he defies the law and takes authority for his own. In the real world, however, the material exigencies of a nation may depend on the unlawful exercise of power. Take, for example, the case in which a swordsman disagrees with the law; one that he considers unjust. What is his course of action?

The swordsman must feel compelled to act in accordance with justice, which, in this circumstance, does not conform to higher modes of behavior. His duty is, therefore, to fight against this law, creating a Pragmatic Struggle in which good behavior must be forced into the codification of law. Because the swordsman's resort to the State of War simply introduces a crude form of idealistic relativism, i.e. one person's preference of justice for another, there is another principle which governs the life and experience of the empowered swordsman — that of sacrifice.

When a minority, an individual or a group, breaks a just law, the swordsman has the moral imperative to exercise coercion in favor of the law. When that minority or majority breaks an unjust law, the swordsman must make a judgment in whether or not to enforce the law. Revolution is often justified in this latter

category. If it is successful, and in accordance with just principles, the revolutionary swordsman gains not only the *de facto*
control of the country, he also re-establishes codes of behavior
that are considered just. This recourse, because it is done in defi-
ance of existing laws, must be accomplished with deliberate
thought for fear of elevating a State of War without replacing it
with a State of Civility & Honor. If honor is equated with self-
interest, it results in personal preference — a dictatorship. If
honor is equated with simply the judgment of a select few, it
results in a larger form of personal preference — an oligarchy.
For the State of Civility & Honor to take reign (a just society), the
swordsman must eventually yield his power.

If the swordsman attempts to use his sword to restore justice,
he cannot fail in his attempt. By winning the Pragmatic Struggle,
he will install a just regime. By loosing, though he may not survive, his sacrifice is still considered noble and enlightened. This
Noble Sacrifice, while tragic and romantic, may seem a futile
exercise, it still remains that the swordsman must chose to use
his power of coercion in the name of justice.

This difference separates a Ferdinand Marcos from a George
Washington. Both are men who struggled against what each believed were injustices in the system. Marcos, a lawyer by training, came up with an elaborate justification which installed
himself as the *de facto* ruler of his country. But subverting justice
through the abolishment of the freedoms and rights of his own
citizens when he refused to lift martial law, Marcos became a
thug unworthy of properly exercising power. Washington, in his
struggle, fought not only out of the self-interest of his fellow
Patriots, but in the name of justice against laws of a king and
parliament which took away the freedoms and rights of its very
own subjects. Washington, an honorable man, upon the attainment of a Pragmatic Struggle for justice, stepped down from his
position as swordsman and let others rule on behalf of just laws,
and not simply because they had the means to rule.

The Case of Japan

Examples of the Pragmatic Struggle (a Just War) can be found in both the swordsmanship traditions of Western cultures as well as that of Japan, the two biggest influences on the Jedi of *Star Wars*. Chivalry, principally a Christian ethic of warriors, and *bushido*, the samurai ethic which holds honor as the highest social obligation.

In Japan, bushido, translated as the "way of Japanese men-at-arms," reflected a fluid and evolving code of behavior. Unlike the Point of Honor system which found expression in legalistic treatises of European jurisprudence, bushido reflected general precepts that lacked specificity in details. Bushido was, as in Europe, a military concept of honor which had a profound impact on the way samurai behaved in society. Today, bushido like its Western counterpart, exists conceptually, having given way to the written rule of law.

The Jedi of *Star Wars* were partially inspired by the samurai whom George Lucas encountered during his formative years studying film at the University of Southern California. Especially informative were the movies of Akira Kurosawa to whom Lucas readily admits a positive influence. The plot for *A New Hope* is borrowed directly from the Kurosawa movie *Hidden Fortress*, while sword fighting, by way of the two-handed manner Obi-Wan and Darth Vader fight in *Episode IV*, is indebted to samurai sword play. The name of Lucas' Jedi Knights, if the children's book *The Phantom Menace Scrapbook* is to be believed, is derived from the Japanese samurai era of swordsman called *jidai geki* (literally "the era of plays") which refers to the samurai inspired settings and themes of many Japanese books, plays, and movies based on that historical period.

Much of Japanese history is often dominated by the rise of the generalissimo called *shogun*. While at the outset the shogun, motivated primarily by self-interest and dynastic ambitions, does not fit neatly into my definition of an honorable swordsman who sets aside his sword in the name of justice, there are corollaries that demonstrate the existence of the Pragmatic Struggle within the context of Japanese history. Shoguns, realists and believers in the State of War, were ruled by a strong tradition which sought justification of their own authority according to principles and customs of Japanese law.

Despite the *de facto* elevation of military leaders to the highest level of rule in Japan, shoguns continually struggled to maintain the pretense that they ruled on behalf of the Emperor, who was considered the divine ruler in whom proper authority rested. In the Heian Period (794-1190), it was the noble aristocracy (*kuge*) which looked down on the crude warrior whom it thought of as unsophisticated and barbarian. Their prerogatives rested, however, on the support of the military class which was elevated in society as "protectors" of the aristocracy. As long as the army could be convinced to support the nobles, the *kuge* could maintain its cultural and military monopoly of the government. The Court Nobles asserted their authority for hundreds of years, but as the military learned the refinement of the court, they began to consider themselves equally capable of managing the culture and authority of the Japanese government which expressed itself in the exalted position of the emperor. At this point, referred to as the Kamakura Period (1192-1333), the samurai class under Minamoto no Yoritomo established the first shogunate in which the military took over the country.

For three hundred years, the leadership of Japan rested with the shoguns who established their own hegemony through force of arms and the manipulation of the Emperor who, while he held moral authority, was confined to rubber stamping the decisions of the reigning shogun. It was under the Ieyasu Tokugawa who ushered in the Edo Period (1603-1867), a two-hundred fifty year dynasty of relative peace and stability in the country in which a new kind of samurai was to develop. Though the methods of the Tokugawa rulers would be considered authoritarian if not draconian by Western standards, this was the period when the role of the samurai evolved from one of warrior-servant to that of citizen-warrior.

Conscious of the threat armed forces posed to his own government, Ieyasu established a society which would create a virtual barracks state that allowed him to control the countryside by the establishment of frontier posts to keep an eye on the movement of competing feudal lords, called *daimyo*. To further check the influence of enemy daimyo, Ieyasu formulated a complicated patronage system which required all important lords to maintain residences for part of the year in Edo, modern Tokyo. If a lord were to leave the capital, his family was required to stay in the city as a hostage should the lord conduct any affairs that went counter to the shogunate's interests.

Following previous periods after a shogun had established himself as master of Japan, the problems of recently unemployed samurai caused minor and even major consternations for the shogunate. Inequities between classes and within classes were the simple fact of life, and when masterless samurai, called *ronin*, or peasants felt they had an opportunity to gain some concession through open rebellion, the shogunate had to be quick in stamping out the insurrection which could spark greater discontent among individuals and regions that chaffed under Tokugawa rule. So in order to give new focus to samurai who no longer had wars to fight, laws were established that required samurai to behave as custodians of feudal domains and to pursue a life that imitated the graces of the Imperial Court. The samurai class was a disciplined and self-regulating military force, and now they were required to learn courtly skills like refined behavior, poetry, and calligraphy. Their martial skills, which were still necessary in case of challenges to the shogunate, were also transformed into less violent expressions.

During the Edo Period, schools of swordsmanship, called *ryu*, trained samurai in the fighting arts of various weapons, the curved *katana* being the predominant weapon of the military class. Instead of training to fight on the battlefield, samurai were encouraged to demonstrate the superiority of their skills using protective gear that simulated the arms and armor of the samurai. The art of *kendo* was born.

Kendo required the use of lighter armor and the use of a

practice sword made of bamboo slats (*shinai*). Instead of temper-
ing practice as they did with wooden practice swords called
bokken, the new shinai allowed the samurai to engage in a more
vigorous combat without the danger of using the bokken or live-
blade katana. Though there were controversies on whether the
new shinai style was indeed true Japanese swordsmanship, the
prevailing consensus that a new form of Japanese sword practice
was soon to become a permanent fixture in the study of Japanese
martial arts.

Faith in the peaceful era also led to the change in attitude
toward the sword. Instead of using the sword as merely an instrument of power, practice of the sword was now used as a way
to develop the spirit and martial ardor within the context of a
peaceful society. *Kenjutsu*, the use of the sword as a killing
weapon, became kendo, the way of developing personal spirit
through swordsmanship. The State of Civility & Honor came to
replace the perpetual State of War.

It also evolved into a new method of reaching personal enlightenment in a new religion called Zen Buddhism, which
taught that enlightenment could be attained during an epiphany
which resulted from austere physical practices. Enlightenment,
according to Zen philosophy could be obtained by the tea ceremony, meditation, and even sword work. According to the philosopher Sato, Zen was "thought to have had a special appeal to
the warrior because of its stress on a highly regulated way of life,
simplicity, discipline, and the equation of life and death." By
contemplating and mastering his fear of death, the swordsman
then became free to live a fulfilling good life; one that served the
highest ends of Japanese culture itself.

Mastering the Fear of Death

The refinement of both Western and Japanese swordsmanship is an idealized and recent development of the cult of the
sword. It plays on a heroic tradition in which the swordsman can
find the courage to suppress his personal fears and allow him to
engage in the horrific melee of a clash of steel. The plain fact,

however, is that the battlefield is really a stand of men together to suppress the natural urge to flee. Higher thoughts of country, justice, and honor do not enter the mind when self-preservation, that basest of human functions, seems the only guiding principle.

It is only when given the moment to think — either during a lull in the battle or a period of civil peace — does the warrior contemplate lofty ideals. Loyalty to one's country spurs him forward, memories of family and thoughts of their protection egg the soldier to proceed, and love of justice drives the knight to bloody his sword so that he may then sheath it at the end of the battle. Peace and security from invasion tends to diminish the reliance on weapons, but in an emotional attempt to justify training with a sword, the soldier must find a rational justification that redeems his barbaric exercise, for war and battle when reflected upon become a romanticized abstraction that overshadows the deadly violence for which the sword is most properly used.

Some swordsmen break the self-justifying circle of violence — to make peace one must make war — by delving deeply into their own soul. The actions of their art lead to a self-examination that questions the very reliance on the sword as a means to an end. When this happens, swordsmanship then becomes a road toward a virtuous and compassionate life.

The paradox of religions professing doctrines of both peace and war are foreign to pacifists. But acts of terror, brutality, and inhumanity may sometimes convert the pacifist who becomes so disgusted by human atrocity that he can no longer tolerate the thought of inaction that would allow the continuance of unspeakable slaughter. Whether it is the slaying of innocent civilians, deliberate and planned genocide, or the injustice of subjugation, the man or woman feels a burning fire to right wrong and dispense personal justice.

His antithesis, by the very nature of his profession, is the warrior who must act according to training and doctrine. Luck willing, there will be a higher authority which tames his mind and spirit of the corruption and lure of power. Swordsmen by their very nature act and react in the world, and it is by the laws of nature or by the laws of men that he keeps his sword sheathed until the proper cause and proper authority release the stay on his gauntlet-covered hand.

Without justice, there is little reason to perpetuate the training with a sword. Thoughtful men and women use their training as a way to inform and enrich their lives. With the fragility of life and the body's permeability to violence, practice with the sword is preparation for death. Montaigne, crediting Cicero, says in his essay "That to Think as a Philosopher Is to Learn to Die" says,

> Foreknowledge of death is foreknowledge of liberty. He who has learned to die has unlearned servitude. To know how to die frees us from all subjection and compulsion. There is nothing evil in life for him who clearly understands that the loss of life is not an evil.

Montaigne admonishes the reader to train his soul and educate her to meet the force of the adversary of death.

The fencer is always an actor. He has the power to impose his will, but there still is the question of how to live one's life. Hamlet in his famous "To be or not to be" soliloquy ponders the struggle of mortality and man's natural fear of death. Is it better to bear the grief and suffering of life — "outrageous fortune" — or are we to take action to improve our existence by fighting against our miserable life? Hamlet knows that he could take the dagger into his own hands by slaying his mother's murderer, effectively obliterating the passionate desire of a soul burning for revenge. He fears death — that "undiscovered country" — as well as the potential penalty of an agonizing hell as God's retribution for murder.

Because the swordsman, the actor, has the power to command, rule, and dole out death, he must ask himself the question of how he will exercise his power. With the world offered on a platter, the will to a corrupt and decadent rule is a sweet dish easily tasted. This is the story of Anakin and Luke — both swordsmen with the power to shape the universe with the lightsaber. Will their rule be one of the good life or that of the corrupt and evil life? The lightsaber is the tool at their disposal, but in the end it is the heart and soul that is an even more powerful force.

As Anakin falls to the Dark Side of the Force, his hate and anger lead him along a path that brings order to the universe but at the price of liberty and freedom. In his quest to make himself even more powerful, Vader then embraces the potential of his son who is both powerful and innocent. Luke knows of the destructiveness of the Dark Side of the Force, but can he resist his father's temptation? While Anakin is the Chosen One who will bring balance to the Force, Luke is a "new hope" who harbors a burning faith in the goodness of his father. It is the son who will release the father from the slavery of wielding power with a lightsaber in hand.

In their climactic battle in *Return of the Jedi*, Luke defeats Vader with the lightsaber, a weapon that brought Vader to the height of his glory. Seeing the reflection of himself in the dismembered stump of his father's hand, Luke realizes that he was on the edge of becoming his father. Suddenly the meaning of the test on Dagobah when he defeated the phantom Vader becomes clear. It is a test about our life behind masks; masks which, according to Montaigne, scares innocent children. Luke is no longer the child, and at the moment of his father's death, he removes the mask Anakin has worn since his fateful transformation into Vader. Montaigne continues:

We must remove the mask from things as from persons. When it is removed, we shall find underneath only the self-same death that a man-servant or mere chambermaid met but now without fear.

There is no longer any romantic notion of the sword, for when Luke sees his father's face for the first time there is solace in his soul. The lightsaber loses all value, for naked before Luke's eyes, Anakin has defeated death and can face it fearlessly. If

Anakin can conquer death, to which all men are utterly defenseless, Luke, too, can begin to live life unfettered by a reliance on the lightsaber. He can face life as Anakin faced death — without fear.

Chapter

3

Nature of the Sword

Three characteristics distinguish the manner in which the sword can be used as an effective weapon: 1) the sword must hit its target either as a slash or a thrust, 2) the blade must penetrate to do physical damage, and 3) the swordsman needs enough physical space in which to wield his weapon. Similarly, the lightsaber, owing its unquestionable inspiration from the sword, can be better understood and appreciated when seen in the context of real fighting experience, which goes much farther than a simple slash, thrust, and draw.

Indeed, the plain simplicity of the sword belies a complexity that even the general historian often fails to understand. Instead of focusing on the sword's interaction with defensive armor and the military culture that trained soldiers in the art of swordsmanship, curators and hoplologists alike endlessly emphasize the evolution of the hilt and the blade or the sword's role in courtly fashion as parade and dress accessories. What is needed, however, (and is of more interest to the general reader) is a discussion on how the physical properties of the sword affected the manner in which the swordsman fought.

On both the dueling green and battlefield, the sword is the weapon *par excellence* employed by pre-explosive societies. No matter the person's height, weight, and age, the sword serves as an equalizer without rival. Strength matters less than skill, and experience easily outperforms the vim and vigor of the young man or woman who joins the ranks of the sword armed soldiery. And while individual and natural talent seem to receive the lion's share of attention, common drilling and regular practice create better swordsmen than natural talent or ability alone. In the hands of an exceptional swordsman, honed skill can be manipulated in any number of ways to inflict a slight graze of the skin, a non-lethal penetration of a limb, the deadly pierce of the torso, or the sanguinary chopping of a limb. Though most literary portrayals of the sword shine light on the individual hero's use of the sword, the true heroic skill of the swordsman was its basic and coordinated use at the front of the battle line.

Physical Properties of the Sword

Function Defines Form

The sword's shape, length, size, weight, and edge both allow and limit the sword's utility. Recognizing the need for a cutting instrument, the basic shape of a blade with a handle — a knife — was developed tens of thousands of years ago. Extending the knife by tying it to a long shaft — a spear — gave the additional distance between the hunter and its prey. It also gave the blade an added grip, allowing even greater reach when thrown. With the need for a simple hand-to-hand weapon to be used against other humans in war, the extension of the knife blade into a sword was a natural development. Not only could it inflict considerable damage to flesh, but the severe trauma of a laceration had a more potent psychological advantage than clubbing with a blunt weapon. And unlike the spear or bow, the sword could be used without limit until it broke.

The invention of the sword was no feat of cleverness, but elements of its design and construction were often extremely sophisticated examples of creativity, if not outright genius. The search for unbreakability, rigidity, and cutting power in a blade led to a variety of forging techniques that attempted to blend the best balance of these three universal qualities. A good sword should not snap when used against flesh and bone, and should hold together when striking hard surfaces — an enemy blade, metal armor, a steel or wooden shield. It needed both rigidity to hold its shape and the ability to flex or bend with the pressure of thrusts and slashes. Finally, the sword's cutting power depends on the blade's ability to hold its edge while the cut or strike cleaved into its target, which included toughened leather, the fabric of metal rings, and plate armor.

As armor evolved, so too did the sword, developing into more specialized shapes which allowed more effective penetration. Specialization, however, tended to weaken the overall strength of the sword, leaving it less capable against certain types of armor or fencing styles. Because the swordsman relied so heavily on the sword, a stronger all-purpose sword was more desirable than a specialized weapon. This explains the relatively long history for the simple double-edged sword and the sabre. Its basic shape would dominate swordsmanship until the cultural requirement of courtly fashion and the development of thrusting styles of sword play led to the lighter, faster moving small swords.

The development and evolution of a weapon like the sword did not occur in such logical steps, however, and was influenced by external factors such as available materials, group organization, and a tribe or village's cultural and scientific development. A severe climate and threat of incursions from hostile neighbors propelled successful tribes into a more disciplined, belligerent, and/or military existence. Survival depended on securing food, sheltering against the weather, and defending one's territory, even if it only amounted to the space of one's encampment. Not all cultures developed and used the sword, but like the wheel, its universal simplicity made it an invention that transcended cultures around the globe.

The typical medieval footman of Europe carried a small falchion that was suitable for hand-to-hand combat. Knights carried the long sword with a strong point that could be employed only by the best of swordsmen, as did the typical Chinese warrior. Many nomadic tribes of Asia employed the curved sabre as their preference because of its crescent shape, as did Japan which is of course known for its curve shape of the *tachi* and *katana*.

While there are examples of cultures which used the straight blade, mounted warriors often chose the sabre as their principal weapon because of its easier use in the slash and draw. Mongols, Huns, and Persians, preferred the curved sabre, as did many European cavalry troops like the Cossacks and Hussars whose curved swords would be later adopted by French, British, and even American cavalry.

In the case of the lightsaber, the development of a focused energy source capable of deflecting blaster fire, the principle weapon the *Star Wars* universe, was a technological feat that has remained unchanged apparently for millennia. It was inevitable that a sword of this kind would become relegated to the hands of a few elites because it followed the same patterns of evolution that marked the sword on Earth.

Before the gun, extensive training was required of any weapon. Swordsmen had to be drilled endlessly by experienced swordsmen, and many saw barracks training as considerably less instructive than an actual battle. Only a dedicated soldiery would have the time to devote to the military skill of swordsmanship because it imitated no other civilian job. Even the bow, the first democratic weapon for the masses, required extensive training. Laws in England forbade the practice of any weapon on Sunday other than the long bow to encourage and develop training in bow & arrow marksmanship. And even in the constricted cities like Venice and Genoa, open plazas were often reserved for crossbow practice.

In a universe where even the least technologically sophisticated societies could get their hands on the blaster, only the specialized and disciplined training of a group of warriors like the Jedi could develop the skills to effectively wield their light sword against blaster fire. Were the steel sword able to deflect the slug of a bullet, there is no doubt that the sword would have remained an essential weapon today as the lightsaber does in the *Star Wars* universe.

Construction

The construction of a metal sword was a combination of combining metals and then forming the blade into its shape. Early techniques consisted of a simple process of hammering metals together to shape it into a blade. Later techniques combined metals in a molten process and then pouring its liquid form into a metal cast. Smiths using this casting technique could manufacture many more weapons than in a hammering process and achieved a high degree of consistency in the qualities of their products. Cast metal, however, because of its high degree of homogeneous content, does not fully meet the needs of the exceptional blade.

A rigid blade may give strength to the sword, but it also leaves it susceptible to shattering or chipping when pushed to its integral limits. Too soft a blade allows the blade to bend under stress but it quickly dulls. The answer to these seemingly exclusive qualities was to combine soft metals with harder metals. Bronze is a combination of copper and tin, and can be formed and shaped by either cold or hot pounding, a process called deforming. Iron is a tough material, but when shaped into a sword it had a propensity to bend. Steel, a combination of iron and carbon, was too brittle and was prone to snapping when stressed. The logical step, then, was to combine the steel and iron in a forging technique called pattern welding, which produced a strong and durable weapon.

An alternative to pattern welding, which was a physically demanding process of hammering and folding, was the development of wootz steel, most commonly referred to as Damascus steel. The process was developed in India, though its use was quickly spread by nomadic conquests throughout Asia and westward into the Middle East and North Africa. Because Damascus was one of the centers of Islamic culture which depended heavily on the production of bladed weapons, the city became synonymous with weapons of exceptional quality. While still requiring hammering, wootz steel gets its strength during the solidification process of the steel which creates a patterned effect that is characteristic of Damascus blades. It does not, however, have the toughness of pattern welded blades, but does keep a very sharp edge.

Blades from Japan provide probably one of the best examples in weapon forging techniques. Not only do they have exceptional durability and utility on the battlefield, but the sword's status among Japanese crafts is regarded equally as art. A complex nomenclature and plethora of foundry histories in Japan speaks to the quality of sword making in that country. Blade making in Japan is a ritualized activity which takes on the trappings of an outward religious expression. Purification rituals from Shinto origin are part of the sword making process, as are the traditional garbs of the most illustrious blade making families.

Japanese blade makers responded to the necessity of both a rigidity and resilience by creating a blade with a soft core (which allows the blade to flex) surrounded by an outer skin that holds an edge of exceptional sharpness. The secret to its strength is the process of manufacture which consists of hammering down the steel and folding it back over itself, creating an exponential number of microscopic steel layers that give the steel extreme resilience. Folding a billet of steel ten times resulted in over a thousand laminations, and it was not unusual for a blade a quarter of an inch in thickness to consist of more than a million laminates. Since weapons of such quality demanded such intense labor, it became the custom of families to hand down their weapons to succeeding generations as venerated family treasures. Even today there is an etiquette in the appreciation of a samurai blade when a family heirloom is shown to a visitor.

It is not at all defined how the lightsaber as a technological discovery occurred, though much has been said and made up about its inner mechanisms. Arguments abound: Does the "light" of the blade have the physical properties of light? Does the blade radiate heat? Is the "light" of the blade really plasma? What inner mechanisms power the lightsaber? All of these questions (and others) do have an impact on the definitive properties

of the light blade, but such scientific minutia affect the understanding of the lightsaber in only a minor way for the purposes
of this book. Instead of going into the science of the lightsaber,
it is sufficient to examine the weapon's outward properties as
found in the actual *Star Wars* movies.*

While there is a tendency among fantasy writers in the *Star
Wars* Expanded Universe to mystify the lightsaber as some discovery of a Force-powerful-Jedi, two basic possibilities seem
more likely. The first posits that the technology of the lightsaber
was developed serendipitously during the invention of some
other "light-dependent" experimentation. Perhaps in the search
for a new kind of laser to quarry stone or cut metal the lightsaber
"blade" was discovered. The second is that scientists early in Jedi
history sought the invention of a laser deflecting substance to
replace their metal swords. Die-hard Expanded Universe enthusiasts will reject these theses, arguing that the lightsaber owes its
invention to the ancient Jedi and Sith from the Dark Horse
graphic novels, which shows early lightsabers as attached by a
cable to an energy pack carried on the torso. The scientific leap,
however, to "light energy weapons" without first developing a
sword from the mundane material of metals seems utterly
preposterous.

One interesting conundrum is the manufacture of lightsaber
in *Star Wars*. Based on the single line in *Return of the Jedi* —
Vader: "I see you have constructed a new lightsaber. Your skills
are complete." — the Lucasfilm franchise, with the impetus of
contracted authors, has established the custom that a Jedi, in
order to become a Jedi, must "master" the Force by creating his
or her own lightsaber.

While circumstances necessitated Luke's need to create his
own lightsaber when he lost his first during the duel with Vader

---

*Readers interested in scientific analysis of the lightsaber are
directed to Robert Brown's lightsabre website (http://www.synicon.
com.au/sw/ls/sabres.htm#intro) and Jeanne Cavelos's *The Science of
Star Wars* (St. Martin's Press, 1999).

on Bespin, it is hard to believe that he created it singly on his own without the help of others. While Luke seems quite capable of handling the maintenance of droid and skyhopper repair, it seems far-fetched that Luke never consulted with physicists or metallurgical experts in his desire to create his own lightsaber. Yet for lack of a better explanation, magical events and mystical experiences are used to explain lightsaber technology. The recent book *Jedi Quest** sidesteps the question altogether when Anakin "unconsciously" constructs his lightsaber during a vision about the threatening Darth Maul.

While this theory is quite in line with a school of thought that says a Jedi must be so versed in his lightsaber that he is required to create one on his own, a less romantic and plausible notion is that Luke did seek the advice, help, and skill of others to help him fashion what most citizens of the galaxy might consider an antiquated weapon. Certainly the lightsaber cannot, in theory, fight the blast of a plasma concussion grenade, but its quaint usefulness is as relevant in a firefight with blasters as a bootstrap knife would be in the hands of a Delta force member or SAS operative in a hand-to-hand combat situation scouting the interior of a building.

Without contradicting Vader's canon statement from *Return of the Jedi*, "I see you have constructed a new lightsaber. Your skills are complete." Luke could still be responsible for the construction of his own lightsaber, if even by supervising the making of its component pieces and then putting them together on his own. Rather than a clandestine quest for crystals, hard to find metallic fuses, and rare electrical wiring, why not take advantage of the greatest minds and resources available to the Rebel Alliance and its network of sympathizers to create the best possible lightsaber since the extinction of the Jedi order a decade earlier?

In the time of the Jedi, it is hard to believe that every Jedi had

---

*It tells of one of Anakin's adventures at 13, before the events of *Attack of the Clones*.

to scrounge up pieces and parts in order to construct their own lightsaber. Did every Jedi have to reinvent the wheel when it came to the construction of the lightsaber? Did the Jedi temple not have dedicated lightsaber workshops? And were apprentices barred from knighthood if they couldn't construct one? The simple calculation of procuring materials for thousands of Jedi and pre-pubescent students not yet even at the Padawan level requires deliberate thought and inventory. With a weapon as dangerous as the lightsaber where even the slightest miscalculation or absentmindedness could mean the loss of a finger or even a limb, it would seem that the construction of a lightsaber is best left to the manufacture of specialists.

During the opulent and extravagant times of Anakin's youth, the expressed Galactic style of designed regalia in *The Phantom Menace* is that of a craftsman's world. Likewise, in our own Terran history, while blades may have been stamped out in presses for mass consumption, aristocratic swords were considered a necessary accessory to the gentleman's ensemble. It was paramount to have a sword that both functioned and demonstrated an elegance for courtly and parade situations. Weapons had to have an aesthetic design that impressed one's friends *and* adversaries of the culture and richness of the sword wearer. So too for the Jedi swordsman who was a regular visitor to the courts and governments of the Galactic Republic.

Function Follows Form

Shape Relates to Slice, Chop, & Thrust

Apart from the construction of the blade, a great deal of sophistication was devoted to shaping the blade and adorning it with decoration. On a practical level, the shape of the blade had an impact on the cutting, slicing, and chopping power of the blade, as did the point which allowed the tip of the weapon to become a useful part of the sword.

Swords are generally divided into curved and straight edged blades. Straight edges are of simplest manufacture and are found throughout the world from Asia, especially China, Europe, and Africa. Curved swords are the staple of many cultures, including India, Persia, and the Islamic lands of North African and the Middle East. On a cultural note, the religions of Christianity and Islam have had a deep effect on the shapes of their swords. Christians preferred the cruciform weapon which echoed the shape of the cross on which Jesus died, while the scimitar imitated the crescent shape that is sacred to Muslim iconography. Even today competitive Western fencing begins with a salute that imitates the Christian kissing his blade before battle.

The shape of the sword has a subtle impact on the effective cutting power of the weapon. And depending on the skill of the sword wielder, its cutting effectiveness could be used to greater efficiency. If a sword is balanced properly, the proper striking edge of the sword, called the center of percussion, is found a little above the center of the blade toward the sword tip. When a blade strikes a target at this point, there is no jar during collision, effectively permitting an efficient cut that uses the weight of the sword, added momentum from the swing of the arm, and the slicing action of the blade.

Properly speaking, there are two kinds of cuts that are impacted by the shape of the blade — the chop and the slice.

The chop is the cut of a blade directly perpendicular to the target, usually made by a straight blade. The blade touches the outer skin, pushing it downward until it braces against bone. The elastic nature of skin spreads until the epidermis breaks along the line of the sword's edge. If there is enough force, the edge smashes through bone (and possibly through to the other side of the appendage) or lodges itself into the flesh or bone.

The slice can be achieved by both the straight and the curved blade, though it is more easily achieved by the latter. A slice is made when an edged blade tears into the skin at an angle, pulling or pushing at the flesh and ripping into the epidermis. The pull of the flesh in the downward slope is enhanced by a curved blade, but most straight blades, because of the angle created from a dropping arm, pull naturally toward the swordsman's body, slicing into flesh, though not as easily as with a curved blade.

Generally a blade edge is straight (i.e. it is not serrated) and follows the curve of the sword so that the width of the sword remains constant along the length before tapering off at the tip in either a point or a flat, though often rounded end. Most swords are distinguished by the shape of the flat of the blade. A straight edge cuts with greater facility though, as has already been mentioned, the cut is really the microscopic tearing of the skin.

Serrated edges have also been used, very often for aesthetic effects of an undulating or wavy appearance. Blades of this kind are not generally as effective as a straight edge because the ridges tend to impede the slice because of its added friction. The wavy edge of the flamberge, which takes its name from the French root for fire, is a huge two-handed sword, some five to six feet in height, and is carried without a scabbard upright as if like a rifle on the shoulder. When used in battle the rounded notches prevented the blade from digging into the wooden hafts of pikes, slightly preventing them from sliding down the length of the blade toward the wielder. This type of wavy edge has a very pleasing aspect and can be seen on many dirks and daggers which relied less on serration than thrusts. The kris is an excellent example of a serrated stabbing knife.

The second use of the sword in attacking is to thrust. While modern styles of fencing seem to emphasize the thrust in its extreme, the use of the point has always been an effective way of attacking an opponent. Armor has always been the primary means of thwarting a slash, but no armor short of a sealed box is immune from penetration. The thrust into the joints of an opponent's armor has, therefore, become a secondary method of attack. Attacks to the arms or legs will immobilize the appendage (the muscles, ligaments, or tendons will rendered the muscles too weak to carry on the battle) while attacks to the torso will result in a soft kill if it does not hit a vital organ.

The lightsaber has particular qualities which seem to depend more on technical requirements of film that reflect a "common sense" approach to lightsaber characteristics than they do on a reliance to any scientific properties of the physical world.

In the Original Trilogy, the lightsaber was used against two living beings (the Walrus Man and Luke) and a host of metal objects, including Darth Vader's armor and right hand. In the first case, there was no cauterization as evident from the blood spread around the arm's socket joint. In *The Empire Strikes Back*, Luke's hand is burned cleanly, sealing body fluids behind a cauterized stump. In the case of objects, the lightsaber seems to burn into metal with a blinding flash and a burning cut. In all instances, the lightsaber, while it is said to penetrate "almost any substance," depends on inertia to penetrate into harder substances. Following an expectation of common sense, slicing through biological material is far easier than cutting through metal, which hinders the lightsaber blade with visible resistance. Vader's shoulder plate also demonstrates a resistance to the lightsaber blade or else it would have unremarkably cut to Vader's neck.

Lightsaber fights in *The Phantom Menace* provide a new set of circumstances under which lightsaber scenes were filmed. The lightsaber was used twice against living beings, as well as a host of metal objects (primarily Trade Federation battle droids and the blast doors of the Trade Federation Control Ship bridge) which are penetrated without any resistance at all. It was as if the lightsaber sliced through thin air, which was, in actuality the very case. The lightsaber scenes were in reality blue screen fights in which Neeson and McGregor wielded lightsaber props with short flourescent stumps which served as guides to Industrial Light and Magic (ILM) animators who digitally created all of the Trade Federation droids. In the case of lightsaber fights, the lightsaber cuts through flesh and metal with the same cutting power.

When used against Qui-Gon at the end of *The Phantom Menace*, Darth Maul's double-bladed lightsaber pierces through the Jedi's chest cavity without any visible resistance. In addition, there is no visible flesh pushed out against Qui-Gon's back, which implies that his flesh is "burned up" when the lightsaber rammed through Qui-Gon's chest. Were this the real world, Qui-Gon probably would have died instantly because his spinal cord would have been too severely traumatized to allow the body to continue functioning. It is a movie, so Lucas is allowed as much creative license as he needs to carry out his story. It is certain that the Prequel Trilogy will provide a host of new footage on which to further explore the physical characteristics of the lightsaber.

Sword Length & Weight

There is, at least in principle, an ideal sword length for each individual. But since swords were not generally constructed with a particular individual in mind, it was difficult to find the "perfect" sword. Standardization also meant a universal design to which the individual had to adapt himself.

The ideal sword was also affected by the purpose and use of the weapon in question. While swords can be quite short, the Roman *gladius* measuring twenty inches typically, there is no firm measure that technically separates a sword from a dirk, dagger, or knife. Shorter bladed weapons usually derive their name by the style of design which was generally associated with its use. The knife was meant for short range cutting, mostly as a utility tool. Daggers and dirks were meant for stabbing at close distance, the latter have a more streamline and light shape. Shorter weapons like the medieval falchion were good basic weapons for close infighting. One can easily imagine the difficultly trying to swing a weapon at the initial clash of the line. The short sword clearly has an advantage. While it does not have the same slashing power of a longer weapon, the clashing lineman's weapon is best used for quick thrusts at weak points in his opponent's armor. The Roman gladius works extremely well precisely because its size allowed legionaries to use their swords in such close quarters.

Longer swords, unless they reach too absurd a length, are generally classified in the same category. Variants are more easily set apart by their manner of grip than by blade length. The hand-and-a-half sword, more commonly known as the bastard sword, is therefore distinguished from the full length two-handed sword, of which, the claymore and flamberge are prime examples.

The success of an attack depends essentially on the ability to reach the target. Added length accords the swordsman a slight advantage over the inferior sword (especially to the knight), and adds weight which contributes to the strength of the blow. A simple rule follows that no matter the distance — whether a millimeter or a mile — if the sword is out of range, it can inflict no damage. Short swords therefore have a slight disadvantage against long swordsmen while suffering a notable disadvantage against mounted horsemen. On the other side, there is a gain in lightness, maneuverability, better balance, and certain advantage in phalanx warfare with a short sword.

The weight of a sword, because of the pull of gravity, contributes to the cutting power of the sword; but with added weight also comes the possibility of increased fatigue more quickly. Certainly the size of the person in relation to the size of the sword, as well as his manner of gripping the weapon — whether one or two handed — affects the relative power to a blow. Unequal men do not employ equal swords in equal manner.

The length and weight of sword is usually designed by a matter of personal preference, but limits on resources, availability of iron ore in particular, affects the manufacture of swords. Simple math shows for every inch in added length to a series of equal swords results in a decrease number of total swords if supplies are limited. An interesting example is Darth Maul's double-bladed lightsaber which has no Terran precedent. Were double-bladed swords to be manufactured in vast quantities, it would presuppose a greater fighting distance between swordsmen because the two ends are equally dangerous to friendly forces as to foes. Similarly, the gain in creating double-bladed swords would necessitate half as many traditional, single-bladed swords. On top of this, at least twice the effort and training would be necessary to learn the double-bladed sword. Of course, it is because of these characteristics that the double-bladed light-saber is ideally suited to the one-man Sith Lord.

Weight, as well as the size of the hilt, also has a tangible bearing on whether a sword is held with one or two hands. If a larger sword is to be employed, increased strength and more specialized technique is required by the person of a smaller stature.

Grip and weight also has bearing on a sword's manner of use. Two-handed swords cannot be effectively used on horses for practical reasons; one hand might be used to control his mount, or, with advanced horse riding skills, the extra hand is used to hold a shield, to brace one's self against the horse for added reach, or to simply act as a counter balance to the stroke of the one-handed slash.

The use of centrifugal force is also paramount to the sophisticated technical use of the sword. Again dependant on the weight of the sword, cutting power can be further enhanced by the controlled "throwing" of the sword toward the target. The sword, if held strongly enough to keep in the grip of the hand and lightly enough to allow for the subtle downward swing of the wrist at the end of a slash, can greatly magnify the speed of the sword. Combined with a quick squeeze just before impact, the slash receives a substantial increase in velocity.

The principle is the same as launching a stone from a sling. By swinging the sling around the head until a comfortable speed is attained, the slinger releases one of the two ends, sending the missile in a straight but descending line toward its target. Timing and the proper technical release of the first string is of utmost importance, else the stone will completely miss or will fall harmlessly to the ground short of its target. Where the consequences of improper technique are evident in the sling, the proper strike of the sword with maximum potential force is equally difficult. If the sword hits to early, an increase in percussion (a jarring) of the cut will hamper the smooth execution of the cut. A strike too late decreases the power of the cut.

Another important consideration is the psychological importance of a substantive weight to the sword, which gives the wielder important feedback as he draws his weapon back for another strike. If a slash feels too light, the wielder is less likely to feel capable of inflicting the maximum potential damage; too heavy a feel will cause him to feel slow and sluggish in the execution of the attack. This poses an interesting problem for the lightsaber wielder.

By all common sense standards, the lightsaber has neither the weight of a steel sword, nor the balance of one. It would then follow that there is less cutting power and a stilted point of percussion in a light energy blade. Since we cannot measure the scientific nature of the lightsaber, observers are forced to make assumptions that may or may not fit with the "reality" of the *Star Wars* universe.

From a swordsman's perspective, the reality is that the lightsaber is simply a Terran sword doctored up by rotoscoping to create the shimmering effect. The lightsabers created by the prop department were made out of light metal or perhaps fiberglass, which means that all movement will be substantially faster than if a person were using a real sword. The weight of an attack will therefore be much lighter than that of a solid metal sword. Since there is no reasonable standard for lightsaber swordsmanship, the stunt coordinator is generally given free reign to create a fencing style that seems plausible to a sword illiterate society. Probably Lucas' best decision in creating a realistic lightsaber fight was the hiring of martial artist Ray Park. He took the choreography and gave it the appearance of believable lightsaber fighting. By knowing the technicalities of real sword fighting, Park was able to successfully teach Neeson and McGregor a true feeling of the sword fight.

Guarding

While the task of protecting the body is generally left to armor and shield, the sword can be used to parry a slash or thrust, serving as effectively as if wearing armor. Indeed, the name given to modern sword play — fencing — conveys the defensive purpose to which the sword can and was often used.

When the sword blade is used as a guard, the blow of an enemy strike had to be absorbed with either the flat of the blade, or, in the case of a sabre, with the back side of the blade.* Some sabres had a cutting edge up half of the back side of the blade, while the traditional long or broad sword had a sharp blade running along both sides of the weapon. The Japanese katana is a good example of a single bladed edge with a strong blunted backside, while many European sabres had a sharp edge along only half of the backside. The styles and variations were numerous and reflect mostly traditional (and often arbitrary) customs of the fighting corps which used the weapon, but in all cases a clash of edge on edge had to be avoided in order to prevent chipping the blade. And while a slightly flattened edge could be sharped with ease, there was little that could be done to fix the jagged teeth of a severely chipped edge. With a sabre, the blunted edge could be used to "catch" the slash of an enemy strike. The only option with a two-edged sword was to use the flat of the blade.

Giving additional protection to the hand was a crossguard. Simple at first, many hand guards later developed into a sophisticated and ornate form of hand protection. Rapiers (a point and slash sword) and broad swords (a straight sword) were increasingly affixed with more protective sword guards, giving protection against the thin-bladed point of a small sword. Others were characterized by the simple extension of prongs that wrapped around the fingers. Cup-hilt rapiers and basket-hilt sabres are the best examples of the sword guards which completely

---

*Of stylistic note is the manner in which theatrical fencing is taught with a double-edged sword. Since, for the sake of safety, the quality of theatrical weapons should always be considered suspect, a guard parry should always be received with the edge of the blade so that the force is absorbed by the strength of the steel. A strike on the flat may stress the blade so much that the defending sword might break in half from a strong slash. Since the theatrical edge is never sharpened, there is little worry about chipping an edge.

protected the hand. Only the Turkish yataghan and Russian shashqa dispensed with the guard altogether, giving particular emphasis to the offensive nature of the sword.

Especially from watching the clean cuts, parries, and counter attacks (technically called a riposte) in movies and theater, the general audience is apt to think that the reliance on the sword blade as a guard is an essential and preferred manner of using the sword. Reinforcing this is the Jedi use of the lightsaber in *The Phantom Menace* as a shield against blaster fire, which demonstrates an exceptional degree of control (especially when turning laser bolts back on its shooter). Unfortunately for the swordsman, too much reliance on defense is a fencer's greatest fault.

If a swordsman never attacks, he can never win the encounter. And by allowing the opponent to keep the initiative, it becomes increasingly likely that the attacker will find an opening in his opponent's defensive blocks. A swordsman can only block one part of the body, which gives the attacker several open areas to which he can strike. Mathematically, the probability that the defending fencer can choose the correct block diminishes with each attack because defense requires more energy and physical strength than an attack.

If a parry or a block is to be made, it must be followed by an immediate attack called a riposte. It may be an immediate attack involving speed, or it may be slightly delayed, which causes the attacker-turned-defender to move prematurely into his own counter defense. When pressed by a strong attacker, the fencer has no choice but to begin a slow retreat in order to maintain proper fencing distance. When there is no room for retreat, the initiative moves completely to the attacker who can attack or feint at the moment of his own choosing.

In *Return of the Jedi*, Luke demonstrates the necessity to attack during the fight scene over the Sarlacc pit. When faced against a host of attackers from every direction, Luke follows a basic rule of engagement that there is a better chance of survival by attacking than by waiting defensively for opponents to attack. By bringing the fight to his attackers, Luke prevents Jabba's henchmen from mounting a concerted effort against the young Jedi.

Qui-Gon and Obi-Wan in the opening scenes of *The Phantom Menace*, demonstrate the need to cut their losses to avoid defeat by retreating from the advancing droidekas. Knowing that every moment defending against the first two destroyer droids, the two Jedi must make a hasty retreat in order to save their own lives. Darth Maul, just after he is forced into the power generator area, makes a strategic retreat in order to get better position against his two adversaries. Retreat, for the sake of retreat; defense, for the sake of defense, without the strategic purpose of gaining better offensive position is a doomed enterprise.

Once the layman understands these basic characteristics of the blade, his logical tendency is immediately to find the sword that best provides the maximum slicing or thrusting power. Such a quest is a useless exercise, for no single blade achieves any specialization without admitting some area of weakness. A two-handed sword will be more effective than against an armored opponent, but the advantage of his weapon evaporates when confronting a nimbler opponent with a lighter rapier.

What serves the swordsman better than any particular blade and its specialization is his skill to adapt to the strengths and weakness of the sword in hand, the protective armor of his opponent, and developing a strategy to exploit the weaknesses of his enemy. Even if one were to find the perfectly balanced weapon with exactly the correct weight and center of percussion, one must never exclude the possibility that the sword might be broken or lost during the melee. More than in any other situation, attachment to one's weapon is an invitation to the devil's doorstep. It is not the sword that wins. It is the swordsman who must win.

Battle

While swordsmen of the dueling days of the Renaissance fought on roughly equal terms, soldiers of the battlefield confronted gross inequalities. Unless a ruler had the power and resources to fully arm his troops, the weapons, armor, and training of melee combatants varied as much within one army as it did between armies. In the duel, the spirit of a level playing field between gentlemen assured that if one used a small sword, the other did as well; if one used armor, so too did his opposite. On the battlefield, however, troops very often armed themselves as well as they could afford or as well as inventories lasted.

When armies opposed each other on the battlefield before the general use of arquebus or musket, the victor was not necessarily the commander with numerical superiority, nor superior weapons. Apart from demoralizing enemy troops with a show of superior troops, victory would go to the commander who could mate superior troops against weaker troops while minimizing or maintaining the strength, position, and moral of the weakest units.

The battle line was designed to be fought on uneven terms, the commander sacrificing one advantage for a weakness in hope that his combination of tactical lines will be strong enough to break and sever the lines of his opponent. Opening volleys of arrow, crossbow, or spear were meant to loosen up the lines, while advancing troops — spearmen, swordsmen, or cavalry — would deliberately advance until the final moments when troops from each side would increase their speed toward their enemies hoping that their momentum would quickly break the enemy rank. Footmen would continue the push against their enemies, while elite troops, usually mounted knights or cavalry, would be advanced to critical points of weakness in the enemy line. When one side's morale breaks, soldiers will begin to think more of their own lives than that of their comrades. Once the rout has begun, there is little that can stop the victor other than his own exhaustion.

The greatest fear of any warrior was the open wound from a piercing weapon. With blades brandished in hands and the shine of the edge glinting in the sun, one of the greatest obstacles in hand-to-hand combat was the fear of exposing one's flesh to an opponent's weapon while at the same time trying to inflict similar damage on an opponent. Especially for soldiers with little or no experience or practice with a weapon, sword combat is a competition of firsts in which one must dispatch the enemy before he can receive an injury.

Preparation ahead of battle by donning the passive protection of armor is a reassurance against the solid blow. But no armor gives maximum protection. Rather, armor's purpose is to give the warrior the chance to deal a decisive blow to one's opponent without being first incapacitated.

Unlike ranged weapons, which prevent face to face exchange of arms, the use of armor in battle has never been considered a dishonorable practice. And where improvements in weapons, such as the superiority of the longbow against chain mail and the crossbow against plate mail, have generally been acknowledged as technological advances which gave victory to one side, the effects of superior armor is rarely acknowledged. Documenting the effectiveness of armor is extremely difficult since no living historian has ever observed with a scientist's eye the chaotic exchange of battlefield sword tactics. Indeed, half of the historian's difficulty is objectively picking through historical accounts and observations in an area where heroic and literary valor take first place to accurate reporting.

The effectiveness of armor can be partially examined by looking at the evolution of weapons as counter measures to armor. Only in the rare battle did armor so completely fail that victory was lost because of it. Even in the famed battle of Agincourt wherein French knights were decimated by English longbow arrow, more blame can be put on the knights who massed themselves so close together that they had little mobility to defend against enemy arrows by spreading out.

Often, more than not, victory or defeat is generally given to troops with the stronger force of will or superior tactics. For Swiss soldiers who clashed with equally armed and trained Imperial landsknecht, victory was determined by those whose determination and iron will was greater. So contemptuous where the Swiss and Germans for each other that both refused to accept surrender from the other. The result were massive casualties from the initial clash, and the determined slaughter of losing troops who refused to surrender. So devastating were such clashes between the Swiss and German landsknecht, that commanders on both sides hesitated to commit their troops to such ill-ending exchanges unless absolutely necessary.

For elite troops, reputation has an unerring positive affect on morale. Not that such troops were unbeatable, but that they fought with the audacity that they were invincible. Zealous and fanatical, the mere mention of their advance has been known to have a chilling effect on troops preparing to meet them in battle. Not only did the Spartan reputation caused fear in the ranks of other Greeks during ancient times, many accounts mention the devastating effect the appearance of the scarlet capes of the Spartans had on morale on troops just about ready to meet them in battle. Even in modern times, stories were told that many Argentine troops in the Falkland War were want to flee upon hearing that Gurkha units were advancing.

Examples of superior tactics abound and need little illustration here, but it becomes clear that apart from the morale and experience of one's troops, battlefield success is generally considered a function of strategic planning and execution — the proper composition of soldiers placed in the proper formation followed by the proper execution of attacks.

Every line of men was generally imbued with certain distinction that were used to exploit the weakness of an opponent army. Spear and pike men held lines against cavalry. Long bow threatened mailed knights at a distance. Crossbows could penetrate plate mail, while cavalry decimated lightly armed bowmen and crossbow at close range. Expert generals could arrange these formations to best exploit the weakness of enemy troops.

Like a game of chess, certain formations may have been used to hold the main force, or even be sacrificed, in order to allow troops elsewhere to penetrate a weakness in the enemy line. Cavalry was a highly mobile shock force, while range weapons of spear, arrow, and bolt could inflict heavy losses on advancing troops. Later, when the use of the cannon was more fully developed, shot and cannon balls were used to break up highly organized formations. It became imperative that cannon be neutralized, if not taken out completely, before the main lines advanced into their range.

Because battle was a creative enterprise, the successful general was he who made the best use of his strengths, while denying exposure of his weaknesses. The ideal was to command a force far superior in numbers to the enemies, but other considerations also affected the quality of his troops, including how well armed they were, their experience, their *esprit de corps*, and, of course, their armor.

Armor

The availability of armor depended on monetary and material resources, manufacturing capabilities, and quality of craftsmen. And while the bulk of most armies were made of men with relatively limited training, armor did make a difference in units trying to resist better armed troops. Greek soldiers purchased their own armor or took it as a trophy from earlier battles. In medieval Europe, knights were obligated to provide for their own arms and armor, while in the 17th centuries, European monarchies, in particular Gustavus Adolphus, a renowned Swedish king, created one of the first European professional armies that had both standard uniforms and equipment as well as training.

Among the principle benefits of armor is the ability to take an attack without being completely incapacitated. The helmet was basic to every army the world over. Some were complete metal masks while others were a simple wagging feather. Body armor was made of the most rudimentary materials (cloth, wood, studs, leather) to heavier and protective metal (mail, plate).

Helmet

The helmet was an easy form of basic protection for any kind of soldier. It came in a variety of shapes and sizes, and afforded reasonable security at a very inexpensive price. From basic metal caps to elaborate helms, the obvious psychological necessity of protecting the face and head cannot be underemphasized. Whether from thin strips of hammered bronze or forged from thick plates of heavy iron, the helmet was essential protection to the head from either minor lacerations that allowed blood to drip down into one's eyes or from powerful cuts that clove through the skull which meant near instantaneous death.

In the ritualized practice of Japanese sword *kata* (precisely determined practice movement), the strike to the head receives the greatest amount of training. Kata involving the wooden swords called bokken, revolved around basic strikes to the head that stop inches from the forehead. These attacks are not pulled strikes, but actual training with the force necessary to split the skull open. A real cut could, therefore, be made if the threshold of the target were simply lowered a mere three to five inches.

Without the helmet, soldiers would feel exceptionally vulnerable to swords cuts that were quite simply designed to traumatize or impede the vital control functions of the brain, including both its eyes and ears. Consequently, there was always an exchange of protection for the ability to use one's sight and hearing. Flat top helmets protected faces from the sun and allowed clear vision and hearing. Conical helmets were superior to the flat type because it allowed blows to glance off the head, and where they covered the ears, diminished hearing was an unintended consequence of better protection.

Helmets could be worn under or over chain mail. Roman legionary helmets had an pivoting side plate that allowed both protection and unobstructed hearing. Larger helms provided greater protection, especially those with a neck skirt of chainmail called an aventail. Unfortunately, they isolated the ears completely and only permitted forward vision through thin slits. Helms that covered the face entirely had to have ventilation holes for breathing, resulting in the last minute lowering of the helm or visor. Other derivations of the helmet included the sallet which covered the head below the ears and was accompanied by a thick metal throat plate called a bevor.

Headgear is to this day a distinguished feature of every military force. Whether for parade or for combat, any type of head protection, whether a quilted cap, a wrapped turban, or a metal or kevlar helmet is therefore the second most important object to the soldier after an offensive weapon. And even the pageant-like ostrich or eagle feather, horsehair crest, or tri-corn hat served as practical impediment that made the visible outline of the head less obvious. So if a helmet, like a quilted jacket or leather suit can stay the clash to the head for just a second, it acts like armor by giving the defender those extra seconds in which to strike back at his opponent decisively.

Leather Armor

The earliest and most basic form of armor were develop by layering thick fabrics. A slightly better were those made from hides of leather. By layering leather, this relatively cheap form of protection was ideal for northern climates. Such "hide smiths" required neither exceptional ability nor exceptional tools, and could be found anywhere leather workers existed.

Sword blows that did not strike a target squarely could prevent deadly lacerations and allow a counter attack. Added protection in the form of circular rings, studs, or metal bars sewn to the outside of the leather, could further absorb the force of the sword edge by distributing the force of blow to a wider area. But such direct hits could not fully prevent penetrations from sword points. The commitment to a penetrating thrust could be a rather difficult task, however, requiring a strong thrust on target. Such a penetration had to be quick (and painful) if it were to prevent an opponent from the several slashes he might possibly muster as a counter attack. Such thrusts could only be made with sharp points with the force of the body weight to prevent the leather from pushing into the soft fat of the skin, absorbing the thrust without being penetrated. Daggers or dirks certainly prove their usefulness in this kind of situation.

When large numbers of individuals are poorly armored (often the case of individual peasants who have to find their own armor), the protection of the group as a unit suffers greatly. Instead of all members of a line benefitting from the possible second or third chance to slash at their opponent, the enemy is more easily able to dispatch the unprotected man in the front line. The general loss of an additional sword strike was significant when the sight of one man falling had a psychological impact on the three to five men standing around him.

One interesting observation regarding leather armor occurred at a time when the gun began to render the full suit of armor obsolete. Because hand guns and muskets have the penetrative power to pierce through even the thickest suits of plate armor, the cost of acquiring and maintaining such specialized and heavy gear became too expensive a purchase. The answer to the decline of plate armor led to the development of the buff coat, which was essentially a newer version of leather armor which protected against most sword cuts and still gave the swordsman excellent mobility both on and off of a horse.

Combined with high leather boots, the buff coat was a good form of protection to the swordsman at a time when armies were becoming increasingly manned by commoners. National movements such as those during the English Civil War and the French Revolution made the clothing of vast armies a top priority. Blacksmith and the increasingly rarer armorer had neither the supplies nor the expertise to produce metal armor in the numbers required by newly formed national armies which amounted to virtually every male citizen.

Asian armies, and to a lesser extent Middle Eastern armies, also made extensive use of leather armor. Nomadic tribes, especially, made use of the hides when they culled their herds. And early in Japanese history, the leather coat was a regular and easy uniform to produce. Indian armies made extensive use of an overcoat very similar to the aketon. While covering the shoulders down to just below the knees, it provided good protection and extensive mobility.

Scale Mail

A common improvement in leather armor was to attach strips of metal to the exterior much like roof shingles with upper layers overlapping the studs used to attach individual plates of metal to the leather coat. Such armor was called scale mail. It created an impressive and often beautiful outer skin which dissipated the cutting power of a sword by distributing the force over the entire plate, small as it was.

A reversed form of scale mail was the coat of plates, which had iron or steel plates riveted to the inside of a tunic or coat. In such instances, rich and expensive fabrics could be used for a nicer, more fashionable appearance. Coats of plates were usually identified by the series of studs that were obvious on the outside of the jacket. Assyrians, Romans, and later medieval Europeans made use of scale mail, though its use fell into disuse when more protective forms of armor were developed. The Japanese made excellent use of scale mail, though it was made of thin slates of wood on a barrel-shaped skirt.

Hauberk of Chain Mail

The introduction of chain mail, also called a hauberk, added even greater protection against the sword cut. Made of interlocking iron or steel ringlets, an "overgarment" of sorts could be fashioned to cover the head, shoulders, torso, and if length allowed, the groin and upper leg. Mail stockings, called chausses, were also developed in the 13th century Europe to protect the legs, allowing the entire body except for the face to be covered.

Individual armorers fashioned a variety of patterns and shapes for the rings, but always the end result was a coat of metal that provided excellent protection against sword blades and points. It provided relatively good protection against arrow heads at great distances, though at closer range its strength diminished. Since chain mail did not allow arrows to glance off as it did with full body armor, large shields were still widely used with mail during the 11th and 12th centuries among European soldier in Europe and in the Middle East.

Mail armor's biggest drawback was the uneven distribution of the weight on the shoulders. Its weight depended on the construction and length of the armor and typically varied as little as 25 lbs to 35 lbs including the weight of padded undergarments to cushion blows against the skin. Mail worn under a padded tunic called an aketon was somewhat cumbersome (it could weight upwards of 60-70 lbs) and did tax the swordsman's stamina. Still, it was a weight to which the swordsman could easily adapt himself.

While a new set of freshly made chain mail was excellent protection for the swordsman, it did take considerable punishment in combat. Slashes from swords which cut squarely into the mail chipped away at the metal links, allowing subsequent slashes the ability to cut through the corselet of rings. Weather and heat also had detrimental effects on the wearer as well as to the armor. The sun would heat metal making it untouchable with the bare hand. An outer garment, called a surcoat, became a common sight in the 13th century. A surcoat was still little protection against the rust from humidity, rain, poor storage, and even perspiration in the armpit area. Bathing chain mail in a solvent of water and vinegar was one manner of removing the outer layer of rust, but at some point major repairs or the purchase of a new set of mail, after a long campaign, was essential.

Mail did afford the wearer sufficient protection. Combined with a tall shield and movement of the body to reduce the most vulnerable areas, mail was an effective defense which could easily save the wearer's life. As a result, sword cuts had to be made to the unprotected area of the body, which included in early hauberks of mail, the wrist, calves, elbows, and face. Sword cuts, when made directly on the mail, had to be targeted at areas which rested solidly against the body, including the shoulders, upper arm and the thighs. Blows to hanging mail around the neck and at the sides would catch a series of links before the pressure of the sword edge could dig into individual links when it pushed against the body.

If opportunity allowed, thrusts instead of cuts could be made to the face and armpits. Great axes, those used as two-handed weapons (like those of the Vikings and the Saxons at the Battle of Hastings), because of the greater force at the impact of the cutting edge, were even more effective at cutting through mail than a sword. War hammers, with either the small head on one side or the sharp pick on the other, also did considerable damage piercing through mail. Bow and arrow, with its 60 to 80 lbs pull, did considerable damage at close range, while crossbow bolts could easily penetrate mail.

Mail was so simple to design and construct that warriors from Europe to as far east as India and China made regular employ of chain mail according to their own customs and tactics. Saracens employed coats of mail when it was available, as did Turkish and Indian warriors. Its use, however, would not only go out of fashion, but it would be replaced by a more protective cover pieces that would eventually make up the full-body plate mail.

Plate Armor

Plate armor evolved over a period of hundreds of years from developments in technology and the need for increasing protection against superior weapons and battle field tactics. The "invention" of individual parts of what would eventually become a full suit of plate mail, also referred to as a harness, can never be dated precisely.

The individual looking for regularity and consistency in the development of armor will be sorely disappointed. Not only was the use of armor haphazard among national or regional armed forces, personal armor differed greatly within armies as well. And at the heart of the problem is that the development of more sophisticated types of armor did not necessarily indicate its use. It does help to examine arms and armor of European troops in relation to the passing of significant battles in European history.

During the 11th century, around the time of the Norman invasion of England in 1066, mail hauberk was the general form of armor worn by the nobles at the Battle of Hastings. Later, during the Crusades in the 12th century, mail was beginning to see threats from the crossbow which could penetrate mail with greater efficiency. In centuries following, Christians, upon their earliest ventures into the Holy Land, brutally defeated lightly armored and armed Saracen troops. In response, the Muslims learned to avoid direct confrontations, choosing instead to fire arrows into the crusader lines until they were sufficiently softened for a direct attack.

Early in the 13th century additional body protection was developed to be worn over chain mail. Greaves were used to protect the leg; first as padding, then metal plates on the front attached over mail or as studded leather coverings, and finally a complete metal covered leg. Surcoats and gambesons, metal plated overcoats, provided additional protection as well as a fashionable medium for heraldry. It is at this time that elbow protection called couters were strapped to the over the mail on the elbows. Espaulers, or shoulder defenses, also came into use. Because of the addition of new metallic components to armor, the sword too began to evolve into a heavier and more pointed weapon than the shorter and lighter swords of the earlier century.

The 14th century led to the development of full sets of armor. The Battle of Crécy, which marked the fall of the outnumbered French nobility to an army of English made up of mostly long-bowmen, was made up of mostly armored knights wearing coats of plate. Other knights wore older armor, which amounted to plate attachments to hauberk, chausses, and metal forearm guards, while the richest wore complete sets of plate that only exposed the under arm, and insides of the elbow and knees, which were still protected by layers of mail.

It was not long after, in the 16th century, that plate armor began to give way to lighter armor because of the threat from guns. The first reaction was to make armor, especially the chest plates, thicker. Eventually guns made plate armor completely obsolete. Despite noble desires to preserve their monopoly on sword fighting skills, the expense and weight of plate armor became too difficult a burden to bear. Like commoners, noble-men began to arm themselves with handguns and muskets while still preserving their skills with the sword for close combat, which was still frequent for elite cavalry and in skirmishes when lines of musketeers got close enough to charge into each other's ranks. Eventually the sword would be replaced by the bayonet which served as a makeshift pole arm and piercing blade.

As the sword began its decline, only aristocrats and officers kept the tradition of wearing a sword. It became fashionable to wear the sword either as part of civilian dress or either as part of the uniformed soldier who often walked the streets of capital cities. In Japan the use of the sword was worn as an essential part of daily dress until the Meiji Restoration in 1868 when the sword and the samurai topknot were banned during the coun-try's new love affair with Western culture.

It the *Star Wars* universe, the use of armor is quite evident in the uniform of the stormtroopers, as well as in Vader's black cos-tume. Not unlike Japanese helmets and face masks, the storm-trooper and Vader's mask take advantage of the power to shock enemies with their menacing appearances.

The stormtrooper was described as fascist white troops, whose pristine and shiny body armor reflected the precision and discipline of modern armies such as those of the Third Reich. Hitler's SS divisions even had a skeleton patch as a sinister sym-bol of their position and potency. The stormtrooper's mask not only resembles the skull, but his entire body was that of the body's skeleton. Lucas conceived stormtroopers as specialized shock troops who only knew how to move forward. In *Return of the Jedi*, he created the scout troopers as a way to distinguish lesser troops from the elite stormtroopers.

Black uniforms, like those of the Imperial gantry officers in *A New Hope*, had a sinister allure. German Panzer division troops even to this day speak fondly of their uniforms which gave them a sense of superiority over the common civilian as well as among other German troops. Even today the use of the black beret, now common to all American army troops, was once a coveted symbol of the elite rangers. It is no mistake that Darth Vader towers over his own troops in a uniform of formidable and impressive black. Anakin, in his transformation, understands that the spectral use of a fearsome appearance had a psychological affect on those under his command. While modern, democratic soldiers of today's armies scoff at a "leader" who uses fear as a tool to get his men to fall into line, the fear of an officer's appearance and punishments were common practices in most armies. The humiliation of public flogging, running a gauntlet, or decommissioning of an officer were cruel, and often effective forms of disciplining an army made up of unchivalrous and uneducated commoners.

Armor such as those worn by stormtroopers and Boba Fett (as well as Jango Fett and the clone troopers from *Attack of the Clones*) served as effective forms of deflection against blaster fire. Not only might laser beams be deflected, it is possible that they might be specially treated by energy absorbing layers of plastic or paint. While seemingly ineffectual against the heroes of the Original Trilogy, the appearance of shock troops like the stormtroopers were fearsome demonstrations of force not unlike that of Soviet troops who disembarked from massive transport planes at the Kabul airport and quickly seized important roads and buildings in the capital. It is with this kind of modern and efficient invasion that elite commando forces make their appearance in civilian locales.

An interesting enigma is the uniform of the Jedi in *The Phantom Menace*. Keeping with the costumes of Ben Kenobi when he lived in Tatooine, the Jedi of the Republic also wear a similar costume. While one would think that a man like Kenobi hiding from the Empire would wear clothes other than those that would immediately identify him to Imperial troops as a Jedi, Lucas creates a continuity problem by using a costume which is already identified with Obi-Wan the Elder, Yoda, and Anakin at the end of *Return of the Jedi*. You immediately know from their clothes that Qui-Gon and Obi-Wan upon their entry onto the Neimoidian control ship are Jedi.

Early conceptual drawings for the Jedi had a more modern militaristic appearance. Working under the assumption that the Republican Jedi were more of a U.N. para-military force, Jedi uniforms had a sharper more urban appearance that would have suited troops in a capital city than an old reclusive hermit hiding in the Dune Sea. With Anakin's new uniform in *Attack of the Clones*, there is more of an urban and flared appearance to his uniform. Made of leather, the pointy shoulders and the shiny curves of his jacket seem more akin to the Germanic tunic jacket called an ulanka. Luke's black Jedi uniform has a similar more modern appearance, though his color is more reflective of the vicar's black than of a gestapo uniform. Lucas' sixth, and final episode will shed even more light on the evolving role of the Jedi as they fight off an emperor who will wrest control of the universe by destroying the Republic's Jedi guardians.

Battle Formations & Combat

The earliest combat situations were probably little different from a haphazard encounters between rival tribes. But just as quickly there must have been a rapid transformation as bands settled land and become more familiar and want to protect their territories. Tribes may have had direct dealings with nearby tribes or they may have come into conflict as stubborn hardheadedness made men decide to fight for their territory instead of giving it up without a fight.

Even the most tribal cultures of the last five hundred years — pygmies, the indigenous of Easter Island, the Zulu, et al — all demonstrated sophisticated military strategies despite their basic weapons of sword, spear, and blow darts. As culture and societal organization evolved, so too did military forms of organization. When a tribe became large enough to manage troops that numbered into the hundreds, the effectiveness of an organized and disciplined military became apparent. Empires likes those of the Aztecs, the Babylonians, and the Chinese were firmly maintained by the ability to manage large armies that could march out to quell a neighbor or to extend their borders. Battles were no longer mere skirmishes, but sophisticated forms of warfare.

The most basic type of formation is that of lines of men looking across a battlefield toward their enemies. Since the amassing of armies worked poorly in the confines of woods, marshes, or mountains, most battles took place on the foothills or plains where warriors had ample room to exercise movement of men.

"Citizen" warriors (i.e. unprofessional soldiers) were more likely to form themselves into ranks alongside of family or neighborhood friendships. Athenians fought next too family, Scotsmen with their kinsmen, and Perugians with friends from their neighborhood. Professional elites, often aristocrats, fought with not only with an *esprit de corps*, but also with superior weapons and armor. Very often they were mounted; the only members of society able to raise enough money to pay for their expensive mounts. For obvious reasons, citizen soldiers or commoners were generally footmen, while the cream of the army were mounted aristocrats.

Unless warriors trained together specifically as a fighting class of soldiers, the tendency for foot soldiers was to mass up in a line and begin an approach toward their enemy. The clash of troops would then determine the victor by sheer stamina and determinations. It would not be too soon after this kind of battle that survivors, especially commanders, learned that organization and discipline would permit a more efficient use of the troops.

Once weapons (and armor) are accounted for, it then became clear that more disciplined units had a better chance of surviving than simply letting troops march out and then sprint towards their opponents. The march was a common and daily event for all troops on campaign. It taught men to rely on each other and it served as impetus to those of a unit who might have straggled behind. It was in numbers that safety was best assured. Even today, the outdated skill of marching is a training tool to instill a military attitude into the behavior of new recruits. It teaches discipline, trains them in the ability to follow orders, and gives them a sense of belonging.

Troops may also have been organized into groups of similar weapons, or into squares or phalanxes (rectangular formation). Troops, like German 16th century cavalry, were organized into wedges, with greater numbers massed more on one side than the other. In strict lines, it was hoped that cohesion could be maintained by a mathematical arrangement and the psychological reassurance of organized comrades. Certainly civilized countries felt organization was more decisive than a disorderly approach.

Despite the order, once battle was engaged, the order of neat lines were thrown completely into disarray. While lines were important at the onset, it then became crucial in maintaining a sense of movement toward their enemies. With men surging forward and back under the muted conditions of men under helmet and the din of battle, it was important for warriors to know that for every man their side lost, more of the enemy were being killed.

For the swordsman, this clash was the ideal situation for their weapon. Even after long spears had crashed into the first ranks, swords were drawn to continue the battle on an intimate and personal level. It is here that the three rules from the beginning of the chapter that characterize sword fighting come into play. One, the sword must hit its target. Two, the blade must penetrate to do physical damage. Three, the swordsman needs enough physical space in which to wield his weapon.

Within all battles is the fear of being attacked from some unknown direction. In the front line, there is no fear of attack from behind or the flank. It is a fear from a blade edge or point that comes out of a direction where the swordsman cannot effectively wield his sword for either a parry or a counter thrust. It is the push of men forward or the shove to the side which distorts and impedes the swordsman from employing his weapon in the way he trained in its use; with enough room to swing his weapon. And when shields are used at the front lines, it becomes even more difficult to effectively wield the sword. The swordsman cannot senselessly strike or thrust with the sword. He must push and shove until a crack in the enemy wall of shields has opened enough for him to thrust his sword.

As troops drop from the initial clash, weaknesses in the line begin to open up. Here the largest men are best suited to pushing into breaks in the line. With a large warrior's momentum, even the smallest and most timid of men are willing to walk in his wake. It is at this point that there is enough space to begin wielding the sword by slashing with its edge. Slashes are answered by parries or counter slashes. The best attacks are those which meet no enemy blade at all and strike the enemy directly. Ideally, the opponent's armor will be insufficient to resist the thrust or slash. In the next best of situations, a second thrust or slash will penetrate enemy armor.

It is this chaos which reigns on the battlefield which defines whether a man is a coward or a not. In the heat of the battle, all fear is put to the test. Will a warrior die valiantly as a hero? Or will he flee the sight of the enemy? While harsh and on the surface counter intuitive, it is this kind of natural selection which becomes a human form of survival-of-the-fittest. Collectively, over tens of thousands of years, war has acted as a method of rooting out the weakest in a tribe or nation. And in the spirit of even the ancient, honor and glory become synonymous with survival on the battlefield, the place where the swordsman learns that power is the ultimate decisive characteristic of human societies.

The clash, however, did not have to be the only way of conducting combat on the field of honor. In the same way that the citizens of Greek city-states resolved to settle their differences on the battlefield in lines that would run headlong into the enemy, the Japanese of the Heian period sustained their combat by individually engaging an opponent in a one-on-one contest for victory. Soldiers aristocrats would march out to the battlefield and call out their lineage and history to challenge an opponent with equal rank and valor to a duel. Couched in niceties of noble insults, the two swordsmen, once they had finished their discourses on their pedigree, then fought in combat. When one survived, he might mark his fallen adversary by sticking a pin into

his dead opponent's ankle to later lay stake to his claim. After
the Mongol invasions of the thirteen hundreds, Japanese battles
would evolved into pitch warfare similar to the other parts of the
great continents.

The 15th century led to more organized military systems. The
Wars of the Roses in England led to a neo-feudal system of Liv-
ery and Maintenance, a patronage system in which a soldier took
service with a great land owners. In France, Charles VII reorga-
nized his forces into 15 *compagnies d'ordonnance*, which was made
up of 100 units of *bande d'ordonnance*, called a lance in English.

The lance was a basic unit that described an individual
knight and his retainers. Often this differed slightly from country
to country. In Germany, a lance referred to the nobleman and his
retainers which was made up of a squire, two bowmen, and
pikeman. In France, it typically included the nobleman in heavy
armor (a *gendarme*), a mounted page called a *coustillier** (an armed
servant), three mounted archers, a crossbowman, culverineer
(handgunner), and pikeman. Spanish lances omitted the *coustillier* and page, while Burgundian lances included a knight, a
mounted page, a mounted light spearman, three mounted archers, and on foot a crosbowman, handgunner, and pikeman.

At first, the burden of arming one's self and his retainers
were left to individual nobles. Not only did the knight have to
have some royal pedigree, he also had to be able to afford the
ostentatiousness of his position. He had to purchase his own
armor, which may have cost the equivalent of three months
wages, as well as those of his retainers. Obviously few could
afford to purchase a full harness for his military servants.
Instead, each was armored as befitted their participation on the
battlefield: coats of mail for mounted horsemen and light
cavalry, brigandines for pike, arquebus, and landed archers. The
cost of war mounts was also a heavy burden. A good destrier
cost twice the price of a harness of armor and availability was
dependant on proximity of qualified stables.

---

*Translated as "finishers off of the unhorsed."

At the same time, monarchs and great lords also recruited soldiers from the lower ranks of society to fill the lines of infantry that supported cavalry action. Increasingly, despite their organization into lances, the knight saw threats from the ranks of commoner armies, like pikemen, billmen, archers, and handgunners, which developed into a semi-professional status. For the nobleman, the lofty ideal of chivalry still ruled their purpose. Commoners, often from the lowest strata of that class, fought for their lives and dispensed with rules of chivalry when necessary. They had no problem cutting the horse from under a knight, pulling the *gendarme* from his saddle, or tearing to pieces the shiny nobleman with their arrows, quarrels, and shot. Survival was at the peak of their minds, and to take down a noble who looked down on them with disgust, made the knight's demise at their hands even more palatable in their eyes.

Despite these new methods of military organization, the ingenious construct of the lance remained an effective manner of organizing field armies which still relied heavily on the massive power of cavalry charges. The lance specified clearly a noble's obligations, and as a matter of practically, preserved the feudal system of continental nobility. The page served as a fetch boy and herald, while the other armed retainers traveled essentially as support and infantry to protect the knight. The lance was in essence a Renaissance "tank" with support horsemen and footmen for protection.

Lances, however, did not roam the battlefield as individual knights searching for adversaries. Retainers were, for accounting purposes, a method of calling up troops in proportional strengths. And on the battlefield, troops would be massed with soldiers of a similar type: knights with knights, pikemen with pikemen, archers with archers. Such units became very disciplined groups and were deployed on the battlefield according to the strategy of their commanders. French and Spanish knights formed lines in single ranks, called *en haie*, in front of archers or *coustilliers*, while Germans formed deep wedges designed to push into enemy lies and maintain the momentum by pouring through the broken ranks.

The evolution to full plate harnesses was completed in the 15th century. Referred to as "white armor," plate over aketon or arming doublet, which had chain mail at articulated areas of the body called gussets, and heavy sheets of metal provided such complete protection that the shield was dispensed with altogether except for the joust. Lines were sometimes carved into the armor, called fluting, which guided arrows and quarrels off of the armor. While missiles are most effected when it strikes armor at a 90° angle, fluting now made it a virtual requirement if any penetration were to occur.

Swords too evolved with the times. Because horses were particularly vulnerable to missiles and pole arms, knights sometimes dismounted before engaging the enemy. With both hands free, the hand-and-a-half sword came into use. This sword could be used either with one hand, or with two hands for close quarters fighting. The poleaxe, a spear with a hammer, beak, or blade, also became popular with knights fighting on foot. Taking various forms, they had names such as ravensbill, *bec de corbin*, guisarme, and voulge. Their long shaft and piercing edges could be wielded with great strength, shattering or breaking apart plate armor. The butt end was often encased in steel so that it could be used to crush feet, armored or not. Such polaxes were very popular in the lists, the tournament battlefield, behind which knights would compete for pride and glory in friendly combat. Such tourneys sometimes resulted in severe injuries when participants got carried away in the heat of the exchange. Other popular weapons included the mace and war hammer which were very effective in smashing through armor and causing trauma in the form of bruising and concussions.

Supplementing the sword were thrusting daggers like the cinqueda, supposedly five fingers wide. These finishing daggers were used to dispatch opponents with thrusts to vital areas in plate armor — neck, arm pits, elbows, and knee joints.

The eventual end of the mailed-covered knight was the increasing sophistication of the gun. The crossbow was earlier supplanted by the effectiveness of the longbow, which in turn, was supplanted by the gunner, who could take down knights in a single shot without the eight years and more of training that was needed to develop an English archer.

The knight's charge would continue well into the 16th century, but with better armed and armored footmen, the knight was facing even greater threat on the battlefield. The impact of cavalry would not loose its psychological impact for centuries more; the world's last known cavalry charge taking place on Polish plains as cavalry, in a heroic stand, faced German Panzer divisions at the opening hours of World War II.

The 16th century did serve as a watershed period that led into the modern era both militarily and culturally. This was the opening of the era that would usher in the blow that would end the age of the plate armored knight. The defeat of the French and Swiss halberdiers at Bicocca, Switzerland, at the hands of firearms was the opening salvo. Three years later, at the Battle of Pavia in 1525 between Imperial and French forces, the knight when cornered by pike and arquebus died in an easy slaughter of nobility. The power of cannon had been demonstrated thirty years earlier when Charles VII invaded Italy virtually unimpeded as he shot down curtain wall after curtain wall in his furious campaign through the peninsula. A revolution in military construction would soon follow.

Warfare during this century would be marked by advances in tactics that required less armor. Swiss hedgehog tactics, followed by phalanx pike warfare, were recent models for the rise of the Spanish on the continent. The Spanish tercio organized into squares of 1,500 to 3,000 mixed pike and arquebusiers. At the threat of cavalry charge, the pikes measuring in excess of 15' were lowered. Mixed within their ranks were lines of arquebusiers who fired their shots in a steady stream. Once a line fired, another line would move up and allow the first rank to withdraw into the protection of the pikemen to reload.

Spanish soldiery was armored with lighter armor, either steel plated brigandines, breast plates, and a steel cap. Their added mobility would prove advantageous, allowing the tercio formation to move at a pace that preserved their formation but crossed the battlefield in short order.

The armor for armies composed more of commoners were relatively light, but effective. Infantry armor consisted mainly of the cuirass, also termed corselet, which included the gorget, breastplate (and sometimes a backplate) and armplates. When available and permitted by the regiment, leg armor, mail, and various helmets would be worn.

Knights still wore full harness, though the armor became increasingly decorative and was used as parade armor. Two styles evolved at this time: those in a German style, called Maximillian, recognized by its fluting or the imitative puffed and slashed style, or the Italian style which was more plain and rounded, better to deflect sword blows.

The medieval sword did not evolve much further during this time period other than adding more protection for the hand in the form of crossing guards and a knucklebow to cover the fingers. Societal influences also had their effect as the sword became a fashion accessory for the civilian gentleman. Not only were swords to be used on the battlefield, but also in cities between lightly or completely unarmored opponents. Invariably, this led to the evolution of the sword from a cut and thrust weapon to an more exclusively point oriented weapon.

While the Jedi have as yet to be seen in full combat mode, it is clear that the unique characteristics of the lightsaber would make battlefield combat different from Terran battles. If there ever were (or is going to be) a situation in which the Jedi fight against an army of lightsaber armed opponents, the pitched fights would still present a danger to its participants. With Jedi armed in traditional robes, pitch battle would be a horrific struggle. Shields would be virtually useless as would traditional armor used on historical battlefields.

It will be clear from *Attack of the Clones* that superior numbers will be the decisive factor going against the Jedi Order as the

Republic Senate decides on whether to raise a military levy in anticipation of a successionist movement in the Galactic Senate. No longer do their diplomatic skills and prestige or presence sufficiently serve the state of galactic order. It will be necessary to raise troops that can sustain huge losses without loosing its own cohesion.

Perhaps the lesson from the Jedi battles at the end of *Attack of the Clones* will lead to a new interpretation of the Jedi Order and their apparent aversion for military technology. When the war breaks out, it seems utter folly that outdated sword fighting can be an effective method for quelling forces which, through rudimentary training, can defeat Jedi Knights and even Jedi Masters. With Jango Fett's influence on the clone troopers, is it possible that there will also be an evolution of Jedi ludditism?

It would be a natural step to see Jedi forego their traditional robes and equip and arm themselves with range weapons in addition to their traditional lightsaber. Better yet, that there could be lightsaber wielding troops (perhaps cloned Jedi) that meet head-to-head with Jedi Knights in a massive sword fight. It is more than plausible that the final episode may yet contain the possibility of an all lightsaber conflict. A finale of this epic struggle would indeed be a climactic end to the story of lightsaber swordsmen.

4

Fencing Style

"How real is the lightsaber fight in *Star Wars*?"

That was the question most asked of me during the talks I gave comparing *Star Wars* lightsaber fighting with Terran fencing just after the release of *The Phantom Menace*. The quick answer is that it is very real, but to truly understand the sword fight, one needs to first understand the nature of swordsmanship which centers on the ability to defeat an opponent.

While the nature of the sword (the subject of Chapter Three) focuses on the cutting ability of a sword, swordsmanship focuses on the manner in which a swordsman uses his weapon; whether with one or two hands, with a wide or narrow stance, with rapid successive strikes or with a single heavy blow, just to name but a few considerations. While it is obvious to the non-fencer that different cultures and different time periods had their own styles of fighting, the fencer of any time or place has to be able to distinguish not only between different schools of swordsmanship in order to defeat an opponent, but he must be able to discern the individual's particular style. In its most specific terms, swordsmanship is a combination of mastery of technique and strategy, and sheer determination of mind and spirit. For the swordsman and the Jedi alike, it is not enough to have mere possession of a sword or lightsaber. The swordsman had to have the ability to use his weapon efficiently and without delay, while simultaneously recognizing the limits of his skills and that of his sword.

The Phantom Menace provides ample evidence of a swordsman's need to adapt himself to the ever changing situation of a fight. While battle droids could only move about and shoot their

blasters, Qui-Gon and Obi-Wan readily adapted to the circumstances in which they found themselves. On the Neimoidian
Control Ship at the beginning of the movie, Obi-Wan and Qui-
Gon retreated from attacking Droidekas, the rolling battle droids,
when they recognized that their lightsabers were no match for
the droid's repeating blaster fire and defensive shielding. Far
from being defeated, their actions were in actuality a strategic
retreat which assured their survival and allowed them to re-
group for another attack. Darth Maul, in a similar move, retreated from the Theed Hangar bay to get better positioning against
Qui-Gon and Obi-Wan. His patience paid off when he isolated
Qui-Gon and was then able to dispatch the Jedi Knight without
the threat of his Padawan Apprentice.

A swordsman's style of fighting was primarily dependent on
the training he received, but more immediately it was affected by
the fighting style of an attacker and the kind of armor he wore.
This continual evolution presents historians with the difficulty
of trying to reconstruct sword fighting styles. Unlike the sword,
which can be physically dug up in archeological sites, the manner in which the sword was historically employed disappeared
with the swordsman who perished in combat or died from old
age. Probably 99% of history's sword fighting styles have been
lost to history, and what we know of swordsmanship, especially
Western swordsmanship, is at best supposition distilled from
contemporary expressions. Asian styles, in particular those of Japan and China, are closer expressions of true battlefield swordsmanship because of the strictness in which technique was taught
and conveyed from generation to generation, but those too suffered pacification as they evolved into a sport or from a lack of
new recruits to preserve the body of techniques which made
their styles unique.

While it can be generally said that every culture that used the
sword had their own particular style of sword fighting, it can be
reasonably argued that invaders fought differently with the
sword than a more insular and non-aggressive society. This, in
turn, makes the modern historian confident that Romans fought

differently from the Visigoths, who in their own right fought differently from the Celts. Similarly, it is true within a particular culture that swordsmanship was dissimilar at different times during its history. Therefore, it can be reasonably argued that a samurai from the age of Tokugawa rule fought differently than those who anticipated Mongol invasions centuries earlier. And lastly, while it is difficult to qualitatively compare the effectiveness of one fencing style against another because of the many factors involved in encounters between swordsmen, it is possible to say that there are cultures which, because of their experience and war-like tendencies, fielded inherently better swordsmen than others. It can therefore be said that invading Huns could easily defeat Roman villagers living deep within the Empire who had never had battle experience nor their own garrison, which illustrates the fact that lack of battle experience and a pastoral life are reasons why belligerent and expansive steppe nomads would and could make deep forays into territory controlled for centuries by Roman imperialism.

There is much documentation and iconographic sources which do help the modern historian understand sword fighting. Whether from actual recollection of battle or from images in a woodcut or on an amphora, it is possible to distill the evolution of swordsmanship through the dynamics of battlefield tactics and strategies, as well as by the changes of the shape of the sword itself. An examination of major fencing styles would encompass a lifetime of research and writing, it suffices to explore the two principal influences of *Star Wars* lightsaber fighting — Western fencing and Samurai swordsmanship.

The Evolution of Western & Japanese Swordsmanship

Western Fencing
For thousands of years, swordsmanship had been dominated by the double-edged sword, commonly known as a long or broad sword, but during the Renaissance, the European sword underwent a rapid transformation as culture and the means of

warfare evolved on the continent. With the technological improvement of the fire arms, including arquebus, musket, rifle and cannon, the nature of warfare was at a watershed point in history. While its impact was immediately recognized by the nobility, the gun's permanent, long-lasting impact did not take hold until its use became predominant between armies on the battlefield. Earlier changes in distance weaponry occurred with the bow and crossbow, but because they still required extensive training and lacked the firepower of an explosive, they did not change the course of warfare as gunpowder and nuclear technology would.

Though the speed of the demise of the armored knight differed from country to country, the rise of democratic ideas combined with the easy-to-operate matchlock would eventually make the position and station of the knight and the aristocracy he protected obsolete. Competency in training commoners in the musket was achieved with relative rapidity, and with a huge population base to replenish the lines of musketry, the educated and trained knights of the realm had neither the numbers, nor the cadres of squires to compete with newer democratic militias. Dominance on the field was no longer a question of amassing experienced and well-armored swordsmen. The protection of a complete harness became a liability, and quickly the heaviness of arm and leg plating were discarded to allow greater mobility. Soon a breastplate, a metal cap, and perhaps greaves if they were available became the new standard of protection for the new units of commoners that would make up the body of national armies. When the metal breastplate was not available, a gambeson or jack (a thick quilted jacket), a bringandine (a studded leather garment), or a buff coat (a thick leather jacket) were used to thwart sword cuts.

But the rise of the commoner occurred hundreds of years earlier with the increasing importance of the middle class. It was not unheard of that a noble faced the possibility of losing land through the simple mismanagement of his properties combined with an over-extravagant lifestyle. Merchants, with their coffers full of gold and florins, made natural conjugal allies of the nobility. It would not be too long before ordinary folk began to see themselves more in terms of a citizenry of a nation and not simply the serfs of a landed class. Nobles continued to hold rank in their society, but the commoner pushed upward into higher social strata by their ability to earn money. This competition expressed itself in civilian life as the noble guarded his right and privilege to continue carrying the sword at his side when he walked the streets while commoners still carried a knife for both eating and self-defense.

The sword also followed trends from the battlefield. As armor got lighter, so too did the swordsman's weapon. Swords with finer and more delicate blades were made, and an increased emphasis on the use of the point became a standard among the aristocracy. Refined civilian styles in dress, which consisted of a fancy shirt and light jacket, now permitted effective use of the point, and the nobleman could protect himself against both offending men of his own rank as well as those of commoners, ruffians, and highwaymen.

The rapier was the *sine qua non* weapon for both slashing and piercing. With its two edges and sharp point, the choice weapon of the French musketeers was a valuable offensive and defensive weapon when bullets and powder were exhausted. It was the Italians, however, who led Europe in the delicate civil and cultural arts of the Renaissance. Quite different from the heavy handed slashes of the broad sword, Italian masters developed a subtle form of point combat that emphasized the advantage of a quick thrust over a slashing sword which had to travel as much as five times the distance the point took to reach its target. Not only did they systematize their art, they published books and traveled to teach foreigners outside of the peninsula. Marozzo, Agrippa, and di Grassi are well represented because of the manuals they published. Others hid their art by taking on students and obliging them to hide their fencing style and refrain from teaching it to others. A kind of mystical reputation developed among fencing masters, who were said to have learned secret moves and attacks that could defeat any fencer.

The rise of the fencing *salle*, which amounted to nothing more than a civic club much akin to a modern country club, was created out of the increasing urbanization of the capitals of rising European nation-states. A master's reputation depended on his ability and skill, which was subsequently nourished and eventually advanced by the quality and breeding of his students. It was not long after that the state took on the responsibility of authenticating the mastery of the individual club by establishing a national curriculum so that instructors would have to prove their skills by passing a battery of tests and exams in order to officially take the title of *master, maître, fechtsmeister,* or *maestro.*

Another change developed as the rapier gave way to the lighter small sword carried by courtiers of the greatest kings and queens of Europe. The nobility still held political power, and as part of their courtly clothes, more extravagant and lighter blades became the fashion. The heavy and simple robes of the Middle Ages gave way to the decadence of the 17th and 18th centuries. Small swords were still practical arms used for friendly play and combative duels, but the small sword became more of a jewel and ornament among the many accessories of a lace covered courtier.

Eventually the cruciform hilt of the medieval long sword was no longer a standard for public occasions. As heavy and light cavalry units like the Hussars, Grenadiers, the Imperial Guard, and the Life Guards, replaced the knight, the return of the sabre also came to dominate the military costume. With the development of muskets, soldiers relied on banks of men who fired *en masse* at their opponents in a large barrage. Bayonets made the pikeman obsolete, and with both the musket in hand and the sabre at his side, the conversion from warrior to soldier was complete.

The demise of the nobility was far from over, but Adolphus Gustavus, the most famous modern military commander, and his military reforms made professionals out of what used to be the armed flower of a nation's nobility. No more would the caracole, wherein armored cavalry would pace just outside of pike's point, execute a half-turn, and then fire their pistols at the line, be a noble's prerogative of shooting at the enemy army at will. It would become the privilege of highly trained sabre-carrying cavaliers (drawn mostly from humble origins) who would be used as an elite unit to threaten and waste asunder slow moving lines of footmen.

Another sword that caught fashion was the hanger, which was essentially a straighter version of the cavalry sabre. Used initially as a hunting weapon for dealing a death blow to wild pig, buck, or bear, the hanger came to be widely carried by gentlemen and ordinary citizens who needed a practical weapon within easy reach. It may have been carried as a daily accessory or as a traveler's weapon when journeying from his estate to the capital.

The sabre also became the favored weapon of naval troops who needed a short bladed edge to fight on the limited space of their decks. Cutting a thick line, hacking down at boarders at the edge of the deck rail, or parrying a wild cut to the head, the cutlass, as the naval sabre was called, provided marines, pirates, privateers, and buccaneer with an easily adoptable weapon for their decks on which they fought. The musket, the deck cannon, and the light cannon were easily supplemented by the cutlass.

As much as the sword was essential to the general and officers of early 20th century armies, so too does the lightsaber play a significant and symbolic role as guardian of the Galactic Republic. The sword was the embodiment of power and today it reflects many of the values that were no different than in the past: justice, honor, virtue. Though the sword is no longer standard issue for modern soldiers, it is probably the greatest testament to the enduring importance of sword that it still remains an important accessory to the honor guards of most nations.

Japanese Fencing

Unlike Europe where gunpowder and the change in armor had a direct impact on the physical form of the sword, swordsmanship in Japan has focused more on the evolution of the *role* of the sword in battle and in civilian life than on an evolution of shape. Since the style of fencing is always affected by the cultural experience of its practitioners, the relatively constant state of war in Japan assured a predominant role for the samurai feudal lord vying for the coveted position of *de facto* ruler, or shogun. As had occurred in the West, the gun would alter the course of history in Japan as well, but where the European aristocracy failed, the samurai were successful in imposing a retrograde policy that banned the gun.

Though it might seemed hard to believe, early Japanese swords were not the curved kind with which Americans are so accustomed to seeing in Japanese samurai films. The *tsurugi* was a straight sword probably of Chinese origin, that looked very similar to the European broadsword.

Early governments of the Yamato peoples established themselves on the main island of Honshu. An Imperial Court evolved and culture as expressed from that court revolved from its center. Assisting the court were military retainers, many from northern frontiers, who assured the position of the Emperor and the court that served it. Through the early periods of the Jomon, Yayoi, Yamato, Nara, and Heian periods, the relative stability of an Imperial government was maintained with the assistance of armed forces that guarded and expanded frontiers, while quelling rebellions that threatened the Emperor. In the Heian court, the nobles (*kuge*) ruled in the opulent splendor of the capital city. Early soldiers to the Imperial Court were considered rough, vulgar, and untamed armed servants. Contingents supporting one noble might clash with those of a challenging noble, but most retainers refrained from openly taking power for themselves.

Military warfare before the Mongol invasion reflected an insular competition between nobles of one house against another. On the battlefield cavalry would first charge toward their enemy, launching arrows from their bows at a full gallop. Lines would then reform several more times before the horsemen would dismount for hand-to-hand combat on foot. After declaring their background, worthy opponents would approach each other and then personal combat would take place.

During the Heian period, Japanese society was dominated by the Fujiwara family, which built a dynastic relationship with the Imperial family. In exchange for protecting the heir to the throne during a 7th century revolt, the Fujiwara were accorded the privilege of ruling in the name of the Emperor. With rare exception, the empress was drawn from members of the Fujiwara clan, solidifying the *de jure* preeminence of the exalted family.

In the 12th century, pretenders to the throne, however, challenged the Emperor who, according to a long tradition, had retired at an early age from political life to monasteries while the Fujiwaras administrated the country. Intrigue at the court and the later weakness of the Fujiwara convinced samurai of both the Minamoto and the Taira clan to wrest control of the country from the Fujiwara through the use of the powerful armies they had developed after years of cultivating their provinces and military resources. The Taira was temporarily successful in repelling the Minamoto clan, but in answer to the Emperor's request for help, Yoritomo Minamoto, a leader from the defeated clan, raised an army and eventually destroyed the Taira's power forever.

Yoritomo's victory led to the establishment of a seven hundred year period in which real power in Japan laid with the shogun. While beholden to the Emperor's gratitude for naming him shogun, Yoritomo quickly removed himself from the Imperial Court and ran his government from a new court in Kamakura. To the detriment of the dynasty, Yoritomo's children were never successful in controlling the country. Instead, his widow entered the political scene and installed her family, the Hojo, as regents ruling on behalf of the Emperor. They arranged for the appointment of a shogun, but they, like the Emperor at the hands of the shogun, were manipulated as puppets of the Hojo regents.

In 1274, Japan faced its first outside threat from Kublai Khan, grandson of the Mongol conqueror Ghengis Khan, who set his sights on Japan to further increase his prestige and rid the Chinese coast of notorious Japanese pirates. Envoys were sent demanding Japanese submission as vassals to the Mongols. Rebuffed by the Japanese, Khan sent an invasion of fifteen thousand men. Unsuccessful in making a beachhead in Hakata Bay, forces retreated to the safety of their boats. That night a storm destroyed the greater part of the fleet. Remnants hobbled back to China to tell of their defeat. Five years later, after conquering the Chinese Sung emperor, Khan returned with a fleet of over 150,000 men divided into two forces. As before, his forces could not make a beachhead and troops retreated to their ships. Again, as had happened in the first invasion, a massive storm struck the Mongol and Korean fleet which returned for a second time defeated at the hands of the Japanese.

From these two invasion attempts, the Japanese quickly learned that their traditional methods of fighting would not be effective against foreign troops. The Mongols did not respect the challenge, and while victorious, they knew the ultimate defeat of the Mongols was not achieved entirely out of their own efforts. During the limited battles that did occur, the samurai discovered that their swords were vulnerable to breakage and that their armor, while properly suited to cavalry movement, was too heavy for ground fighting. Tactics as well were adjusted to reflect the new state of warfare. Instead of issuing challenges after bow and arrow cavalry charges, troops were organized into lines according to weapon type and deployment was determined by strategic considerations. Polearms were used against cavalry, while archers fired at their enemy from behind large, moveable shields.

The succeeding Muromachi period (1338-1573) led to the development of the *katana* (also called an *uchigatana*), with which most Westerners most closely associate with the Japanese samurai. Instead of hanging their sword in a scabbard at their side as had been done earlier, it became fashionable and practical to place the it within the folds of the samurai's belt with the sword edge upward. Along with the katana, a shorter sword was worn called a *wakizashi*. Together the swords were known as the *daisho*, literally the large and small swords. Eventually national law would restrict the *daisho* to the samurai class which acted as both the police and militia of regional fiefdoms.

The use of the katana led to the development of a new style of fencing which relied on the immediate slicing cut of the sword when drawn. Given the nature of Japanese society when assassination was as close as any passing samurai in the street, the instantaneous use of the sword was vital. Practice in a simultaneous draw/attack was required. Because attacks could come at any moment in the day, daily paraphernalia were used as adjuncts to the sword. A cup or chopsticks may have been thrown at the assassin if attacked while at tea or a meal. A samurai learned to roll across the tatami mat floors while still wearing his short sword in order to escape the initial attack of an intruder. Clothing too, especially the long sleeves that were popular, could be used to a samurai's advantage by pulling his opponent slightly off balance. The samurai's ability to defend himself from attack was the only assurance he had of surviving the tumultuous times of his society.

The Mongol invasions also accelerated the squabbling between Japanese rulers and the lower nobility. Some feudal lords, called *daimyo*, and their retainers went unrewarded for their efforts in maintaining an expensive military presence to fight against possible future Chinese attacks. Outlying fiefs rebelled against the Hojo regents and through open warfare two rival courts were established: one in the north and another in the south. In 1467, the Onin rebellion led to a hundred year period of endless warfare that came to be known as the *Sengoku Jidai*,* the Age of Warring Provinces. Peasants, unable to protect themselves from wandering, masterless soldiers called *ronin* or from armies traveling through their territories, organized themselves into military coalitions which challenged the military class. These groups attacked the capital, waylaid government troops, and even defeated a professional samurai army.

Daimyo, as leaders of the military class, organized against

---

*Jedi is derived from the Japanese word for "age/period."

these rebellions and even co-opted men from the peasant ranks who served as footsoldiers called *ashigaru*. While recognized as essential to society (farmers ranked higher than merchants), the samurai class asserted their prerogatives over what in their eyes was a subservient class. As history would have it, another foreign intervention to the Honshu islands would mean political and military upheaval in Japan.

In the 1540's, Portuguese ships began arriving off the western coast of Japan in search of possible trade ventures. Feudal lords in those provinces soon recognized the potential of purchasing muskets from the Europeans. As was being discovered in Europe, the firearm would become as important a weapon on the Japanese battlefield as it was in Europe. It also proved to be the biggest threat to the samurai, who was easily killed by trained peasant musketeers. Warfare now depended on the musket. Renowned leaders Oda Nobunaga, Toyotomi Hideyoshi, and Tokugawa Ieyasu would use the musket to successfully take power and hold it for themselves.

All recognized the usefulness of the new weapons, but the very state of armed insurgency by both rival lords and the peasantry created a countryside ready to move against any centralizing authority. Under Hideyoshi, a policy of decommissioning of weapons was pursued. Called the Taika Sword Hunt, Hideyoshi, under the pretense of collecting steel for the building of a great Buddha statue, promulgated a law that allowed only the samurai class to carry weapons. Government officials proceeded to disarm peasants and merchants both near the capital and in outward regions. Not only did this hamstring thoughts of rebellion against the government, it allowed officials to collect taxes from the peasantry who no longer had the means to resist the samurai class.

Under a later shogun Tokugawa Ieyasu, a set of sweeping governmental reforms instituted a period of relative peace unheard of in Japanese history, preserving his dynasty for over two hundred fifty years. Upon establishing his government in Edo, he instituted laws that locked his country into a rigid societal structure in which the shogun exerted influence over every aspect of daily life. He quelled rival lords by requiring them to maintain expensive entourages and to spend substantial time in a household in the capital. When the daimyo was away visiting his feudal holdings, his family was required to stay in the capital as virtual hostages. The country was divided into administrative regions that maintained border checks throughout the country so movement of important officials and troops could be kept under surveillance. To prevent peasants from acquiring weapons or organizing against the samurai class, traditional expectations were imposed. And in an unexpected reversal of previous foreign policy, Western Christians were expelled from the country because of the influence they had gained in making converts and in engaging in musket trade which threatened to re-arm outlying daimyo. Tokugawa declared that foreigners would be allowed limited access to the country in the port cities of Nagasaki and Yokohama. And to suppress non-Japanese influences, Japanese citizens were forbidden to travel outside of the country.

Under Tokugawa rule, war, while not completely eliminated, became infrequent and of limited locality during the Edo period. The vast armies now without purpose presented a challenge to Ieyasu's government, so samurai were now required to directly administer and maintain their land or that of their lord, while martial experience had to be maintained in case of state emergencies, but in a tempered way. Religion too was used to Ieyasu's advantage as Confucian ethical principles of strict hierarchy were exalted, respect and observance of Shinto practices was imposed, becoming the state religion. Samurai, in addition to keeping up their skills as swordsmen, were encouraged to cultivate the arts of poetry, calligraphy, and literature.

It was during this time that *kenjutsu*, the killing art of swordsmanship, began to evolve into *kendo*. The skill of the sword was maintained, but pacified into a non-violent exercise by the use of a bamboo sword instead of sharp blades. Kendo armor, based on real armor, was adapted for the new sword fighting style, and etiquette and a set of customary rules were established for this new form of friendly competition.

Zen Buddhism, which extolled a stoic, disciplined, and simple life, also had a large impact on modern swordsmanship. Not only did the rigidity of religious life appeal to the austere life of former soldiers, it gave samurai a religious culture in which to express themselves. Zen did not have an overt creed, so by combining esoteric religious practices with swordsmanship, Zen sword came to be accepted by samurai of all sorts. Zen swordsmanship is not, however, a religion. Rather, it is the simple and direct process of mastering swordsmanship which allows an individual to achieve a higher level of existence often referred to as enlightenment, when individual purpose and a simple satisfaction with daily life meet in a harmonious convergence.

In 1853, the arrival of American Commodore Perry in his four men-of-war Black Ships at the harbor of Uraga marked a watershed in Japanese history. America was looking for a base of operation in the Pacific, and in order to secure "proper" relations with the Japanese government, impressive sailing ships were dispatched to negotiate trade agreements. The colorful tête-à-tête was a polite exchange, but from that moment onward, the isolationist Japanese knew they could not permanently shut out nations that carried the impressive array of cannon that protected the American Black Ships. Even if these four were taken by force, Japan was in not in any military or political situation to defend herself against a determined, musket- and cannon-armed invader.

The arrival of Americans who demanded the right to trade with Japan opened the country to a cultural lovefest of things Western. In its wake would be a traditional backlash of conservatives clamoring to "expel the barbarians." The Emperor would soon be restored to power and the samurai, once allowed to carry his *daisho* proudly was abolished in favor of Western modes of dress, thought, and education. Japan hurried to catch up with the West in an unprecedented industrialization that led well into the mid-twentieth century. At the conclusion of World War II, Japanese militarism gave way to a peaceful idealism which manifests itself in a constitution that prohibits the creation of a military that may one day be used for expansive purposes. While the samurai became a soldiery of commoners, study of the sword still remains an important expression of Japanese culture.

Star Wars draws from cultures from all over the world, but the influence of Japanese swordsmanship stands out to fencers who have had even a cursory introduction to sword fighting arts of the world. Lucas, like the Japanese of the Meiji Period were for Western culture, was infatuated by Japanese samurai films. And while not imitating it explicitly, it is self-evident that there is much to learn about Star Wars by examining samurai swordsmanship.

Swordsmanship and the Brain

When a fencing student picks up a sword — a foil, epee, long sword, bokken, shinai, iaito, or katana — for the first time, he or she is stepping into a world that is more dependent on the brain than the body. Certainly the initial focus on physical conditioning further emphasizes the physiological aspect of the art of fencing, but disciplining the body is far less important in the long run to a fencer than the physiological changes that will be made in the brain.

As was discussed in Chapter Two, the human being is driven by the primal and necessary instinct of self-preservation. Because of the nature of their art, swordsmen, as is any other practitioner of a combative art, are exposed to the most challenging of situations — combat with another person whose goal is to kill you. There is nothing like the sheer terror a man or woman can experience than that of another human being inches from your body who is willing to kill you, especially one armed with a long shiny blade who can pierce your chest or cut open your skin. It is this fear of another person, combined with the fear of not being able to defend one's self which makes the impending struggle a fearful and terrifying affair. Swordsmanship, in its very essence, seeks to tame these fears so that there can be only one outcome — the swordsman's survival.

Through disciplined training, swordsmanship seeks to alter the physical body and arm it with the executive control of the brain which will lead to optimum functioning during the chaotic struggle of a life and death situation. It is an interplay between the body and mind which must be developed, distinguishing the swordsman from the non-fencer or the inexperienced fencer. Experience will teach the master swordsman that the fencing encounter is more psychological (and cerebral) than it is physical or skill-related. Whether fencing is 90% brains and 10% brawn, or 60% brains and 40% brawn is debatable, and will probably be never known. The importance of the intellect over the body is self-evident, however, to a good fencer.

While most manuals on fencing elucidate the subtleties of posture, control of the weapon, and basic skills, there has been little discussion of the physiological factors that have a major impact on the human brain during the stressful situation of a sword fight, for there exists a body of thought which states that genetics, the body's endocrine system, the structure of the brain, as well as culture have a profound impact on swordsmen.

Following Darwin's theories on natural selection, scientist have argued that over the course of thousands of years, the human being has evolved into a particular kind of being with particular pretensions toward survival. One would go as far as to assert that certain tribes or groups may have a natural predisposition to war-like behavior, while others do not. Though it is doubtful that scientists of the future could ever identify whether Vikings and their blood related Norman descendants were more predisposed to pillage and plunder than a Polynesian culture, there is compelling evidence that because of our sexual genetic make-up men and not women tend to be the warriors.

Behaviorists argue that over thousands of years *homo sapiens* (who are said to have been around from 35,000 - 150,000 years ago) men and women have been imbued with certain physiological differences that make men the warriors and women the home raisers.

Much of this evidence suggests that much of the gender difference is related to the amount of testosterone in a body and how it controls or influences an individual's reaction to outside or emotional stimulus. It is an old saying that "Men are from Mars, Women are from Venus," which, if taken along general terms and not as a specific criteria with which to judge individuals, leads many to conclude that men and women use their brains in different ways, according to the strengths that were needed of people that lived in strong role-driven societies thousands of years ago.

Because of natural selection, males who had better musculature and spatial skills for hunting and fighting, and women who had better childbearing ability and perceptual skills for foraging survived to procreate. These gender differences also affect both an individual's education, as well as how the brain functions during a life-threatening sword fight.

Our genetic make-up also influences how the brain is able to learn. Males are on average more capable of right brain functions like spacial, visual, gross motor, and gestalt* skills. Women, on the other hand, start out with more advanced left-brain skills such as auditory, language, fine motor, and detailed-sequential thinking. This can be one factor in explaining why boys gravitate toward aggressive and competitive sports, while girls tend to be quieter, more attentive, and disciplined students in the classroom.

While such assertions may seem sexist and inappropriate in today's modern societies which advocate the equal abilities of men and women to perform similar jobs, predispositions do not in of themselves explain the development of individuals as we encounter them. While this thesis posits that certain predispositions in men and women start out at birth, the growth and development of individuals does not necessarily predetermine that all

---

*They have good overview abilities, like seeing the significance of an event over a long period of time. The ability to look at the "big picture."

men will be neanderthal sports lovers or all women soft, feminine home makers. Biological predispositions can be enhanced or diminished through training and acculturation, which had tremendous implications for fencers.

In the early, pre-adolescent years, the brain is still in the stages of developing the network of connections that allow the flow of electricity through the brain in what is typically called "thinking." Different part of the brain control different functions. Brain mass is made up of neurons which are connected to each other by dendrites. One key to improving a person's thinking skills is to build up the mass of dendrites connecting the neurons of the brain. This is accomplished by performing activities that stimulate particular parts of the brain associated with specific skills. For example, if a girl participates in activities that rely on gross motor skills such as throwing a ball, corresponding parts of the brain begin creating more dendrites. Not only is the girl developing the musculature for throwing a ball, her brain is developing the ability to coordinate the thinking skills that allow her to more easily accomplish the task. She is learning.

The inherent problems with the educational system today is that it tends to work for the benefit of the boys. If one looks at a boy's tendencies, he generally gravitates towards his stronger abilities: he likes to explore, enjoys the visual stimulus of comics, relishes sports, and looks less at detail than overall purpose which helps him in math and science. Girls start out deficient in these areas and are greatly suited to traditional classroom learning which emphasizes, listening skills, the use of language as a way to express themselves. The physical act of fine motor skills associated with writing is natural to them, and they pay attention more than their male classmates. Girls and young women improve these skills in the classroom, but they don't get as much stimulus in right-brained activities. Boys, however, get the benefit of both right brained activities because they have a tendency to follow their natural talents, while they get the left-brain activities in school.

The implications for fencing from an educational point of

view is that it develops both left and right-brain skills in a manner that puts neither a male or female at a physical or intellectual disadvantage. Fencing, primarily because it is combative, requires a constant readjustment to threats from an opponent. Whereas most weaponless martial arts tend to favor the physical strength of a man, fencing uses a weapon that compensates for the physiological advantages that favor men. With a minimum expense of energy, the woman can relatively easily mortally wound a man endowed with better physical strength. The same can also be said for physically weaker opponents, whether male or female, in that the person with better brains can be a serious threat to the physical brute. Soft martial arts, like aikido and tai chi, also start out from the premise that minimum energy can be used to defeat physically stronger opponents.

Modern Western fencing, by its very nature, already favors the female who has better balance and fine motor skills than his male counterpart. Because of its aggressive nature, a male does have the advantage of being more suited to attacking, which is the primary way of hitting an opponent. Fencing teaches confidence, risk taking, and gives immediate feedback for learning. It also focuses on the right-brained functions that require spacial and visual acuity — to have to physically see an attack and judge proper distance — as well as the physical, gross motor skills and a larger focus on the overall situation of the strategy of the bout. For males, fencing de-emphasizes brute force and requires an attention to subtlety of movement to control the point of the weapon. Sequential thinking and the use of language — fencing has its own vocabulary — are the typical methods of teaching fencing, while the reliance on sound is an aspect too often neglected by fencers.

Fencing is a series of trained responses to a fight or flight situation, employing the sword to attack or defend against an aggressor. Where physiology tends to produce a fight response in men by sending adrenalin[*] through the body and flight in a woman, training hopes to develop reactionary responses to the stimulus of a threat. Without thought, the body reacts to the unexpected by following the training that has been drilled into a person.

Our instincts are not always the best or most efficient means of dealing with threats. Hopefully it is skill as a swordsman, not a determination from chemical functions, which will be used to defeat the opponent. Skill is developed by practicing movements with a sword that will allow the fencer to win in combat. It therefore becomes critical that practice be done with the intention of practicing perfect movement. During a fencing bout, the fencer typically falls back on the instincts that have be trained in him or her. If the fencer continually practices an advance with a slightly turned front foot, it is more likely he will tend to do the same during a real bout, which, in this case, could lead to a twisted ankle during a lunge. This search for attainable perfection is what translates into efficient and instinctual reaction to the stimulus of an attacking aggressor.

Once trained, an ambush by a highwayman is countered by a man or woman's new instinctual reactions to draw the sword and fight. Similarly, when confronted with an attack from arrows or gunfire, the swordsman, knowing his limits against missile attacks, instinctually runs and seeks cover. It is the development of a specialized skills which, once acquired, will protect the life of the swordsman.

The fencing match is a combative situation in which the winner is determined by better cranial capacity. If one relies on fight or flight instincts when a sword is drawn, the match turns into a slugfest in which one attack (a stimulus) is met with a reactionary counter attack (a reaction) from the defender. When a fencer

---

[*] Adrenaline causes blood vessels to constrict, limiting blood loss, stimulates the production of cortisol which decreases weakness, fatigue, and loss of resistence, and causes an increase of conversion of proteins to glucose which help the musculature system.

does not have a technique in his repertoire to counter a particular attack, he tends to ad lib a reaction, often accompanied with the addition of sheer strength to "make the attack work" when the skillful execution of a proper technique requires a fraction of the exertion made in a wholly improvised attack.

When one has the ability to outperform the opponent, choosing attacks and parries is relatively easy. For the undertrained fencer, it seems like the adversary is capable of predicting his movements and countering his moves even before he's begun an attack. The building frustration continues to play into the advanced fencer's advantage as the novice continues to add unnecessary strength to his attacks which tends to slow down the execution of an attack. This is one reason why young fencers in their late teens or early twenties who rely on their youthful reactions and strength are easily bested by men and women in their late fifties and early sixties. Until the body loses its ability to respond to brain stimulus, the more experienced fencer will always defeat the less experienced one.

Fencing Wisdom

The superior fencer does not depend on physical ability when technique and skill can be used. Not only is the reliance on skill more effective, it also tends to be the more efficient movement, which, in turn, lead to less energy being spent. Because the experience fencer has learned how to react, he can remain poised and calm enough to handle the fencing match. Instead of reacting to an attack, a fencer has learned how to best, most efficiently, and quickly exploit his opponent's weaknesses. This is the reason why fencers do not race head-on toward the enemy without first knowing what kind of attack will be successful.

Apart from practicing certain movement in drills and forms, experience from free practice is often considered the next best way of improving one's skills other than engaging in an actual duel or battle. But how does a fencer decide what the movements should be used to defeat an opponent? Common sense would seem to indicate that simply reacting in the proper, prescribed manner will defend against an opponent's attack. Speed, strength, and endurance all seem to be qualities that would determine a victor. Wisdom (knowledge and insight), however, is what really makes one fencer better than another. Wisdom in fencing is an understanding of four fundamental concepts: 1) timing defeats speed, 2) leverage defeats strength, 3) technique defeats instincts, and 4) distance defeats the sword.

While knowledge is helpful in trying to solve a problem of defeating an enemy swordsman, knowledge is only a single competence of a great fencer. Knowing what attack an opponent will use can clearly lead to the proper defensive response, but fencing is too fluid and quick for there to be time to think about the attack and then cognitively plan a defense. It may seem counterintuitive, but fencers engage in the battle *not* with a host of information, but rather with a *lack* of information because it takes too long for the body to act on stimulus from the brain. Instead, the body must act on perceived and actual threats, both anticipating an attack, discerning between feints and real attacks while simultaneously preparing a defense. When attacking, the fencer must make his moves with the ability to anticipate possible counter attacks and prepare a proper response. Such a complex activity does not express cognitive thinking, but more a kind of intuition which is heavily influenced by experience and an understanding of the art of fencing.

Cognitive thinking (the execution of executive brain activity) is used to solve intellectual problems. Involving more senses increases the brain's ability to learn, which is why the educational field has begun to emphasize holistic activities in lower grades to engage as many or all of the students senses as possible. Designing and constructing three-dimensional projects or reading out loud supplement what most have assumed to be the internal process of thinking and learning. The Chinese adage, "I hear and I forget. I see and I remember. I do and I understand," has new meaning. Cognitive learning, as it becomes more difficult, requires more energy from the brain and body. Concentration focuses the mind's attention and senses are used more keenly to inform the mind for a specific, rather than general purpose.

The mind is also capable of associative functions: multitasking, to use a modern word. Doing two or more things at the same time, like driving and talking, is an associative function. Outside factors, however, can make associative functions more cognitive. If, for example, it begins to rain heavily and you drive an older car with balding tires, almost instantly the brain understands that it is in a hazardous situation. It must focus on controlling the car, which, a few minutes earlier, was done without difficulty or thought. Chemically the body's senses become heightened and the brain examines stimulus with increased attentiveness. Extraneous stimulus, like casual talking stops, the driver sits up, turns down the radio, and looks more attentively at his mirrors. Every datum from the five senses is examined for relevance to controlling the car. The driver is learning to handle the situation.

Conversely, the inattentive driver leaves himself in the situation where an accident is more likely to occur. A common experience for urban drivers is that of a driver talking on his cell phone. It is not that a person can't talk, hold the phone, and drive at the same time, which will improve with practice, but that drivers don't adjust their driving to the complexity of their associative activities. Without realizing it, drivers who talk on the phone often dangerously slow down below the speed of traffic, make over-cautious turns, and do not hear ambient noises, like ambulance sirens or the honking car behind them. Worst of all is the act of dialing, which requires complete cognitive ability to recall a phone number and then look for the correct buttons to push.

Cognitive and associative functions are matter of life and death to the swordsman. Not only must he remain focused on the task of fencing (attacking or defending), but he has to also be aware of everything that is going on around him. Glands begin secreting hormones that heighten senses and the body and mind fall back on the training that has prepared the soldier for this moment. Viking berserkers gave all of their energy to emotional rage so that they might begin attacking anyone around them, friend or foe. The one-on-one swordsman, especially the duelist, must have a greater balance, maintaining sufficient adrenaline and testosterone to fight fiercely. Too much of either, on the other hand, would impede the body's cognitive functions during the fight.

This heightened state of battle preparedness on a simple endocrinological level is extremely difficult to maintain. Olympic athletes must not only maintain their physical peak, but the ups and downs of their psychological training tax the body even more than most people realize or understand.

Part of my own training for the World University Games and the World Championships in 1987 included intensive physical conditioning as well as intense mental focusing. Thousands of lunges, ten of thousands of advance and retreat drilling, running, stretching, and then bouting. To prepare myself mentally, I did a lot visualization exercises in which I imagined my movement according to scenarios I created in my head. Practicing defensive guards in the mirror as well as meditation also helped me place myself in a state where I could fight off every attack without fail. I had to dominate my opponent both physically and psychologically, and part of that process meant the vilification of my opponent and the elevation of victory as the most important object of my existence.

At this intensity, fencing was raised to a spiritual level. I was riding the high of my body's hormonal chemistry, allowing my mind to migrate into a different state of mental existence. The perception of time changed; attacks moved at a slow pace and my sense of control over the moment was so euphoric that I craved the rush it brought as if I were on an addictive drug.

Maintaining this intensity also had its inevitable side-effects: the emotional drain, the physical exhaustion, and increased paranoia. The body can only take that heightened alertness for only a limited time. Constantly looking over your shoulder to evaluate every stimulus for its potential danger was not unlike small birds and animals, which live in a constant state of fear, fidgeting, constantly looking for predators, and over-reacting to even the slightest sound. A state necessary for a creature in the wild, but not one the typical citizen wants to have as he lives in his peaceful urban or suburban world. Security and a diminished, if not a nonexistent fear from attack, have thus become prerequisites for inhabitants of modern societies.

The level of training and its associated psychological drain was one reason why I left competitive fencing. There was no romance in maintaining the emotional intensity of being a fencer twenty-four hours a day. And after meeting and fencing the greatest fencers of the world, it became apparent to me that the economic* and psychological costs were not worth it. After giving up fencing completely for two years, I began to refocus my energies toward writing, as well as the Japanese martial art of aikido, which relied on a tempered and even sensibility than the fight or flight mentality of the pitched battle. Only later would kendo, iaido, and jodo rekindle my interest in fencing.

Western & Japanese Styles

The traditional historical book on warfare often looks at warfare in broad strokes as a way to contrast the military culture and tactics of two opposing sides. Examinations of a commander's experience, reliance on battlefield disposition, and a brief vignette of the typical soldier are the usual fare in the discourse of such treatises whose purposes lay in placing the battle in the larger perspective of the war. And when discussion of battlefield technique is found, it focuses on the tactical movement of bodies of troops in relation to enemy units on the other side of the battlefield. What one does not find is a description of the specific techniques of the weapons used. This dearth stems from the fact that most historians are not or were not soldiers themselves, or there is no actual historical source which recounts such details.

---

*Fencers usually pay the full costs of training and travel for competition themselves.

And even when such documentation does exist in the form of a treatise, guide, or manual, the historian must read them with the understanding that 1) treatises did not necessarily describe the general manner of fighting within a particular body of troops, 2) it was propaganda for one particular style of fighting, and 3) the subtleties of pictographic and textual explanation do not substitute for direct training or practice. So where traditional histories of warfare are lacking in the manual technique in sword fencing, this section hopes to give the reader a better sense of the swordsman's actual fight by comparing Western and Japanese fencing.

As has already been seen, Western fencing has been one of an evolution of style appropriate to the physical transformation of the sword from a slashing weapon into a point weapon, while Japanese fencing is best described as an adaptation to the conditions of the battlefield and civilian life. In most cases, Western fencing styles were forgotten as instruction in new methods of warfare were developed. Unlike Japan, where strict observance of precise movement led to the complete transmission of the style to later, contemporary generations, Europeans focused on new methods of organizing firepower rather than devoting nostalgic attention to the art of swordsmanship which was quickly in decline.

Japan's isolation prevented open warfare, and while new styles of fighting did not develop, established methods of fighting systematized their style in face of the increasingly peaceful state of the country. Head instructors of kenjutsu quickly realized that an era of peace meant less support from the ruling government, which inevitably meant the end of the style through lack of attention. Fencing *ryu* (style) faced the scrutiny of the government because they were sources of education that might train future armies that would challenge the government. Samurai disaffected by the changed in the shogunate would return to their home province and train a new generation of samurai to overthrow the shogun.

In both Europe and Japan students would be first found among the nobility. Because their numbers would always remain limited, there was a natural impetus for commanders to begin to look to the commoner class for recruits. Knighthood and the priesthood were traditionally the two ways of entering higher levels of society, but commoners who demonstrated fighting ability and the sensibilities to adjust to the upper class were only accepted out of military necessity. In Japan, fencing halls trained a new generation of samurai through the patronage of noble families, while in Europe swordplay was a skill expected of all officers during their postings at a garrison barracks.

The fencing hall was the haven of a military culture, so initial training included basic etiquette toward their superiors. A soldier would often begin with physical training to toughen the body and prepare the mind for instruction. Often instruction was harsh and punishing. Officers or lead instructors, like the modern drill sergeant, gave their charges difficult and physically demanding jobs, believing that difficult tasks would break new recruits of the laziness of civilian life and prepared them for the battlefield.

In Japan, since the samurai was servant of a lord, learning the humbling skills of serving tea was another task that emphasized attention to detail needed during exercise. Because the subtle movement were required in fencing, the small and precise manner of holding a utensil or pouring water had the unintended effect of teaching fine motor skills. Since tea, as in the West, involved polite conversation, it also became a way of introducing the student to honored and respected instructors and individuals. For noble children, it taught them not to expect instant privilege, and for commoners, it served as a way to learn the refined social etiquette of the upper class.

In the training halls, called *dojo* in Japan and a *salle d'escrime* in Europe, instruction began by teaching stances which are the starting and stopping points for any martial art. Mastery of footwork is crucial to a fencer's movement and are essential to the proper execution of any movement. Once the feet are in place, the upper body is then free to perform the thrusting or slashing required of the fencer. So distinctive are stances that it is easy to recognize the type of training a person has received through his footwork. Sometimes it is possible to identify not only a particular style within a school of fencing or martial art, it may be possible to identify an individual instructor.

In competition, the stance indicates to judges when participants are ready to begin. In the street, when threatened by muggers, a stance will indicate the potential "victim's" knowledge of self-defense. A martial artist, caught in such a situation, has the choice of hiding his ability in order to surprise the assailant or he can take an overtly recognizable stance as a way to scare off the aggressor. Between competing martial arts, as well as styles within a particular art, the stance serves as a distinctive declaration of their fighting style.

In swordsmanship, stances not only serve as a starting point, it predefines the movement of the art. Kendo stances are characterized by parallel feet meant to allow the kendoka* to maintain a forward position opposite his opponent. Traditional kenjustu, which anticipates an attack from any direction, places his feet in a V-shape, which allows the swordsman to turn in any direction instantly. Western fencing has the feet at 90° angles, which best permits the fencer to move up and down along a thin strip that designates the bouting area.

Placement of the hands also has an impact on the way the sword is held. The extended forearm and opposite arm hanging out behind the head are characteristic of Western fencers. Japanese swordsmen can be recognized by the two-handed grip with their weapon's point aimed at the opponent. Not only does the stance allow the swordsman to initiate an attack quickly, it permits him to block enemy attacks with little or no movement.

Contrary to what most would assume, there is no single perfect stance. Basic stances, however, do act as an initial defensive postures which allow a person to quickly attack or defend according to the circumstances of the situation. Each stance has both advantages and disadvantages, the easiest example being the foil

---

*A kendo fencer.

and epee whose guard protects only one side of the body more completely than if the weapon were placed squarely in the middle of the body. If the foil or epee is placed along the center line of the body, the entire torso is partially open to attack. In the reality of a fencing duel, there is no single stance, but a series of stances appropriate to the opponents attack.

The manner of holding the sword is probably the most obvious difference between Western and Japanese fencing. Again, each style reflects the culture in which they lived as well as the manner in which they will initiate an attack or parry. The Western foil and epee emphasize subtle movement of the point toward the opponent which obviates the fact that both fencers would probably be in civilian dress which would allow penetrations to the torso and the body's appendages. Japanese stances, being still more closely linked to the attack of an armored opponent, relied on the penetrating strength of two hands. In both Japan and the West, the single-handed use of a sabre or its equivalent Heian *tachi* reflected the necessity to use the non-fencing arm to control the horse or to act as a counter balance to the outward sweep of the sword. Earlier European knights actually carried a shield which served both as a counter balance and defensive shielding.

Attack and Defense

Fencing, whether Western, Japanese, or any other, depends on the swordsman's ability to both defend and attack. Victory, however, is almost entirely dependant on the ability to attack.

In Western fencing, the body is customarily divided into four basic target areas that protect the most vital part of a human's anatomy — the torso. The body is divided across a vertical line through the middle of the torso; the side closest to the fencing arm being called the "inside line," while the other is the "outside line." Another line, this one horizontal, bisects the torso into an upper and lower half, creating, in effect, four squares that need to be protected.

The defensive parries in foil and epee are divided into four basic parries which protect each of the four torso areas. These parries are further divided into two grips called supination, in which the palm faces up, and pronation, in which the palm faces down. Together there are a total of eight parries, two for each part of the torso. While all parries move upward or laterally, supinated parries are inherently stronger in that the downward force of the arm acts as a stronger brace and allows for an easier push through the opponent's blade. The supinated hand allow the muscles of the arm to extend more quickly for attacks. Additionally, supinated parries allow the blade to lift an opponent's blade upward and away from the larger torso area.

Because of the blade's thin profile, it is only possible to defend a single line at a time. This is accomplished by holding a guard that deflects attacks past the body on the inside line, while twisting the torso to reduce the openness of the outside line. When threats or attacks are made to the outside line, a simple shift in the wrist allows the fencer to take a parry on the opposite, outside line.

Kendo takes a different approach to defensive postures. Because the grip of the shinai* is with two hands, the body forms a frontward stance toward the opponent. This stance is much like that of a golfer who lifts the head of his club upward to eye-level with the top of the club aimed at his naval. Instead of dividing the body into four parts, the kendoka uses the tip of the sword as the forward end of a triangular shield. Any attack, whether a thrust or a cut, must pass on either side of the blade. As the attacking moves toward the kendoka, he pulls his shinai slightly toward the side of the attacking blade, forcing the opponent's point away from the center line. A slash is caught in mid-cut before it has a chance to reach the kendoka's body. Low parries are made in the same way except that the point is lowered. More traditional Japanese fencing styles pull one shoulder back behind the other, in much the same manner as the

*A bamboo practice sword.

Western fencer turns his torso to limit body exposure.

Swordsmanship, however, is learning to properly attack, whether it is from a direct attack, which strikes unopposed at an undefended area, or pushes through a defensive parry. An attack may also be done immediately after a defensive parry (a riposte) has been made to block an attack, though the psychological training of swordsmen must continually focus on the advance and attack, de-emphasizing defensive tactics which will never emerge victorious.

While the strategy of biding time may be necessary to catch one's breath or to wear down the opponent, it must always be done with the strategic goal of preparing for an attack. Giving more time to the enemy to prepare their own attack during the short encounter with an armed opponent in hand-to-hand combat allows the enemy to take and use the initiative for his own. The press of a concerted attack allows the fencer to expend minimal energy while imposing a disproportionate expense of energy on the opponent. Consequently, it is always to the fencer's advantage to maintain an attacking posture, especially on the battlefield when opponents may attack from any direction. Even during a regulated duel when there is no fear of surprise attack, "toying" with lesser skilled fencer allows the opponent to plan an attack as the better fencer slowly lowers his guard in an arrogant and misguided sense of confidence. The most expert swordsmen understands that *he* has more to lose against desperate fencers, who have nothing to lose and everything to gain.

Apart from the gentleman's duel in which the goal is to be the first to draw blood on their opponent, the ultimate goal of the swordsman is to incapacitate the enemy to prevent him from temporarily or permanently returning an attack. While the former involves disarming, knocking unconscious, or causing the enemy to flee, the battlefield encounter requires the efficient killing of the enemy. The brutal truth is that sword fighting that merely injures the opponent gives the injured another opportunity to kill the attacker.

There are two ways of killing with a sword: the first using

the edge of the blade called a hard kill, the second using the point called a soft kill. The hard kill relies on the cutting of the limbs, trunk, and head that results in instantaneous death in the case of decapitation or the eventual loss of blood that quickly leads to death if left untreated. The soft kill uses the point to kill by piercing vital organs like the brain and heart. Penetrations to a non-vital organ may, in time, kill the opponent either through the eventual failure of vital body systems or from possible infection. Ideally, a slow kill will at least prevent the opponent from continuing to attack. Superficial cuts, if allowed to heal free of infection, do little permanent damage to the injured apart from obvious scarring.

Without question, the most important area of the body is the head. Injury to the executive controls of the body — the brain — impact not only the five senses, but the body's autonomic and reflexive controls. Striking at the head is a psychologically important attack that cannot be underestimated. An anecdotal incident in which I accidentally struck at my opponent's head during a Dagohir mock combat simulation emphasizes the point that trauma to the head, or even perceived trauma, can have profound consequences on a warrior. Every moment leading up to the encounter is the psychological building of fear — fear of pain and fear of death. From the beat of enemy drums, the drawing of swords, and the march forward, a climax in a person's life reaches a crescendo. Add the limited vision of lowering one's helmet and the echoing sounds of the interior, the uncertainty of battle becomes even more acute.

When the first hit strikes at the head, a swordsman's vulnerability becomes evident in the quality of the attack. Did the sword cut penetrate the helmet or bounce off? If it penetrated, did it damage the scalp? And to what degree?

An attack on the head has two purposes: to disorient the opponent so another, more fatal attack may be made, or to penetrate the skull decisively and kill the opponent instantly. An attack on a bare head has even greater implications; cleaving into the skull is more likely to kill, and if even a graze is made on the

scalp, the subsequent blood which drips down to the face and into the eyes has a demoralizing impact on the defending swordsman. Not only does blood impede a swordsman's visual perception, it makes him conscious that he had been hit when, because
his sense of touch has been dulled by adrenaline pumping
through the body, he might not have even noticed his injury.

After six years of study under two exceptional Japanese instructors, I trained to make the strike to the head with the bokken so fast and efficient, that I can make a wooden sword slice
through the air and "sing" like a metal sword. When combined
with the precision of an attack that stops inches from one's eyes
and ears, the most experienced and toughest partners with
whom I have practiced expressed an uneasy nervousness that I
might make a mistake in my strike. The control needed to stop
a wooden sword, much less a live blade, so quickly without losing cutting power is an incredible combination of the natural use
of gravity and a very focused coordination of the arms' and
hands' muscles. At such intensity, practice evolves into sheer
acts of faith that an attack will stop short of the head each and
every time.

In one occasion, an instructor with whom I was training
failed to properly brace a block to his head when I did a head
cut. Realizing I had smashed through his guard, I immediately
attempted to pull my strike. Though with considerably less force,
I still hit him on the bare head with my blunt wooden edge. He
grabbed his head for a second to feel the bump, when suddenly
it began bleeding profusely. Despite my pulled attack, the impact
with a blunt wooden sword was still strong enough to break skin
at the point of impact.

In the already mentioned example of Dagohir-rules mock
fighting with stiff but padded weapons, I inadvertently caused
several nasty, though non-life threatening injuries to the head of
my opponents. The rules prohibit attacks to the head, but as
medieval-clad opponents bore down on me with their mock
weapons in the air, my instincts returned to my kendo training.
I responded by making blocks and then instinctually making a

counter stroke to my attacker's unprotected head. Dagohir weapons were padded enough to prevent the interior wooden or fiberglass shaft from being felt, but the force of being hit on the head or face was shockingly similar to being hit in the face with a tennis ball shot out of an automatic tennis ball server. The outer canvas of my mock sword smashed into ears, knocked heads solidly, and, in one case, smashed the lips of one guy into his teeth, cutting the inside of his mouth. In that last instance, my opponent instantly dropped his sword and shield and began screaming in agony as he grabbed the outside of his bleeding gums. After profuse apologies, I had to change my fencing tactics to avoid hitting my opponents in the head.

With a real sword, the potential for permanent damage is even more evident. In kendo, the strike with the two-handed katana is made with a frightening quickness. Within one and a half seconds the sword can be raised above the head and then thrust forward at the enemy. Once the attack has been launched, there is not enough time to consciously make a block. Only tell-tale signs of tensing hands or arm muscles, or the intuition that a head strike will be made allows the recipient of a head attack to raise his sword for a block.

Attacking with the point is also an effective, though more difficult method of hitting the head. Many European treatises display points made to the eye of an opponent in order to penetrate the brain through the eyes, nose, or mouth. Because of their location and the anatomically round shape of the head, eyes are rarely pierced by a sword. The side of the head is an easy target for a sabre cut, however. And penetrating into the skull has immediate and devastating consequences. In one instance during an Olympic fencing tournament, a foil broke during a rough exchange and penetrated the mask of one fencer, lodging into the man's brain. Though he did not die instantly, the penetration was so severe that he expired soon after.

Below the head is an area that is particularly vulnerable to attack — the neck. While it is the softest and most exposed area of the body, because of its size and location near the head, it is probably one of the most difficult areas of the body to hit. Blocking attacks to the throat must be extremely swift and precise in its timing because the body's natural instinct is to raise the arms up to protect the throat and head.* Not only is the carotid artery located in the neck, but a crushed trachea or blood from a punctured artery could literally drown an opponent in his own blood.

Aiming for the throat with a rapier or court sword is extremely difficult and rarely worth the effort. Not only must the point lodge exactly on either side of the Adam's apple, but it must puncture deeply enough to pass through the neck to either slice through the trachea or cut through the neck's artery. Turning the blade so that it cuts horizontally or twisting it as it passes into the flesh are also necessary to properly penetrate the throat. Only a hard and direct hit into the spine can sever the backbone. An extremely difficult task indeed.

The target areas of Western competitive fencing do not lend themselves to attacks on the throat. The foil (a descendant of the court sword) targets the torso. The epee, because the whole body is target, targets the wrist and arm, while sabre practice emphasizes cuts to the top and side of head. Kendo teaches a powerful and direct thrust to the throat that must be used very rarely so it can be used as a surprise attack.

Severing the head, made famous by the *Highlander* movies starring Christophe Lambert is a strike that can only effectively be made when the opponent does not wear armor. Timing must be perfect — the enemy has to have just made a large swing and have lost his balance in order to allow an opening that allows sufficient time to cut to the neck. The neck might also be exposed if an earlier attack causes the body to double over.

---

*It is interesting to note that in weaponless fights in the movies, punches to the head are routinely made with little obvious trauma. While inflicting a series of concussion seems to fit the expected male pretension of brawling, the fighter intent on killing his opponent ought to strike to the throat where the Adam's apple and trachea are easily crushed.

This kind of *coup de grâce* is rare and is only accomplished by the complete domination of the opponent. Beheading serves as an effective propaganda tool as a way to terrorize a local population. The beheading might also have served as a victory trophy, as was the case of in feudal Japan. The tale of the Forty-seven Ronin illustrated the cultural etiquette of bringing the enemy's head to the samurai's master. In this case, the head is brought to the grave of their dead master. Bringing heads as proof of killing an enemy are common trophies of many cultures. Herodias asked for John the Baptist's head on a silver platter. Wampanoag King Philip's head was cut off by the Pilgrims, placed on top of a spear, and planted in the center of Plymouth, following a cruel tradition common to many European cities. Even the scalping of native Americans in exchange for a bounty at government offices perpetuated the same barbaric act. Tamerlane supposedly left ten foot high mounds of severed heads. In some instances, he used them to build towers as a legacy of terror to make unconquered enemies cower before his army. It was said among diplomatic circles that the KGB sent the severed corpse of an Iranian operative to Teheran as a warning not to take over the Soviet embassy in the wake of the American embassy attack in 1979.

The Japanese saw beheading as the last step in ritual suicide called seppuku.[*] Under particular social circumstances, self-inflicted suicide was the culturally respectable manner of proving an individual's inner mettle by dying in the dignity at one's own hands. The ritual is a carefully prescribed affair which results with the samurai piercing his own abdomen and then pulling it across his belly in two distinct cuts. Recognizing the difficulty of the act (an act which one never gets to practice), a swordsman trusted by the samurai committing suicide is expected to strike down at his friend's neck at the very moment when the victim was about to lose control of his motor functions. Proper technique requires the swordsman giving the *coup de grâce* to slice off the head in a single cut leaving a thin piece of skin at the

---

[*]*Hara kiri* is the commoner's term, meaning "belly cutting."

throat to prevent the head from rolling away from the body. Not only did the samurai preserve his own personal dignity by taking his own life, but it served as a final test of his strength and discipline as he fought the grueling pain of his bloody task.

Slicing through the spine was a skill in which Japanese swordsman formally trained. Called *tameshi giri*, the swordsman would practice cutting through a thick bamboo pole surrounded by thick straw that had been tied together and soaked in water. The bamboo simulated the spine or bone, while the heavy, water logged straw represented the flesh. An alternate method involves taking old tatami mats and rolling them up to the thickness of the neck. The rolls would then be put on a vertical stick to be chopped down with a live blade. A more difficult practice would be to go out into a bamboo grove and cut down shafts in clean strokes. In both kinds of practice, the swordsman quickly learns that it is not the strength of the muscles that makes the cut, but the edge of the blade which slices through the "flesh." The hardest cuts are the horizontal slash and the upward cut, which require the blade to move in a perfect plane to avoid lodging the blade in the flesh. During a session of *tameshi giri*, a friend of mine improperly hit the rolled up mat, causing the steel blade to bend at a steep angle. It was eventually straightened out, but any such damage may potentially break a blade.

Apart from slashing at the upper body, the body's appendages are more easily hit. Striking at the limbs is ideally done by shattering the cartilage of the kneecaps, ankles, and elbows. Not only is it easier to cut through, but even minor penetrations will have a greater affect on a limb by severing ligaments and tendons than if cut between the joints. Muscles, because of its fibrous nature, are more difficult to cut. A cut through the tendon allows the muscles to move, but prevents execution of the body movement desired. If the tendons in the forearm can be cut, an attack that requires swiftness and only a minimum of force, the fencer will be completely prevented from controlling his wrist. Superficial damage to muscle will heal over time, but tendons or ligaments, unless reattached, will permanently disable or damage fine motor skills.

In striking to the torso, the fencer must consider the anatomy of the opponent. Ribs and the sternum will stop a sword cut, so thrusts to the mid-section must be made between ribs by twisting a flat-bladed sword into a horizontal position just before piercing the opponent's trunk. A blade that penetrates the chest can hit any number of vital organs, some of which when hit may cause instant death — a hit to the heart for example. Soft hits to other organs, while not immediately fatal, may eventually cause the body to go into shock. A hit to the stomach is a nasty penetration that releases acids which begin to eat away at the linings of the internal organs. If not stopped, the damage to other internal organs will become permanent. Puncturing the lungs will similarly releases fluids that will internally drown the injured swordsman.

Because of the rudimentary state of internal medicine or the lack of medical attention on the battlefield, the damage inflicted on a soldier was often quick and swift. Whether from shock of massive hemorrhage or exposure to the elements, severe lacerations or internal puncturing of the organs meant eventual death. While some armies supported either a small unit of surgeons or other medical personal, their knowledge was limited, their equipment basic, and their skill too undeveloped to save all but the least wounded of the injured. It was often the responsibility of the light infantry, or even noncombatants who assisted in moving the army's baggage train, to follow in the wake of the front line's offensive to finish off the wounded that still lingered from their wounds. In other instances, armed servants dealt the death blow after his horse bound master dealt a devastating blow.

At the end of a battle, the traditions varied from culture to culture. The Greeks ceased further operations when it was apparent the enemy had retreated and then made obsequies before taking armor from the dead as part of their trophy panoply. Others buried troops in mass graves with their full arms and armor, at other times without. Whatever the custom, the aftermath was a gruesome scene even for the victor as friends and comrades were counted for national registers. Battlefield warfare in its minutest detail is a senseless event of brutality, but when faced with the alternative of invasion and possible annihilation, war on these terms justifies the necessity of the swordsman's art.

Comparing Styles

Once one learns some of the subtleties that distinguish Western fencing from samurai fencing, the most immediate question that springs to mind is who would win if a European and a samurai were to engage in a fight. While it is hard to say exactly because there are so many factors to consider, including the armor each wears, the sword they use, the time period from which they come, et al, it is possible to share some generalities.

Certainly the swordsman who is used to fighting opponents of varying cultures has the advantage over the swordsman who is only used to fighting similarly armed and armored opponents. Likewise, the swordsman who is not dependent on armor will have an advantage over the man who is used to compensating for technique with the help of armor. The discrepancy in ability and skill, however, are impossible to quantify in an activity like swordsmanship except by actual combat. Swordsmen did have a way of measuring their skill, though it rarely crossed cultural lines and was limited to combat with swordsmen in neighboring regions.

The traditional method of seeing who was better was to send out a member of the school and challenge a member of the opposition. A member of a Barcelona fencing school might travel to France and challenge a swordsman in Paris, for example. In Japan, students of one dojo would sometimes traveled to other dojo in search of challengers. If the challenged school accepted, it would send its best student to meet the visitor. Rules would be decided and then the "friendly" duel took place. If the school's representative won, he preserved the honor of the school. If the visitor won, he would take the placard on which the name of the dojo was written as a trophy. Challenges could be made to the death, but such serious encounters were unheard of except in the case of a personal feud. Challenges served both the challenger and the challenged by providing fresh sparing partners against whom they could test their fighting skills. On occasion, the feuds did get personal, especially between nearby rival schools.

But still the question remains as to which is better: the Western or Japanese fencing style? Or, in broader terms, which swordsmen were technically superior to others?

One cannot respond without first saying (as had been done in the previous chapter) that armor played a crucial role in combat. For all of the emphasis on fencing style, not even the best technique amounted to anything if it could not penetrate an opponent's defensive armor. Next, given the divergent evolution of Western fencing and kendo, there is a clear difference in the martial applications of each competitive sport. The foil and epee were developed for courtly encounters, while kendo came out of a more recent and practical history in which the katana was actively used by the samurai class late into the 19th century. And while a comparison might be made between the modern sabre and the katana, technique in the light sabre of Olympic-style fencing does not have the same martial application as kendo, much less kenjutsu.

History does provide circumstances in which European sailors encountered Japanese pirates. Yet the examples are neither decisive in favor of one style. Chance encounters did exists, but explanations of one culture's victory over swordsmen of another is not definitively explained in terms of better swordsmanship. Samurai boarders may have been successful swordsmen who could have easily been cut down by Western pistols and muskets, but even novice samurai could have been bested by Western sailors and nobles experienced in boarding enemy ships, though this feat was rather a rare occurrence.

While anecdotes are rare, there is one historical report of the quality of Japanese hosts who personally drew their own swords and dispatched several renegade samurai attempting to assassinate several European diplomats. But given the fact that Euro-

peans had already gone past the sword and employed the musket and pistol, it was increasingly rare that Europeans would allow themselves to fall into a situation where a talented samurai
might draw his sword. While one-sided in terms of fairness,
survival in combat eventually depended more on technology
than it did on fencing skills. It is this very reason that Europeans
were able to extend their empires all the way to the opposite side
of the globe.

On a practical level, there have been many informal exchanges in the past century between Western fencers and Japanese kendoka. In my humble opinion, based on a purely anecdotal level, Japanese kendo, strike for strike, attack for attack,
bests any of the three forms of modern fencing which has been
so refined for international competition as to be useless. While
the Western foil fencer practices to depress a point with only 500
grams, the kendoka practices the slicing cut that can easily be
transferred to a live blade. Put a katana in the hands of a kendoka and a rapier in the hands of the foilist, the physical nature
of kendo easily smashes through the Westerner who is not used
to the infighting the katana favors with its blade length edge.
Even when a live blade sabre is placed in the hands of a Western
sabre fencer, the strength in his arm for one-handed parries
cannot sustain itself against the heavy and rapid attacks of the
two-handed kendoka.

That is not to say that there are not advantages to fencers of
the Western style. The lighter saber also has a speed that allows
for a rapid counter attack if the two-handed samurai misses with
his first attack. The Western fencer is also quick and agile in
advancing and retreating when compared to the sure-footed and
deliberate samurai warrior. Subtle movements of the point also
allow the rapier to plunge into an on-rushing samurai who
might fail to catch the Western blade. A rapier point in the eye,
throat, or chest was as deadly as any slicing motion of the
katana.

So is there an answer to the initial question does not really
apply to which style is better than the other. The ultimate ans-

wer, however, ultimately depends on a more important question: Who is the better swordsman? For it is the swordsman who best adapts to the situation, making the best of his offensive capabilities and denying access to his obvious weaknesses, that will win any sword fight encounter.

In terms of comparing modern fencers to their historical predecessors, quality of swordsmanship is heavily dependent on experience. It can probably be argued that modern fencers are more physically capable than swordsmen of earlier generations. Similarly, the modern swordsman, if he trained in order to fight with a real sword, he could in time readily adapt to its use in this fashion.

There is also the tendency to ascribe more weight and credibility to sword fighting styles of earlier periods. The age of a style, however, does not necessarily indicate a superior style; more that the style was more successful in finding talented students to continue transmission of the style from one generation to the next. And were moderns somehow required to use the sword in hand-to-hand combative situations, there is no doubt in my mind that with modern attitudes and training methods, the modern would be able to acquire skills and abilities equal to or surpassing those of historical swordsmen under similar circumstances. It is by luck and fortune that contemporary men and women will never need to learn the art of swordsmanship, and that its activity is best appreciated by fencing afficionado as well as the *Star Wars* fan interested in learning about lightsaber fighting.

Terran and Lightsaber Fencing

Given the number of martial artists practicing Western Fencing and Asian forms of sword fighting, it is of note that most are equally impressed with the lightsaber fighting that took place in *The Phantom Menace*. A remarkable feat when one considers the plethora of sword fighting films that have come out in recent years. The enduring presence of *Star Wars* lightsaber fighting will always exist in its service to the story of the Jedi as George Lucas has envisioned them in his cinematic saga.

More so in the Original Trilogy, the sword fight helped tell the story of the rise of a young boy to Jedi mastery. Every action was choreographed with the dialogue that conveyed the Luke's temptation to power and the eventual redemption of Darth Vader at the end of *Return of the Jedi*. It should be especially clear from this chapter that sword fighting, if properly done, is bereft of the dramatic presence found in theater and cinema. A successful swordsman had to win instantly or be overpowered by the sheer numbers of enemy swordsmen looking for an adversary to kill. Even the modern competition which takes place over a period of ten minutes according to strict rules attracts small audiences usually limited to friends and family of the competitors. Fencing is too refined, too subtle, and too quick for modern audiences to appreciate its beauty. It is rather unfortunate that fencing, which has existed longer than the history of all modern sports combined, attracts less attention than the teenager's passion for skate boarding. You will never find a copy of *American Fencing*, the U.S. Fencing Association's bi-monthly magazine, in any store, while any number skateboarder magazines can be found in the local magazine rack.

Perhaps it is because of how uncommon and so outside of our modern experiences that the sword fight continues to amaze us. But unlike most historical movies whose genre seems stilted and so far out of our experiences, *Star Wars* has endured and will remain a permanent fixture in the experiences of the many generations that have been around since its debut in 1997. Of interesting note is the apparent intolerance of adult fans who criticized *The Phantom Menace* for being too much geared to children when they, themselves, became hooked on *Star Wars* when they were the same age.

Many were let down when they actually saw *The Phantom Menace*, but any movie would be hard pressed to live up to the hype that preceded its May 1999 premiere. But what everyone remembers, as was evident during my talks in the summer after the release of *The Phantom Menace*, was that the sword fight was more memorable than any other part of the visual feast that was that movie. Certainly what set the sword fight in the Original Trilogy apart from the Prequel Trilogy is the focus not so much on a fighting conversation, but the sheer energy of Jedi Knights fighting a Sith Lord. No one can forget the impression Darth Maul made when he makes his appearance in the Theed Hangar as trumpets in John William's musical score blare into the theater.

While non-fencers have expressed their enthusiasm for the *Star Wars* sword fight, there are serious discussions among martial artists about the new style created by stunt coordinator Nick Gillard. Their criticism isn't focused so much on the technical abilities of all the actors and stunt men who created the sword fight in *The Phantom Menace*, but the gratuitous use of the sword fight. In *The Empire Strikes Back* and *Return of the Jedi*, so much of the characters' emotions were conveyed by the very lightsaber fight itself. While still impressive, the silent battle between the Jedi and Darth Maul lacked the same presence of the duels in earlier films.

Fencing by its very nature is defined by the ability of a swordsman to survive combat. Heroism and idealism have little bearing the swordsman engaged in a fight for his life. For the Jedi on screen, however, the sword fight is choreography created as entertainment for the masses. It should consequently be used to tell the story and not simply satisfy our appetite for action. It certainly draws on the basics of Terran sword fighting, which it must if it is to be believed by audiences accustomed to the swashbuckling adventure of historical films like *The Mask of Zorro* and the surprise hit of the Chinese genre *Hidden Dragon, Crouching Tiger*, but a prize fight without a story is simply a prize fight.

If the *Star Wars* lightsaber fight has succeeded in anything, it is that proper fencing does give the modern actor an added edge in authenticity in modern films. Achieving actual realism with fake swords in a fictitious combat for film has a powerful presence when projected on the silver screen. Up until only the last thirty years, cultural films relied exclusively on the sword fighting of their region. The swashbuckler film had cutlass fights that simulated modern sabre and ancient and medieval films used rough broadsword techniques. In Asia, sword fighting was defined by the cultural traditions that existed within that country. Japanese sword techniques could only be use in samurai films and wu shu broad sword and spear could only be used in movies of Chinese origins. It was with the advent of *Star Wars* that East would meet West in a style of sword fighting that was both Terran and other-worldly.

Up until *Star Wars*, the cultural divide of Eastern martial arts and Western martial arts remained separate historical traditions. In *Red Sun*, Toshiro Mifune plays a samurai in the Wild West and in *Enter the Dragon*, Bruce Lee popularized kung fu for a Western audience. Today, many American films have seamlessly imported Asian fighting techniques into completely Western films. Steve Seagal, Steven Douglas, and Keanu Reaves have gone far past the Sixties and Seventies cliché of a karate chop to the shoulder. *Star Wars* brought Eastern sword fighting to Western cinema in a way that both Orientals and Occidentals appreciate, making Lucas' hit a blockbuster in every nation of the world.

Inherent in this bonding of Eastern and Western fencing is the fact that there are fundamentals to all fencing that transcend cultural expressions. Starting in the Fifties when American soldiers found themselves living in Asia at the end of World War II, Americans began learning the traditional martial arts that native Asians had developed and refined for centuries. If their martial arts were not filled with profound skill, discipline, and wisdom, no outsiders would have seen much value in learning what have come to be popular martial arts like kung fu, pa kua, karate, judo, aikido, and hundreds of others. On a practical level, Westerners appreciated the fighting efficiency of Asian fighting styles that they have been formally taught as forms of self-defense in many Western military forces.

The intellectual movement reached a threshold with Eugene Herrigal's *The Art of Archery* which exposed Westerners to both a spiritual and intellectual level of martial practice. Not only did the "way" of the martial arts begin to formulate in Western minds, it reflected a growing interest in non-Western methods of thought in an increasingly consumer world. In Japan, the diminished emphasis on killing technique found formal expressing during the early Edo period when peaceful justifications of the sword became the subject of open writing. The "Way" of the sword was to find a sword that served peaceful ends, while the "Art" of the sword became a series of techniques that were used for the practical ends of killing.

While many of my contemporaries would argue otherwise, it is my belief that a true understanding of the "Way" of swordsmanship — the sword as a tool of peace — cannot be found without first developing the technique of the "Art" of the sword — the sword used in war. Despite the terrible thought that one is learning how to kill with a sword, the lesson of truly understanding how peace wins out over anger and aggression is learned when one fully understands the horror of the skill which the swordsman has learned through severe and disciplined training.

It has been my experience that students who do not face the difficult challenge of making technique effective delude themselves into thinking they are learning the peaceful martial art. Students of this sort, while well-intentioned, desire to learn art for self-development, but they do not learn the iron discipline that informs and challenges the mastery of a martial art. This is what separates the barbaric soldier who fights on emotion from the warrior-intellectual who understands that there is a medium in life that defines men and women as members of a society. The education of warfare for the simple use of winning battles builds an expansionist mind set which justifies the domination of the strongest over the weakest. What the intellect and technology (and sword fighting is a living technology) best illustrate is not what one does to win the battlefield, but what one does to build the world after the battle.

It therefore behooves the student to practice his art with utmost diligence under a wise and thoughtful instructor. Without this, the focus of war becomes the end product inculcated in a generation of fencers. Far from it, *Star Wars* is a lesson in the triumph of good over evil as so clearly illustrated by the lightsaber duel. With a fuller understanding of the skills that are necessary for Terran sword fighting, the *Star Wars* lightsaber fight, and its focus on settling our fears, can be even better appreciated.

5

Jedi Precedents

Unlike most modern and futuristic films, George Lucas turns away from the special ops and secret government agent when he looks for heros to his epic *Star Wars* saga. Part knight, part monk, the Jedi Lucas created are an order of swordsmen that help rule the universe in accordance with law and lofty principles. In his own words, the Jedi are swordsmen, ambassadors, negotiators, and, as he facetiously puts it, "intergalactic therapists." They are not strictly enforcers, but men of action who are as wise as they are trained swordsmen. The Jedi don't simply sit in the context of *Star Wars* as mere police men on call to answer emergencies across the galaxy when needed. Instead, they have a more substantive culture to their organization which finds precedence in the life of the religious (that of monks and nuns), military warrior knights, and in enslaved soldier armies. This chapter focuses on influences of various cultures that were historical examples of warrior monks — Jedi of the past.

All societies have had to come to terms with the expression of military values within society. Governments need a military to maintain order. Sometimes it imposes it. In most instances, it enforces it. When the military did not rule openly and outright, societal and social pressures help to soften the hard edge of barracks life which is often characterized by harsh discipline and a brutish survival-of-the-fittest existence. A nation needs soldiers to fight a wars of defense and offense, but what does one do with them once the war is won?

The nature of the Jedi Order, as can be parsed from eight hours of film and a plethora of primary and secondary sources, is an amalgam of *gendarme*, monk, and diplomat. He has the skills of the warrior, makes a professed commitment to a regulated life according to a common rule, and he must have the education and training to advise men and women of authority on how to act in their leadership role. Though skilled as martial artists, they are wise enough to understand that their power lays more in their ability to convince than to coerce. As Qui-Gon Jinn says to Queen Amidala in *Episode I* about his limited powers, "I can only protect you. I cannot win a war for you."

As servants of the Supreme Chancellor, the Jedi are duty bound to carry out the wishes of legally elected officials in the Galactic Senate. As respecters of the law, they are bound by their function as public servants, dedicated to the service of others far beyond their own needs. Yet the Jedi, as inferred by the existence of a Jedi temple, live a severe life of strictness and discipline. Sometimes they recede into their temples to be free of the world and to be free of its temptations. At other times they must engage the world, often being full participants in the unfurling of history. Not unaware of their role, the Jedi face hardships and obstacles in life that common and ordinary people would perceive as unnecessary, and even self-absorbed. Yet it is assumed during the time of *The Phantom Menace*, when the Jedi are still at the height of their power, that they play an honorable and worthy role as soldiers of the galaxy, protectors of the Galactic Republic.

We know for a fact that the Jedi are trained while very young. Their force abilities are detected around the time of their birth in hospitals; presumably the Jedi test is one of a series of standard procedures for the recently born. Anakin, even at the tender age of nine, is already too old to begin Jedi training, and if he had entered the Jedi order in the traditional method, he would have taken the title Padawan and served an apprenticeship to a Jedi knight before taking Trials which would demonstrate his ability and skills before being conferred the full title of Jedi Knight. And had he served the order well in some function, whether as a front line fighter or a diligent administrator, he may have had the opportunity to become the greatest of all Jedi, a Jedi

Master.

While details of training are left for the next chapter, Terran examples of Jedi Knights span broad historical and cultural paths in human history. By drawing not only on the fabled story of King Arthur and his knights, but on historical examples, Lucas makes the Jedi order even more compelling than if he had simply affixed a noble sounding name and a multiparti beast on a shield. The voluntary knights of European military orders, the priests, monk, and nuns of the Middle Ages, the warrior-monks of Japan, and the slave warriors of Islam have deep histories whose depths have been transferred to the imaginary Jedi Order. Without detailing every historical precedent for the Jedi, I focus in this chapter on knights of the Templar, Hospitaller, and Teutonic orders, priests and religious of the Christian faith, the fighting monks of Japan called *Sohei*, and the Janissaries and Mamelukes of Islam.

Religious Life

Though the Jedi are not explicitly a religious order professing a specific culture of faith that overtly dictates the belief in a monotheistic God (the concept of midi-chlorians is very animistic), the organization of the order resembles that of the Catholic Church which predominated Western Europe for the past two thousand years. Similarly, the Protestant reformation in which predominantly German speaking Catholics in the late 15th century rebelled against the Church because of the pope's insistence of his recognized authority, the selling of indulgences (purchased guarantees of entry to heaven), the poor quality of the clergy, and the absentee nature of church land holdings which siphoned money off to Rome, provide historical examples of how sincerely professing Roman Catholics came to be reviled by break-away Catholics,[*] and how each truly believed in the righteousness of

---

[*] The comparison of Catholic/Protestant wars to the Jedi/Sith antagonism is superficial at best, and no intention of equating one faith or the other with the Sith is made except for the fact that

its own cause. For over two hundred years, the religious struggles led to uncountable atrocities and tens of thousands of deaths on both sides of the wars that rocked Europe during the Reformation and its subsequent Catholic Counter Reformation.

Apart from the macro example of faiths in conflict as analogous to the confrontation between the Jedi and the Sith, the heart of religious life starts on two basic ideas: the worship of God and the purification of the soul. In order to achieve these two goals, three traditions of life were developed for those who wished to leave the secular world and their non-religious societal functions for an existence devoted daily to the worship of God. Within those turbulent times of continual war and strife, it was easy to understand why those seeking a better communication with God would seek isolation from the world. Not only did this give the man or woman the freedom and time to devote to prayer, he or she was also removed from the world of temptation that often led to a life of sin.

The hermitage was the easiest form of obtaining the time and isolation needed for a serious contemplation of God. Their life was to be a constant reflection of their relationship with God and their solitude a daily reminder of God's omnipotence and their relative powerlessness. Even today, there is no official set of rules for the hermitage; each hermit, which can be a man or woman, submits him or herself to an austere regimen that allows for spiritual reflection. This isolated life may be wholly self-imposed or it may be official sanctioned by an outside authority as it still is in the Catholic Church today. Hermits formally submit in writing the purpose of their retreat from the world and the list of rules they will follow in order to fulfill their objective. The Church in the Vatican then keeps an official list as a way of recognizing those who dedicated their life to what is probably the most difficult relationship with God.

Part of the hermit's life is a commitment to poverty and a

---

during this time, it is clear that each group saw the dependence of its survival on the extermination of the rival, heretical church.

closeness to nature which is often perceived as God in her fullest. While hermits work or cultivate as a means to provide for their sustenance, mendicants wander from place to place, relying on the charity of individuals and the community to provide both shelter and food. For an unspecified time, the monk, perhaps in the company of companion monks, would then work to assist the poor by alleviating spiritual pain, the thirst for drink, and the hunger of the starving who suffered miserable lives in medieval Europe. At appropriate times, though there is no specific pre-scription, wandering monks might settle down in communities with which they developed a close relationship and bond. Such communities then ceased to become mendicant but retained the namesake of their origins by referring to their permanent lodg-ing as friaries.

Capuchin monks, a branch of the Franciscans who based their devotion to God by giving special recognition to Nature — God's creation — were such an order. Monks traveled the Euro-pean continent and led a life of devotion by example to the secu-lar world. They gave up their possessions and worked to assist the needy. While it might be thought that a mendicant lifestyle was free from politics, very often the time spent in a community caused local feathers to ruffle either from jealous envy of their charitable acts or because of political differences. Not everyone in the world was willing have the word of God brought to their very door step. The life of one Bernadino Ochino demonstrated the political dangers in which mendicant monks might find themselves. Ochino was unschooled, but became through personal effort an inspired Capuchin. He came to befriend John Calvin who openly spoke out against problems within the Catholic Church. Because of Ochino's closeness to the heretical priest, the entire Capuchin order was almost disbanded by the pope. Were it not for their history of untarnished service, their actual extinc-tion might have actually come to pass.

Monastic life of men (brothers) and women (nuns) religious was another alternative to those seeking communication with

God. Unlike the often lonely life of the mendicant, communal life, though still austere, was another way to devote one's self to God as well as the community around it. Monastic life of the religious is distinguished by commitment to a shared common rule recognized by the pope. Like the hermit and the friar, the religious did not usually take priestly vows. The common rules, however, were quite strict and were meant to assist the brother or sister in fulfilling their commitment to God. All orders wore simple clothing called a habit, they usually did menial labor around the monastery (anything from cooking, to cleaning, to farming), and attended prayer services. Some orders made a vow of silence (except in recognized emergency situations), others gave up shoes (the discalced wore simple sandals), while yet others performed voluntary self-flagellation. The heart of monastic common rule were the vows of poverty, chastity, and obedience. Poverty was direct imitation of the life of Christ. Chastity was meant to deprive both man and woman of sinful carnal lust. While obedience to their abbot or abbotess was essential for discipline in their difficult life.

Monasteries were usually established by devoted individuals who won the support of the community. St. Benedict and St. Augustine are the most well-known rules followed by monasteries around the world. Money may have come from the head of the order's head, but usually it was the community which donated land, supervised construction, and granted them exemption from taxation or allowed them certain rights to collect tithes. Many monastery were build on high overlooks to symbolize their closeness to God, but it also served to isolate them from secular citizens who had to trek up the winding paths to the entrance of the abbey. Monasteries were run by an abbot, and through their dedication some monasteries became quite well to do in either raising its own funds in the production of a local craft such as wine or champagne making (Dom Perignon was a champagne created by monks) or in the baking of bread (a service directly related to their care for the poor).

Monasteries during the Protestant Reformation came under

increasing criticism for the wealth that they had obtained from their constant diligence. Local rulers, when they canvassed the properties monasteries held, were often shocked to discover great areas of monastic land paid no tax to the local authorities. Jealous of these fixed exemptions and plagued by the need to raise money or the desire to penalize the Catholic Church led to pressure to return land to local rulers. Sometimes their land was confiscated outright.

Other religious orders did not cloister themselves from the world and devoted their daily lives to the service of humanity. In terms of comparison, the Jesuits stand out as a prime example of Terran Jedi Knights. The Society of Jesus' founder, St. Ignatius, was a Spanish nobleman and knight from the Basque region. After a battle, as he was recovering in convalescence, he examined his life and concluded that he could best serve God by leaving the military life for a priestly one. Without training, however, he realized he could not hope to fulfill his duty in service to God so he decided to attend the University of Paris, one of the most prestigious universities at the time, to become a priest. He made friends quickly and others who shared Ignatius' vision of service began to act as a team. He and seven companions vowed to dedicate their lives to the service of others by engaging the world, unlike the cloistered life of a monk. Working in Rome for a period before continuing to Palestine, Ignatius and his followers were soon noticed for their unswerving charity. It was not long before Pope Paul III formally recognized their order. Ignatius' Society of Jesus, as the Jesuit order was called, was unlike other priestly orders. In addition to the priestly vows of poverty, chastity, and obedience, all Jesuits had to take a direct vow to serve the General of the Society as well as the pope.

Ignatius held a deep respect for education and he felt it crucial if the Christians were to lead a full, expressive life. Acts of charity in imitation of Christ were esteemed, but knowledge and self-reflection were equally valued. Following a military style of organization, Ignatius established the common rule in his *Consti-*

tutions in which there were several levels of achievement, the highest of which (called "solemnly professed") could achieve full standing in the order. Those who were not deemed both spiritually and academically suitable could still serve the order under the title of "co-adjator." Ignatius disparaged the Jesuit who self-servingly cloistered himself instead of serving others, and as a way to preserve the dedication of the order to duty, Ignatius prohibited Jesuits from taking high, official positions unless so ordered by the pope. He could head a school in order to assure proper Catholic upbringing, but taking a ministerial position or mayorship was forbidden.

At the heart of their formation was a practice called the *Spiritual Exercises*, which was a vague outline of a spiritual journey toward contemplation of God led by an experienced Jesuit. The purpose was for a believer to reach a higher relationship with God. It may have included meditation, menial duties, a series of guided instructions. It differed from Jesuit to Jesuit, the one focus being the necessity to emotionally move the person's spirit through the exercise. So fashionable was the desire to partake in the *Exercises*, that the European aristocracy came to see their journey through a Jesuit led exercise as a social badge of distinction.

The Jesuits, being an intellectual order of the highest caliber, trained not to bully converts into belief through guilt or promises of paradise. Instead, Ignatius chose a conversational style to engage the potential Christian (or Protestant) into coming over to the Jesuit's point of view. The Jesuit did not focus on an individual's faults (and sins), but praised and encouraged the virtues of an individual. It was a long and difficult process, but the Jesuit could be satisfied that if he did make a convert it was one in which the individual's mind and spirit chose for him or herself to embrace Catholic Christianity. This manner of proselyting through intellectual discourse worked extremely well for the educated nobility of Europe. It was equally successful with the Chinese emperors in Asia who admired the Jesuit's ability to learn the language and culture of the court, beating even native Mandarin courtiers in their own arguments.

Especially during the religious wars when the faith of the people of a territory changed with the sovereign, the Jesuits became the front line in trying to assuage Roman Catholic leaders from joining the Protestant movement whether from personal or political reasons. Jesuits were only allowed to serve one "client" at a time, traveling with this count or that prince, serving both as spiritual advisor and confessor to the elite and powerful of Europe. They played a significant role in preventing the whole of Europe from becoming completely Protestant. Their presence in the courts of Europe also served as an important source of information to the Vatican. While priests could not divulge direct secrets, Jesuits, who were probably the best in documenting their travels and deeds in reports to the General of the Society, could easily share political and social pretensions of their "clients" with papal bureaus without breaking their vow to keep confessions confidential.

Seeing Jesuits in a regular pattern of attendance at noble courts, it is no wonder Protestants saw the Jesuits as their evil antithesis. The diatribes and invectives slung at the Jesuits goes without mention, being reviled as servants to a devil-pope armed with a cursed tongue that could magically ensnare a listener. The *Spiritual Exercises* were spoken of as if words from the very devil himself by Protestant propagandists, and the pressure of politics on the papacy even led to the temporary disbandment of the order in the 18th century. Regardless of one's perspective on the Jesuits, Protestants and Catholics understood the importance they played in stemming growing Protestantism. Today, the moderate Jesuits have fallen out of favor with the reigning pope who has sought allies with more conservative elements of the Catholic Church.

It is certainly clear how the personal search for a connection to the spiritual can take many forms of expression, be it the hermit, the member religious, or a member of a priestly order like the Jesuits. The Jedi too in their areligious order similarly bear the trappings of the religious life which is admired by secular populations because these individuals willingly give up freedoms that most assume to be their God-given rights.

Military Orders

Contrary to Christian thinking regarding activities of war, the Catholic Church has always held the position that fighting may be necessary for self-defense. The days of Roman martyrdom were over when Constantine, a pagan ruler of the Eastern remnants of the once glorious Roman Empire, converted to Christianity after seeing a cross in a vision just before his battle with German barbarians. Overnight, Christianity was transformed from the religion of the poor and needy to the official religion of the state. Christianity, however, saw a challenge unlike none in its seven hundred year history. Muslim advances in the Holy Land, modern Israel and Palestine, were advances for the "Infidel," and for 600 years, Turkish expansion would remain a troublesome threat for European Christendom.

News of losses in territory to the Muslims was seen in Europe as the opening volley in a greater expansion of the Islamic threat to predominantly Christian Europe. So sentimental was the loss of Palestine and Jerusalem to Muslim invaders that calls were made out by Pope and king for worthy nobles to go to the Holy Land on crusade to "rid the Infidel" of its possession of Christ's birthplace. Nobles marching off to war was a sincere answer to Christian calls for assistance in the Holy Land. It also had the consequence of ridding countries of the rival nobility which might claimed rights to various sovereign titles in their home country.

Among the most grievous of news coming from the Middle East was that of Christian pilgrims falling victim to Muslim attacks. Not only were they being captured and held for ransom until European families could raise and send money in exchange for their loved ones, innocent pilgrims were being attacked and

murdered by Muslims who believed in the wrong God.[*] Knights
from Europe traveled to the Holy Land, and upon finding com-
radeship among men of equal rank and religious piety, it only
became natural that these European knights organized their
service under military forms. Originally, many of these knights
sought communal ties for the purpose of assisting and aiding the
sick and wounded from clashes with Muslim raiders. These men
formed themselves into bands that imitated the communal codes
of monastic orders and the customs of chivalric knighthood.
Voluntarily these men adhered to the customs of religious orders, mostly the Benedictine and Augustinian communal rules.
They took vows of poverty, chastity, and obedience which they
gave to a governing head. After a period of service in the cities
of the Holy Land like Acre and Jerusalem, they sought recognition of their organization from the pope in Rome. Their lives
simple, their piety unswerving, knights that took part in these
orders were fulfilling personal dreams that satisfied both a
spiritual yearning and fidelity to a faith that was crucial in the
mostly illiterate societies of medieval Europe. While their methods of expressing their faith seem barbaric and violent today,
the threat and fear of a violent death by the sword was for many
people a real possibility. Unlike modern cities and nations where
a police force and army are specifically trained to fight in place
of the ordinary citizens, medieval men and women often had to
fight tooth and nail for their own protection. Recourse to a court
system was rarely an option for the poor, and enforcement from
civil officials depended on gaining the favor of important digni-
taries of the city who may or may not have had the best interest
of the public when they exercised their authority.

Knights were men of action. They lived in a culture where
demonstration of one's military prowess was a cultural norm,
and as protectors of authority they understood the relationship

---

[*] Muslims, in their perception, saw invaders from Europe
establishing bridgeheads that would eventually lead to their own
enslavement or death.

between the rulers and those who carried out their laws. Knights were the backbone of rulers and it was important to create a culture which supported and justified the preeminent rule of the noble class. In the illiterate society of the Middle Ages, fanfare and open declaration was the method and manner of presenting one's heart and soul to others. Men displayed their social and political prowess, therefore, by attracting the attention of others — either through good speech or through good deeds. Knights excelled in the latter as long as they lived up to the lofty social graces of the aristocratic class.

In an illiterate society, the skill of the educated, which often mean they could read, was of grave importance to the successful administration of any government. Especially when European countries, now numbered in the hundreds of thousands, the maintenance of written communication was central to the greatest of governments. But one only got an education if one were born into a noble family. Both knights and priests, however, had access to the upper class by the very fact that the nobility needed them. Knights pledged their fealty and died for their lord, while priests advised and disseminated the law of the sovereign while reminding their patron of their obligations to their church. Both knights and priests did not have to be born into their position. They obtained their privilege and were deferred to by the common populace and aristocracy simply on the merit of their actions or ability.

Knights of crusading Europe sought the best of both vocations: that of warrior and monk. Canon law in principle forbade the spilling of blood by a cleric.* Knights were laymen, however, which allowed them to use the sword on behalf of their Christian God. In answering a personal call by God, as well as that of pilgrims under siege and attack in the Holy Land, pious knights journeyed to the Middle East and took on the role of protector

---

*Some priests circumvented this rule by using the bludgeoning mace. Others like Pope Julius and Cardinal Richelieu actually carried a sword on their person.

and assistants of the Christian poor and injured. These warrior-monks took the religious vow of poverty, chastity, and obedience, and committed themselves to communal rules based on abbey rules which stressed a disciplined hierarchical organization. Without going through the education to become a priests as Ignatius Loyola had done, these knights took a middle ground that served the interests not only of the poor and needy, but also that of the pope which was quick in sanctioning the establishment of military orders. Though there was some expressed question of whether fighting was compatible with Christian values, no popular cause oppose their formation. Quite to the contrary, their deeds were celebrated in both oral and written form during the centuries at the height of their power. Nothing was more honorable than to serve society as both knight and pious Christian.

The Knights Templar are the best known and celebrated in Christian chronicles and histories. Like the Jesuits, the available literature on Templars far exceeds those of the other two military orders which basically amounts better PR for their order. Templars took their name from the land which they were given, which was supposedly located near the Temple Mount of Jerusalem. They began as knights who were commanded by the Patriarch Warmund of Jerusalem to protect the routes pilgrims used through the Holy Land. Taking the simple color of white, their surcoat would be distinguished by its red cross. Members were to exhibit piety and love of God at all times. A single blanket was deemed sufficient for their comfort, they were to sleep in their clothes, and at night, to assure others that they did not take the company of women, they were to keep a lamp lit until morning. Templar knights were required to have a tonsure (the bald circle cut into the tops of their head), and communication, even during meals, were to be limited to vital or necessary speech. While expected to bring their own horse, armor, and weapons, their possessions were considered communal and could be taken and shared as deemed by the appropriate authority in the order. Among pilgrims and Christian priests in the

Holy Land, the sight of Templars was reassuring as they traveled or went about their business in the town and cities in which they lived.

The Templars, probably because of the fame of their success, led to their greatest fall from grace. Because of political intrigue, French king, Philip IV, brought charges to Pope Clement V that Templar knights had become corrupt and heretical. Charges were brought against the order, and knights all over Christendom were arrested, interrogated, and put on trial. Charges included allegations that they conspired with Muslims, refused to assist pilgrims when asked, and committed homosexual practices. Some charges of heresy alleged that they denied the redemption of humanity of sin, the divinity of Christ, and that they worshiped a false idol. Despite the many testimonies supporting their pious practices, the order was found guilty of many heresies, and Templars wherever they could be arrested were burned at the stake as heretics. Regardless, it was clear that the success of their piety led to a resentment that Templar knights from many who had reason to personally or politically despise them. The Templar were accused of abusing their position in that they refused to submit to local authorities (though they would submit to the pope), that they became greedy and quarrelsome (they did quarrel with rival military orders), and that they failed to live up to the expressed and spiritual purpose of their order (they did refuse to assist pilgrims when their journeys were ill-conceived). Much scholarly work suggests that a combination of jealously of their wealth (they had accumulated vast tracts of land from donations) and the political challenges they presented to many local authorities who called for dispersal of their land and disbandment of the order led to the demise of this once respected order.

The second military order to appear in the Holy Land was that of the Hospitallers which derives its name from the Hospital of St. John of Jerusalem which served and cared for injured pilgrims visiting the Holy Sepulcher where Jesus' body had been laid before rising from the dead. In the eleven hundreds, the hospital took to employing mercenaries to protect the hospital in a city which was the first line of defense against Muslim attacks. Hospitallers, like the Templars with whom they sometimes fought alongside, were devoted to assisting Christian pilgrims and their journeys. The Hospital of St. John won great praise for its care of the sick in Outremer (French: other side of the sea) which employed many sophisticated medical techniques developed by remarkable Arab doctors.

Early members of the order were French, though membership in the confraternity drew from devoted individuals from all over Europe. Early knights were expected to be of the aristocracy and today membership is reserved to those with officially recognized noble titles. Such families would then be able to provide their son with the appropriate mount, armor, and weapons needed for his participation in Hospitaller campaigns. Their ability to fight off the Muslim was generally known (their most famous fortress is the Krak des Chevaliers) though with the loss of Acre in 1291, their headquarters was removed to Malta, and then later to the Island of Rhodes, where the eight pointed Maltese cross on red became their symbol.

Less about the Hospitaller's actual battles and campaigns is known than of the Templars, but it is clear from contemporary literature that knights of this order were held in the same esteem as the Templars. Ballads and songs about their order did not make rounds in Europe, however, until later in the 13th century, almost a hundred years after the order's establishment. Like the Templars, the Hospitallers accumulated wealth and land that was the envy of local political figures. The Hospitallers did not receive the severe political punishment of the Templars, and in the wake of their fall many Templar properties were transferred to the Hospitaller order. Today the order is one of a related network that includes Catholic, Protestant, and non-denominational orders which still serve to help the suffering of the world. Their hospital is now a modern building that serve people of all religions.

The third crusading order of renown in the Holy Land was that of the Teutonic order, established by German knights. Like Hospitallers, the Teutonic order began as a medical corps in the service of injured or wounded German pilgrims. Based in the Hospital of St. Mary of the Germans of Jerusalem, the order also had obligations to assist Christians. Supported by the German Emperor Frederick II and the popes, the Teutonic knights gained official recognition and support from the Catholic hierarchy. They too became the object of land and monetary benefices which allowed them to develop a soldiery that rivaled that of the first two orders, though they were establish some eighty years after them.

Even is less is known about specific battles than even the Hospitallers, though the Teutonic knights would become most widely known in Europe from their work administrating pagan areas of the Baltic region. Quelling the barbarians became an important function in northern Germany and what is now parts of Poland. After establishing themselves in key cities, they proceeded in the construction of castles which served as headquarters for local chapters of the order. Their battles with pagans were celebrated and their success in bringing prosperity to their region is reflected by the establishment of thousands of towns and villages and its participation in the lucrative Hanseatic League by becoming an important exporter of grain to the rest of Europe. The order did face defeats, and with the Protestant Reformation the order's military efforts essentially ended with the conversion of its grandmaster to the Protestant faith.

The Teutonic order did propagate itself in forms in many countries around Europe, but with the religious wars of the Reformation much doubt was cast on the order's ability to find itself a solid purpose. Ever since the early 16th century, various forms of the Teutonic order have been established with the purpose of assisting others, much of it dedicated to caring for soldiers wounded in the many European wars of the continent, working out of its present headquarters in Vienna, Austria.

The legacy of these three orders has made an unmistakable impression on students of European history. Despite criticisms that have plagued these orders, it is unquestionable that knights of these orders did have the highest regard for both their religion and its commitment to assist others in need. Their original creeds were particularly xenophobic, however, reflecting the orthodox view that their religion could do no wrong. Muslims despised these knights as carriers of a hateful religion, though on the battlefield commanders of both Muslim and Christian faiths sometimes learned to respect a common code of warfare which could today be described as chivalrous. Without belittling the atrocities committed by both Christian and Muslim at times during the 11th-14th centuries, let it be said that within the context of exploring precursors to the Jedi knights, these three orders — Templar, Hospitaller, and Teutonic — are instances of a manner of living that is not dissimilar to that of the Jedi in *Star Wars*.

Sohei of Japan

Lucas' influence from Japanese film not only includes samurai that served the feudal lords of the Nippon, it also included the much romanticized and revered warrior-monks of the mountains. Similar to the Jedi who live in their pinnacle temple on a man made pyramid in the heart of the capital, the Japanese monastic warriors, called *sohei*, lived in elevated Buddhist temples constructed in the mountains surrounding the former capitals of Nara and Kyoto. Among the sohei were powerful swordsmen who retired to the cloister of the temple serving their abbot as well as the Imperial Court to whom various priests acted as advisors to the Emperor and his court. Like the Jedi, these men of faith were trusted because they openly gave up the self-interested lives of normal citizens for the benefit of their spiritual well-being.

The influence of monasteries in the history of the country focused not on doctrine and belief as had been the case in 17th and 18th centuries Europe, but on influence and power. The sohei were fiercely independent and were mastered by a spiritual outlook that completely subordinated their perspective on the world inward. They were respected by both commoners and the aristocracy and were disposed of a belief expressed in the Western saying that "God was on their side." The sohei were also extremely territorial and became jealous of rival monasteries who threatened the prestige and influence of serving as direct advisors to the imperial person. Sometimes these warrior monks turned even on the Emperor when their position had been slighted or insulted. Ex-Emperor Go Shirakawa-In, as quoted from the *Heiki Monogatari*, Japan's most celebrated history, lamented, "There are three things which are beyond my control: the rapids of the Mano river, the dice at gambling, and the monks of the mountain."

Buddhism was first imported from China and was quickly adapted to the temperament and needs of the Japanese Imperial Court. It has an outlook on life as an existence of perpetual suffering. Founded by Siddhartha Guatama in south Nepal, he was raised in the joyous world of the prince's court. It was not until he dared to venture out of the palace gates that he discovered the miserable lives of the common people. Forsaking his birthright, he traveled the land devoted to living the life of the suffering and quickly gained a following of disciples. Through meditation and the practice of a good, moral life, Buddhism teaches that Nirvana, a state of enlightenment can be achieved. With thought and reflection, those who devoted their lives to the search for enlightenment came to be trusted by both courtier and commoner alike.

While the general doctrines of Buddhism remain static across plain and from mountain top to the oceans reaches, various interpretations led to the evolution of divergent sects, which was especially true of its Japanese expression. These sects usually maintained working relations, though if threatened by the rise of another sect, rival sects were not above taking up arms against the other.

Priests and monks in Japan did not have the Christian prescription against spilling blood, and, therefore, did not need lay knight-protectors like the Templar. Japanese Buddhist monks protected themselves when they could not secure or rely on the patronage of a nearby samurai *daimyo*. Itinerant monks might have to defend themselves when traveling, while the need of permanent protection of the temples ultimately rested on the clergy that lived in or near the temples in which they served. In extreme circumstances, entire armies of monks could be used for political ends. And so successful did they sometimes become, that both the Imperial Court and their appointed guardian samurai clans sometimes found the existence of sohei untenable to the point that they were militarily suppressed.

During the Kamakura period, Zen Buddhism came to be practiced by samurai of the court. An anti-intellectual and non-doctrinaire sect, adherents of Zen Buddhism believed that enlightenment could be achieved by the severe focus of some practice or art. One could be perfecting tea ceremony, flower arranging, painting, and, especially among the samurai, swordsmanship. Zen stressed an austere simplicity which appealed to the military class which was used to the discipline of barracks life. By trying to understand unfathomable koans (senseless tales with no logical resolution) or through the art of focusing on the wielding the blade, it was hoped that the samurai could come into his own enlightenment. Precepts like emptying the mind and allowing the blade to act on its own in the hands of a swordsman were concepts that also led to the mastery of the sword. Most of all, Zen taught that life ultimately was meaningless, and that facing death stoically would lead to its conquering. And if death *were* inevitable, the swordsman would then also be ready for his obliteration.

Because of the attraction Buddhism had on soldiers looking for some spiritual meaning to a harsh and difficult life that demanded unswerving loyalty even unto death, it was not unheard of for a samurai to retire to a monastery after a battle-filled life of serving a feudal lord. Retired soldiers could be found in various monasteries and served in times of crisis as instructors in defensive arts for the abbey's monks. In some cases, a retired lord might bring his entire retinue of samurai with him to serve in the monastery. Sohei practiced the martial arts, wore armor when available though with a cowl, and employed the sword, bow, and were renowned by the use of the halberd, called the naginata.

Abbots and appointed priests had strong ties to the Imperial Court, serving as spiritual advisors who informed the court of astrological and religious obligations vital to the proper exercise of authority by the Emperor. In an age when astrology and geomancy were considered vital to commanding favor with the gods, the court had a deep interest in maintaining strong relations with Buddhist priests.

On occasion, disputes between an abbey and the court would arise. Often these conflicts revolved around taxation and funding of the monasteries, which relied heavily on patronage from visitors, gifts from aristocrats, and the legacies of those who served in the monastery itself. An imperial decision could profoundly affect the monetary base on which temples needed to survive and prosper. In other instances, the appointment of an abbot might cause political consternation among the members of a particular temple or its rivals.

When claims against the imperial officials could not be settled through negotiation, monasteries might send their armies of monks, literally an armed contingent of religious, down from the mountain to clamor in the streets, engage the populace to their cause, and even physically approach the divine emperor himself. The sight of masses of monks chanting in the streets was an impressive sight to behold. In one extreme circumstance, seven thousand sohei entered Kyoto demanding the government hand over Kiyomori as samurai-protector to the Emperor after he had defiled a moveable shrine called an *omikoshi* by shooting an arrow at it. Because Kiyomori and the Taira was considered vital to the existence of the Imperial Court, his act of sacrilege was amended by the payment of a nominal fine. Kiyomori would later attack a Buddhist temple in which three thousand five-hundred civilians and monks died. Not only was the temple burned down, but the heads of a thousand monks were carried away as trophies.

Sometimes the appeals from the monks to the commoners met great success, threatening to foment civil violence through peasant riots. Afraid of the curses monks were able to make on citizens, the city inhabitant feared the uncertainty of a temple or shrine in open conflict with the secular authorities.

One manner of rallying public outrage against the government was to bring down an omikoshi from the temple. Usually used during festivals, the irregular use of an omikoshi no longer safe in the sanctity of the temple was a harbinger of bad times. Citizens disturbed by an omikoshi found sitting the streets unprotected in the street would quickly appeal to secular authorities to appease the monks. This practice of open blackmail was similar to the Catholic church's imposition of the interdict, which suspended the carrying out of sacraments on either an individual or an area or region. Local populations fearful of their souls, would similarly pressure officials to appease the church. When under the interdict, the Eucharist could not be celebrated, last rites could not be given, and if you died, you could not be buried in holy ground. The interdict also absolved vassals of their obligations of fealty to their lords, thus allowing them to rightfully overthrow their lords.

In the Japanese court, such deference was given to Buddhist priests and monks that the Emperor might be cowed into capitulating to the monk's demands. If not, the sohei might even attack the imperial palace or its associative administrative buildings. In one instance, when a contingent of sohei accompanied by an omikoshi approached a gate leading to the high court, Yorimasa, the commander of the palace guard, leapt down from his mount, took off his helmet, and washed out his mouth with water out of respect for the monks. Impressed with his deference, the monks continued to another gate where they were duly attacked by the commander. Several monks were killed and others wounded before the monks arrived back at their temple.

Competing sects too could also be reason for the need to raise military monks. When the capital moved from Nara to Heian (modern Kyoto) in 894, the Nara temple lost power, prestige, influence, and wealth at the expense of the Tendai sect who developed a complex of eight thousand religious buildings. Mount Hiei, because of its geophysical position, served as a physical ward against evil that might affect the Imperial Court. In another example, a new sect, the Lotus sect of Nichiren, openly challenged and denounced the priests of Mt. Hiei. The abbot sought allies with samurai lords who, out of their own self-interest, openly attacked temples of the new, populist sect. Monks were killed and sometimes buildings, even the principal temple itself, were burned to the ground.

Government rivalry continued intermittently through Japanese history, but none as fierce and lasting as Shogun Oda Nobunaga's eleven year struggle against the religious-populist Ikko-ikki group. It's leader Rennyo organized a revolt in 1488 in which the Kaga Province came to be ruled by the religious order and Mikawa Province seemed on the road to follow a similar fate. Supplied with muskets, the Ikko-ikki proved a fierce challenge to samurai authorities. Over the course of years, Nobunaga attempted to thwart the influence of the Ikko-ikki movement, and in 1471, relations had become so poor that he ordered an attack on Mt. Hiei's monastic complex. Encircling the mountain, his troops killed every man, woman, child, priest, and monk that had taken refuge at the mountain's heights. Twenty thousand people were killed and the complex was burned to the ground. Later, in Nagashi, Nobunaga again attacked a temple and burned it, killing another twenty thousand. And in his final campaign against the Ikko-ikki, he surrounded the Ishiyama Hongan Temple after thwarting the Mori clan's attempt to break the naval blockage Nobunaga had imposed. The fate of the temple had been sealed, however, when relief forces did not respond to the temple's plight. A messenger from the Emperor then arrived advising a peaceful surrender of the temple. Pressured by Nobunaga, the garrison did surrender, though the temple itself was burned down.

When determined samurai were determined to stop the monastic orders and their troops, the eventuality of the outcome could only mean victory for the samurai. Despite their influence on both the Imperial Court and the commoners, the samurai were so well positioned to fight the sometimes violent influence of the warrior monks that eventually the sohei would cease to field armies of their own. Samurai troops were too numerous and well trained to let a small number of monks, fanatical though they were, to defeat the wealth and experience of Japan's vassal armies. So too would the Jedi meet its extinction at the hands of troops that far outnumbered the ten thousand Jedi of its order.

Muslim Warriors

The scene in which Qui-Gon Jinn and Shmi discuss Anakin reveals the fact that Jedi are identified in the Republic when then are very young. "He (Anakin) has the way," Qui-Gon says in the *Episode I* script. And in the Jedi council, Yoda reveals that even a boy like Anakin at the age of nine was already too told to begin training. Especially for a boy gifted with powers of the force, it is important to begin training as early as possible. Practitioners of *go* and chess (both strategy board games) agree that the best players require training from the youngest age in order to properly develop the brain connections that will make the child into a master.

History has its own version of the child trained warrior. Taking children in their youth as the Jedi do, was something Muslim commanders did after the initial conquests of the Islamic faith in north Africa and the Middle East. Mamelukes and Janissaries took slave children and trained them to become the powerful fighting forces of Islam. Slavery, while typically thought of as a complete deprivation of freedom and rights, held an important economic and social role in Muslim societies, as it does in *Star Wars*, especially in the upcoming *Attack of the Clones* where slavery will be an issue Anakin must come to grips with in his journey to the Dark Side.

It has only been in the last three hundred years that modern concepts of total emancipation of the human population came to be accepted by church, the state, and the general populace. The concept of human rights did not exist in the form it does today. Freedom, and freedmen, however, were constructs which did exist in ancient societies in which slavery was common place. Despite modern prejudices against permanent servitude and ownership of humans, slavery had been a fact of life among all of the civilized cultures of the world. Especially in the high cultures of Greece, Rome, Persia, and Egypt, slavery could just as easily mean an improved and even privileged position as it might have been total subservience to a master.

Slave soldiers eventually became the principal military force which propped many Muslims controlled territories. It seems contradictory that slaves armed with their own weapons would not forcibly overthrow their masters. In fact, the culture of the military slave became the backbone of military forces for many Islamic leaders. Most slaves were non-Muslims, often Christian, who were brought as young children to Muslim countries and trained to soldiers of Islam.

The need for non-Muslim military forces came from the desire of Muslim leaders to consolidate their authority after successful campaigns against rival Muslim leaders. War against the Infidel was unhesitatingly permitted, while war between Muslims was abhorrent to the Koran, which told of a single kind of war; that of jihad against non-Muslims. The struggle for authority came when caliphs — leaders linked directly to Mohammed's supporters — and secular rulers tried to justify their authority and control of governing institutions.

This difference plays itself out in the two main branches of the Muslim religion; that of Sunnis and Shi'ites. Sunni and Shi'ite both hold the Koran as spiritual doctrine, but each interprets other cultural facets of Islam in different ways. Sunnis, the more numerous branch, accept the first four caliphs as successors to Mohammed and admit the importance of the Umma, or the collective of Muslim people. Shi'ites have a stricter outlook, rejecting the first three caliphs and regard Ali as the legitimate successor to Mohamed. Links to Mohammed are held in the highest level, imams, or religious leaders, being directly linked to Mohammed. The Shi'ite branch, because of its more conservative interpretation, tends to be the more militant and fundamentalist of the two Muslim branches.

Since warring against a brother Muslim was blasphemous in the eyes of God, foreign troops were established as a way to circumvent Muslim fratricide. Their practice was not without precedent either: Athens had its own Scythian troops, numbering around three hundred, who were directly owned by the state. Numerous European monarchy kept paid Swiss Guards as palace troops. The use of foreign troops was meant to assure loyalty from a military force which would not be swayed by the factionalism that populist movements brought to Muslim countries. Umayyad Caliph al-Hamim of Cordova and Abbasid Caliph al-Mu'tasim of Iraq all had their own slave palace guards. In time, a soldiery of free Arab soldiers would become an anachronism among Muslim leaders.

The creation of slave armies depended completely on the indoctrination process which re-educated the children for an Islamic society and established a code of behavior that would assure loyalty to the aristocratic leaders to whom these troops had been garrisoned. Discipline was strict, members being expected to follow order exactly without regard for their own interests. In return, their numbers would become a privileged and elite class who were the protectors of the state and of Islam. Muslim leaders had a soldiery which did not follow popular whims, though there would be moments when the slaves did wrest power for themselves. Such take overs were uncommon, and in the end, resulted in the total elimination of the slave soldiery altogether.

The Mamelukes of the Abbasid Caliphate of Egypt came to power after the Mongols conquered the Baghdad caliphate that ruled Cairo at the battle of Ain Jalut in 1260. Many of the Mongol horsemen were of the same Turkish and Circassian ethnic stock that would make up the Mameluke troops that served the Egyptian sultanate.

Mamelukes started out their military lives first as slaves from the Steppe areas of the Black Sea and were then brought to Cairo where they would follow barracks rule. They developed into an elite corps which both served as slaves and as protectors to sultan. Being steppe nomads, their culture was one of nomadic horsemen who lived on basic staples of milk and meat. It said that Steppe nomads were conceived and birthed on horseback. These Turkish and Circassian children were taught the basics of Islamic culture and were trained in the *furusiyya*, the sword and archery skills of the mounted Steppe warrior. So convinced were the Mamelukes of their military prowess that they held an open contempt for the firearm when it began to appear in the armies that marched out against them. From the east Portuguese and Ottomans from the north, both armed with muskets, became significant threats to the sultanate, which quickly engaged black African troops in the ways of the firearm. In response, the Mamelukes renewed their study of the *furusiyya*, giving them a false sense of confidence in their military ability. While the Mamelukes shared a similar loathing for the gun as did the samurai, the latter quickly recognized when Commodore Perry's ships arrived in Japan that superior weapons were at the heart of a new army. The Mamelukes would eventually be defeated by the new weapon.

In the battles of Marj Dabiz and Raydaniya, Ottoman armies with their rifles would defeat the Mameluke pride. At Darj Dabiz, troops were deployed in typical crescent formation. Mamelukes fought fiercely but Ottoman firepower drove the Mamelukes back to Cairo. Seven thousand of their number died in the battle. When the Ottoman army advanced on Cairo and routed the Mamelukes, Kurbay, one of their leaders lamented the fall of the Mamelukes, saying that three Mamelukes can defeat your army of 200,000. He dares the Ottomans to see, if only they would put down their musket, that treacherous weapon, he describes, as that which even a woman can bring down a mighty Mameluke.

The Mameluke institution did survive the Ottoman conquest, but they still refused to take up the musket. Napoleon and his modern army would have little difficulty defeating them at the Battle of the Pyramids. Chafing under Christian domination, they maintained their disdain for Western weapons and training. As servants under new rulers, the Mamelukes kept their elite superiority but eventually their institution would become anachronistic in an age of cannon and rifles.

The Ottomans were not so intransigent in their acceptance of the new weapon. Indeed their army of Janissaries would become one of the strongest in Europe. Not only did the Janissary form the bulk of the Ottoman military, important administrative positions would be drawn from their ranks, serving in the highest levels of government. Their fate, while heroic, would end as tragically as that of the sohei monks at Mt. Hiei.

The Janissaries were first established by Osman who took power in the early 14th century. Lack of manpower led to his open welcome of immigrants fleeing Mongol incursions. Regardless of race, religion, or ethnicity, Osman accepted any who would learn about and accept Turkish customs. This openness also led to a state sponsored military, which was entirely paid for by the state to maintain the power of his sultanate.

The creation of the Janissary forces came from the system of *divsirme* — a customary tribute of Christian children, usually of Slavic or Albanian origin, who were sent to serve in the Sultan's military. The *divsirme* was originally prohibited by sharia (Islamic law), but military needs and tribal customs won out against the arguments of Muslim scholars. According to the practice, every four years, boys between eight and ten (though it sometimes went as old as twenty), were taken by a Janissary commander. In total, one-tenth to one-fourteenth of the male youth population was taken during the quadrennial tribute.

Recruits would be divided into a regular group, which lived in Anatolia (modern Turkey) for acculturation with a Turkish family for three to five years, and an elite group, which was sent directly to the sultan's palace. The elite group trained in the palace for up to fourteen years working in the palace garden or in the shipyards. Recruits, called *kul*, were not allowed to leave the palace or see the outside world, and they engaged in a rigorous education that involved learning Arabic script, literature, and the languages of Turkish, Persian, and Arabic, while still pursuing military and physical training. Though difficult as it was, service in the Janissaries was considered a desirable alternative to rural, peasant life. Some Muslims saw Janissary service as quite honorable, and there are many accounts of Muslims bribing Christians to take their sons during the *divsirme*.

At around twenty, the young man was released from the palace for service in a Janissary corps. They did not get complete freedom, being still required to serve the sultan. Freedom to a Janissary only meant that they could no longer be bought or sold as a slave. At this point, they had the opportunity to join the cavalry where they might have the opportunity to become a respected general. If they were chosen for palace service, the Janissary had the opportunity to serve as governors, viziers, and even grand viziers who administrated the thirty-one provinces of the empire. Under Mehmed II, all governors were products of *divsirme*. Because all were still technically slaves, the Sultan could still easily punish or even execute them without hesitation should they fail in their assigned duties, or even at the slightest hint of disloyalty. Under the *divsirme*, the Janissaries became loyal servants of the sultan.

Originally celibate, eventually Janissaries were allowed to have children, many of whom were later allowed to enlist in their father's units. They were renowned for their orderly use of the musket and were a threat to all potential invaders. Janissaries wore pantaloons and a distinctive white turban. Never was a Janissary allowed to grow a beard, which was a sign of a freed man.

Threats of disloyalty and politicking began to surface in the 17th century when many coups d'etats were organized by the Janissary. Growing from twenty thousand in 1574 to one hundred thirty-five thousand in 1826, sultans and their court came to understand the threat the Janissaries were to their own authority. They lived under their own rules and culture, forming corporations and even making alliances with outsiders.

It was during the Auspicious Incident in 1826 when secular leaders, with the approval of the religious community, began a campaign to break the power of the Janissaries. Sultan Mahmud II began making plans for a Westernized army. Despite their mastery of musket tactics, the Janissary elite was still reluctant to reform their own institution. When the Janissaries heard of the creation of a new, more modern army, they began an open revolt against the sultan. Mahmud ordered the arrest of the rebels. When the Janissaries retreated into their own barracks and refused to surrender, he ordered his cannon to fire directly into the barracks. Those that did survive were either executed or banished. A most inauspicious end to their elite corps.

The Jedi of *Attack of the Clones*

It is now obvious how the Jedi draw from a long and eclectic history of warriors from various times and cultures. Whether it be from the monastic and military rule of Western knights, the sohei tradition of Japan, or the indoctrinated children of Muslim serfdom, it is clear how the unusual upbringing of Jedi novitiates from a tender age is not unknown to actual history. While not a justification of past warrior cultures, the Jedi in their lofty ideas are not without precedent in the world.

Important in all of the histories recounted in this chapter was the ability of a military institution to change with the needs of the world, in this case of the universe. As will be further elucidated in *Attack of the Clones*, and *Episode III*, how will the Jedi ultimately meets its doom? As the name suggests, *Attack of the Clones* will see the advent of a new army of laser rifle carrying troops — clone troopers, the precursor to the stormtroopers — who will be crucial to the movie's climax. How the Jedi respond will affect the very survival of their own hallowed order. Will the Jedi engage and support the creation of a new army, and possibly aid in their own destruction? Or will they openly refuse to change in the wake of an evolving universe?

Chapter

6

Master, Padawan, Apprentice

From the very beginning in *A New Hope*, education has been a commanding theme in what will be Lucas' epic sextology. Luke, the unschooled adopted charge of a moisture farmer on a desert planet, desires to escape his world and go to the Academy and relieve himself of his repetitive and uninteresting life. Like his father Anakin as a boy, he looked up into the heavens with a burning desire to see the stars first hand with his own eyes. Neither, however, expected to receive the education they desired from the likes of Jedi Masters, space warriors charged with the very protection of the galaxy itself. As in many great tales, protagonists do not chose their destiny. It is thrust upon them in a unique master-apprentice relationship which has been the model of education for swordsmen of countless societies. In theory, their obligations are simple — apprentice follows the master's instructions.

The Nature of Education

The duty of a master teacher is to get someone to think well. The duty of a master swordsman is to teach honor. In *The Empires Strikes Back*, Yoda captures the heart of what it means to educate a swordsman: "Only a fully trained Jedi Knight with the Force as his ally will conquer Vader and his Emperor. If you end your training now, if you choose the quick and easy path, as Vader did, you will become an agent of evil." Luke then asks if staying to complete his training is worth sacrificing Han and Leia. Yoda replies, "If you honor what they fight for... yes!"

In societies in which armed fighters walked the street with impunity, their code of honor was what separated them from mere ruffians. Though much maligned in history as a reasoned excuse for bloody excess, the concept of honor still resonates deeply with the human psyche. Honor requires no written contract, a person's public reputation being held as collateral for any transgression. The gentleman's agreement is sealed with a handshake, though words alone seal the commitment until death. In that same conversation, Luke says he will finish the training that he has begun. "You have my word."

In order to best cultivate honor, the swordsman must first have the knowledge of the art in which he is learning; learning not only of skills and technique, but also of the world in which the swordsman is to live. It is therefore critical for the swordsman to begin his training with a wise and experienced teacher who will become for the duration of the apprenticeship his teacher. This master will teach the novice how to *think* and *act*, all in an attempt to impart the obligations of those given the right to wear a sword of power. The swordsman, because of his ability to coerce, must learn how to reign in his passions. He must be trained properly so that the temptation to abuse and exploit that power is circumvented. Sometimes, as in the case of Anakin, a master's instruction fails.

The master-apprentice relationship is a traditional form of instruction that dates back to ancient times. Through trust, affection, and submission, it is hoped that the student's dedication might one day lead to his eventual affection and love for his teacher's instruction. The apprentice system is an intimate relationship quite different from the distant learning found in modern classrooms. Direct instruction is seen as the best method of imparting not only knowledge, but also values. It allows a master to carefully monitor a student's progress and it permits the student the rare opportunity to benefit from the formal guidance of an expert.

Martial arts training speaks loudly to the training that occurs in *Star Wars*, but mentoring also occurs in a variety of other fields: carpenters, brick & tiles layers, painters, sculpture, religious disciples & leaders, teachers, attorneys, and writers & editors. Within fencing, there is no more hallowed individual that the *maître d'armes* (Master of Arms) and the *Sensei* (Japanese for teacher). Masters of Arms in European societies taught the king's men the art of the fence, but they also served as important advisors to the military and the court. Through their skill of arms, they became professionals who demonstrated their knowledge and skill in the instruction of a new generation of soldiers. They were often arbiters on courts of honor and their role, above all else, was to safeguard the sanctity of a gentleman's word. The modern equivalent — the sports coach — draws little from this tradition, but his role is no less important than that of the master fencer. A Naval Academy midshipman lamented about the quality of one of his coaches, "All you need in a coach is that he (or she) be a decent person."

In Japan, as in most of Asia, the teacher is held in the highest esteem. They were wise men and women worthy of society's respect. Without them society would cease to be a society and the richness of their culture would lack the glue to its preservation. After returning from a 4-year stay in Japan, I wrote a letter telling my kendo sensei that I had become a middle school teacher. As an American, I measured my new station in life by the amount of money I earned or by the influence of power I had, but to Kubo Sensei I received a formal congratulations. An instructor in an English language school for four years, it never occurred to me until I received his letter that I could now be addressed by the title Sensei, a title which I learned in my studies of Japanese was reserved only for the most respected individuals.

When Yoda took Luke as a student, an explicit relationship defined by the instructor came into force. Luke first had to pass Yoda's initial test to see if there would be an intensity to his student. Then he had to prove commitment and perseverence as his master looked blithely and indifferently at Luke's struggles. Through time and space, Yoda had kept an eye on Luke's progress on Tatooine — presumably through the use of the Force. Dave Lowry, in his enlightening book *Autumn Lightning*, was turned away at the door countless times until the reclusive swordmaster saw that he was deeply committed to learning the sword and enduring its hardships.

Yoda, similarly does not submit to Luke's initial entreaty for instruction. He does not even know how to ask for a master swordsman's help. But against his own instincts, Yoda, with the words of the ghostly Obi-Wan, accepts Luke into his tutelage. Yoda hesitates because the skills and abilities he will teach must not be taken lightly and must be used properly. The master must ask himself whether the student is ready to learn, whether he has the maturity, and whether he has the potential for wisdom. Yoda sees a lack of focus in Luke who searches for adventure, not discipline. Yoda is fearful of a repeat of Anakin's fall, fearful of the Luke's lack of preparation, especially of his age. It is telling that even the greatest Jedi master is as easily prone to the same fear that may mean the demise of a Padawan Learner, as the Jedi apprentice is called. Yoda is not infallible, but it is for Luke to prove to his master that he can survive the training, and indeed break the cycle of evil that is in his father by turning him from the Dark Side.

Luke's experience, while not normal to a school of fencing, is that of fairy tales. Yoda, originally meant to be a frog-like creature, was supposed to be an insignificant animal whom Luke would happen upon as he passed through the forest in his quest for his master. Luke would have to suppress his human pride and listen to the subtle rambles of a speaking beast. He would have to see the power of nature as a teacher in its smallest forms. The powerful youth would have to submit to what looked to his very eyes was a weak and silly old creature. Luke would have to humble himself, prove he was ready to learn, show that he would have the open mind necessary for severe training. Above all else, he had to obey.

In the real world, the problem in finding a teacher is separating the charlatans from the true masters who are talented, experienced, and professional in their standards. Today, the student looking for a martial art must examine the credentials of the instructor carefully. What is their emphasis in teaching: competition, practice, children, adults, self-defense, making money? How many long-time students does he have? By talking to students, watching practice, discovering where he trained, and asking directly about a teacher's goals give a prospective student of the martial arts clues about an instructor's abilities. Finding the right teachers is often a matter of luck, for those truly committed to learning, it is natural that students will find and seek out the best instructors. As an ancient saying goes: When a student is ready to learn, a teacher appears.

The closest approximation to the Jedi Temple is not a military academy or university, but that of a dojo, the Japanese training hall. Often it is easy to enter. Usually it is simply a matter of filling out a registration form and paying monthly dues. The rest is up to the student who may never catch the eye of the headmaster. Senior students are in charge of beginners who must prove themselves worthy of even their attention through hard training. Even the most experienced martial artist must founder like any new student. And especially for the person with previous martial arts experience, he should not expect anyone to take him under his wing. The more someone expects praise, the less likely he will receive it. Pride is more obvious that anyone would care to admit. Even when classes are a mix of senior and beginning students, the hierarchy of the dojo rules. Sensei looks out for the senior students, who themselves are charged with supervising the progress of their juniors.

In the *Star Wars* universe, Padawans enter the temple as young children, maybe even as babies. Students are raised in a common life with senior Knights supervising the progress of the children into their teens. Yoda himself teaches the young children until the age of thirteen when Jedi Knights will come to observe children's classes to find an apprentice, whom they will groom, hopefully, into full Jedi Knighthood. Those who are not chosen are destined for the Agricultural Corps which serves the needily and poor on planets around the universe.

Similarly among the Jesuits, only the solemnly professed have the potential to reach the highest ranks. The rest, the spiritual co-adjators, still serve honestly within the order. Whether it is God's will or a novice's penury in ability to apply himself to his studies, aspiration into full service is a privilege. To be meek and self-effacing are commitments to service, and unrealistic aspirations are outward signs of pride undesired in higher levels. Though bitter as it may seem, a co-adjator has only the highest respect for his colleagues who meet the highest academic and moral standards of the order. The same is true for the Jedi. While modern lay people may misjudge the inequity of a hierarchical system, they must remember that the goal of a spiritual life is not personal aggrandizement, but service to a greater good. This is indoctrinated in every religious preparatory school as it would be in the Jedi Temple.

Traditional Fencing Instruction

The institution of the martial arts dojo and the manner of its teachers is one of submission. Because the teacher's obligation is already to teach a pupil to his highest potential, the onus of study and his willingness to submit to the master's instructions rest solely on the shoulders of the student. In a dojo, this means giving up your ego and pride to the student who began training even a day before you. And in an environment where a year's training may mean rudimentary instruction in the art's techniques, it is not unlikely that a talented student may feel his skills are superior even to the one-year trainee. Recognition by the headmaster, however, and his affection come only in relation to a person's commitment to study. Often, it may never come at all.

Under the five instructors who have influenced me the most, only two are of a close, informal relationship. Because of an instructor's responsibilities to all of his students, unless there is some individual spark which develops into a friendship, the role of the master to his students is somewhat aloof, though usually kind and caring. To have the kind of direct link like that of a Jedi Knight and a Padawan is an extremely unusual circumstance, especially in modern dojos. While it is common for senior students to circumspectly guide an individual, the formal relationship of a master and student does not occur until a senior student is permitted the privilege of teaching classes of his own.

To be recognized by a teacher requires a commitment and self-effacement that seems contrary to the reward system of modern societies. The apprentice system flies in the face of the university's conference of higher degrees, which amounts to the simple completion of an institution's curriculum. Similarly, the conferrence of a black belt is secondary to the knowledge and skills which a person has mastered. Even in the university system, the greatest learning occurs not from obtaining a degree or multiple degrees, but from studying under the most respected professors in a particular field.

While money is often necessary to care for basic necessities, the idea that a student is paying for one's knowledge is repugnant to the learning process. Fencing masters do need to support themselves, but their goal is the formation of young minds that are the foundation for a future society. It is crass to talk to a headmaster about payment. A student pays a fee for an opportunity, not the right to impose their will on a teacher.

Swordmasters understand implicitly that their obligation is a far greater commitment than the work exerted by even the most diligent students. Not only have they gone through the apprenticeship process, they are now responsible for its proper continuation. No matter how hard the student works to meet his master's expectations, it is far harder for a master to create a curriculum than it is for his students than to follow it. While a minimum standard of knowledge must be met — knowledge of forms (kata), the ability to execute technique, and the proper spirit of mind — the master is constantly adjusting to the needs of this student's strengths and abilities. No mean trick, teaching is a skill that takes years of experience. Even formal instruction in the educational field does not substitute for actual teaching experience.

It is out of selflessness that the greatest teachers answer the calling to become a master. He does not desire a cult of sycophants, nor does he advocate a particular agenda other than the proper training of his students. Abuses of this obligation have led to the establishment of private armies led by warlords, petty princes, praetorian guards, and outright dictators. Perhaps in the politics of the nation in which a fencing master finds himself, he cannot avoid the machinations of the political process unfolding in the land surrounding his school. His commitment to one political side or another will be the greatest test of the master teacher. The survival of his life may hinge on his decision but so does his school of fencing and its students. They may become puppets of politicians, who see their abilities as a means to their political end. The Jedi Council understands this more fully than the casual observer would think. Indeed, it is the allegiance of the Jedi Order to the Republic which will lead to its eventual extermination in *Episodes III*.

All teachers, whether the most experienced or the newest to the profession, must create an environment conducive to learning. Often this is determined by the teacher's demeanor, whether a person is rough, vivacious, petty, hard, considerate, or even inconsiderate. The worst teacher are bullies, unworthy of their title. They goad, annoy, and even threaten their students. The best teacher is both hard and resilient, strong and yet supple in their teaching. They command and their orders are carried out not because of fear, but because of trust.

It is the amygdala in the brain which regulates the body's fear mechanism. When a person fears some situation, the amygdala causes an endocrinological response which begins to shut down the cortex and prepares the body for physical danger. If the student is in a continual state of fear or anxiety when a teacher enters the room, the cortex, the heart of the brain in which learning takes place, is not free to function normally. So from the teacher's first point of contact with a student, confidence and not fear must be the student's initial reaction. This is even more imperative for the swordmaster whose job it is to teach the student to be fearsome in the most fearful of circumstances.

Master teachers must teach competence, critical thinking, and creativity. And whether they start with a formal education in fencing such as that obtained from a nationally licensed body or from informal study and experience in bouting, training, and, though rarely these days, from battlefield experience, the teacher must instruct a body of knowledge and then get the student to apply himself to that instruction. The onus of a master swordsman then is a delicate task of encouraging without patronizing. His students will recognize meaningless and repeated praise. Baby talk or terse instruction that has the appearance of talking down to the student's intelligence also impedes the process. The master must be both intimate and distant, he must lead and not coerce. He must know the specifics of a student's abilities, but he must not give him attention which might make the student think he is getting special consideration. The instructor must demonstrate techniques that are beyond the reach of his students so that they may aspire to what they are not yet ready to accomplish, but he must not give too many advanced techniques which are still beyond the ken of the student's ability to perform. Like a tantalizing apple, techniques must be within site but just a little out of reach in order to move the student forward. Perfect execution of technique is always a requirement of the master, though he must also realize that the student is not any more capable the first time doing a technique than is a baby's first grasp of a mother's finger. In time, all will be accomplished.

The ability to "make" a student do his best is a difficult feat. Quite often it is a question of being firm, yet sometimes indignant at the hint of a student's slacking attitude. A reassuring voice, however, is often the key to soothing an anxious heart. Especially since failure before the eyes of one's teacher is an ever present anxiety in the dojo. Even the student with the most bravado harbors an inward fear, else he would not need to perform so obvious a display. And yet the swordmaster must only give the slightest suggestion or word of advice.

Yoda, in the short dialogue he has in the film, speaks in short aphorisms not dissimilar to Zen koans. Lucas, with Leigh Brackett and Lawrence Kasdan, decided deliberately to have Yoda talk in proverbs and commandments. Irvin Kershner, director of *The Empires Strikes Back*, was personally interested in Zen Buddhism, distilling some of the slight nuances of Yoda's character from what he knew of Zen.

Often instructors on the mat teach in a similar way. During instruction, which usually lasts between one and two hours, the instructor is demonstrating and observing his students. Whatever the format, the martial arts class is a series of supervised drills. The master demonstrates and then watches as students do their best to imitate his example. Each comment a master gives, whether to an individual or the whole class, is an immediate critique of their performance. He gives immediate feedback on their process. The comment may be a suggestion for improvement or it may be criticism of a technique's execution. The student may understand exactly how to correct the problem. Quite often, he knows exactly what to do but does not have the physical skills to execute the movement and fails. The master gives only a lifeline which keeps the student from drowning. He cannot make the student swim, which is up to the student.

An instructor cannot correct every mistake one or every student makes. He must address the most grievous problems, and when spoken by an excellent teacher even the critique meant for an individual sounds to every student as if it applies to them.

In aikido, a student finds extreme satisfaction in being chosen to partner with the teacher for a demonstration. And during regular practice when everyone is practicing a demonstrated movement, an instructor may interrupt a pair practicing together. Certainly the partner feels special attention, as the other must sit quietly watching his partner train with the instructor. Often, however, it is the instructor's intention to show the watching student subtleties in a technique. Clever students realize that every moment of direct instruction, if even of a duration of fifteen seconds, is a gift from the instructor to the student.

Anakin receives this kind of instruction several times in *The Phantom Menace*. When Ric Olié teaches Anakin about his ship's cockpit controls, it is up to Anakin to remember and learn. When Qui-Gon tells Anakin to "be mindful...always remember, your focus determines your reality," Anakin takes Qui-Gon's instructions to heart when he is told to stay in the cockpit of the Naboo fighter which would inevitably carry him into the dog fight above the planet.

Lack of attention, and even indifference, are the greatest anxieties for novices. Without a strong feeling of mastery, a student naturally desires a guide. And for every moment a teacher spends with one particular individual, there is a majority of students who feel as if they are not significant enough to be attended to. The student's inclination is a desire for praise, which underscores their desire to have a master who will give them personal attention. Little do they realize that when an instructor is working with someone else, he is demonstrating to everyone. This is little solace to students who feel neglected, especially those who put out so much effort in trying to do their best. The fact is, however, that not every beginner deserves attention. They must earn attention through humble practice which formalizes their technique before teachers who are observing students more often than they think.

In the first five years of my training in aikido, I kept a journal of memorable practices. Over and over I expressed an unquenchable desire to be recognized by the headmaster, Saotome Sensei. Feelings of accomplishment are not the ordinary staple of regular practice. Experienced students understand this and no longer base the success of a practice on whether or not the instructor pays any attention to them. Improvement is obtained not as a result of praise, but through practice.

In kendo, the custom for beginners is to drill endlessly with seniors. Having purchased armor in the States before I left for Japan, I was looking forward to joining a kendo dojo and finally getting to wear my armor. For nine months, I drilled without armor, participating in exhausting drills. So difficult were some practices that I almost threw up from exertion. And when I could not physically continue with practice I quickly learned to turn away from practice facing a wall for a moment to compose myself before turning back to training. Sometimes drills were so grueling I had to muster every ounce of energy to keep myself from crying. Half expecting pity from sensei, I thought there would be but even an ounce of reprieve in the practice. Instead, I was encouraged to practice even harder than before, and always did I feel that his drive to make me work was more than I could handle. That is the mark of a good teacher.

After drills, senior students were permitted free practice. Juniors without armor could only watch, drill among ourselves, or ask a senior to drill him some more. Over time, I observed that newer students were being asked to bring in their armor, and not soon after, of all the beginners, I was the only one not wearing armor even though I had started before many of them.

One day, rather nonchalantly, Kubo Sensei asked me to bring my armor in for the next practice. I thought he only wanted to take a look at it. I never questioned Sensei about others wearing armor. In fact, I didn't even think I was ready for it. Because of my experience moving too quickly into competitive fencing, I was content to practice. I brought in my armor for the next practice, but was never asked to wear it. Soon I forgot that it was even sitting on a shelf in the back room.

Then, just after the beginning of drills, Sensei asked me to bring my armor downstairs. Moments later I approached him holding my armor the way my seniors did. He told me to take a seat in seiza at the head of the dojo while he continued drilling other students. *Kakari-geiko*, attack practice, began with its typical relentless fury. Sensei then left his students and approached me. Piece by piece, he began to place each part of the armor on my body, tying each cord with efficiency. First the *tare*, the protective skirt, then the breastplate called a *dô*, and finally the mask, called a *men*. He then held out the *kote*, the gloves, for me to push my hands into.

Duly knighted in a way I had never seen Sensei do to any

other student, I took my place at the beginning of the line. All high on myself, I was ready to do some "real" training. Instead, I found myself weighed down with an unbearable load. And where my partners before were never permitted to physically hit me with their *shinai*, the bamboo practice sword, I was now fair game, a lamb sent out to slaughter among the wolves. It was at that point that I realized that I had just begun a new training, and while the months of endless drilling were behind me, it was about to start all over again until my last day of practice before returning to the States, when I was required to do two hundred individual single-touch bouts.

On my last night at the dojo, my kendo friends made a line, and one by one each drew up before me in an attack stance. I would not be allowed to continue to the next match until a definitive hit was scored by either myself or my opponent. At first I held my own against each attacker, but as I got more and more tired, I realized that I would not have the stamina to maintain complicated strategies against successive attacks. Soon, I found myself being slaughtered by every attack. At some point, though, I decided to let my spirit go. I relaxed my body and simply let techniques take over. Like Luke practicing on the *Millennium Falcon* or just before launching his proton torpedo at the Death Star, I let the spirit inside of me guide my actions. By the end, I was scoring points against even the most senior students, including Sensei. It was from such hard bouting that one learns that a fencer cannot wait for an attack and simply fend them off. Every movement must be decisive. Every attack must hit. Hesitation is the path to obliteration. Conversely, if an attack doesn't land, the swordsman is also resigned to the fact that a decisive hit was made on him. It is at that point that the swordsman realizes that there is nothing one can do to change the inevitable.

As that final night at Kubo Sensei's dojo demonstrates, practice is always the moment for the student. It is up to the student to use his time wisely or risk squandering his effort. It makes the student remember that it is not the teacher who must learn, it is the student.

Discipline of Apprenticeship

One the fundamental issues students of a traditional martial arts must grapple with is the need to exert their independent creativity in a system which demands the subordination of one's ego to the will of another person. The dojo's environment seems to fly in the face of the creativity modern students are raised to expect when they endeavor any artistic expression.

All artists believe creativity is the heart of their artistic expression, but not until an artist finds himself under the strict tutelage of a master does he discover the true meaning of creativity, that source of energy which drives the soul forward and compels the artist to create. Georgia O'Keeffe was once asked if discipline was not a hindrance to her artistic creativity. She responded by saying that it was not creativity in the first place if it could survive the test of discipline.

While a master and his strict expectations seems to tell a student to suppress his personal inclinations, the discipline of staying one's natural inclinations, desires, and intuitions push the creative soul to stretch its limits. It forces the artist to put himself in a new box in which he can discover something new or assimilate a manner or method that improves the present state of his "suppressed" creativity. To paraphrase O'Keeffe's retort: if discipline destroys your creativity, you were never meant to have it. Creativity is tenacious and defiant. It knows no master, no matter how hard someone tries to suppress it.

The final expression of any martial art is a test in the uncertainty of a real fight. Unpredictability creates a stress on the intellect and pushes the body to meet the cognitive expectations that are needed to defeat the concerted attack of another person. The act of foiling an opponent trying to kill you with his sword is nothing less than a creative enterprise. It is that fact that makes the combative nature of fighting such a tragic event. Throughout history, around the world, men and women of the greatest potential are training to kill each other when they could have focused all of their energies into peaceful purposes.

The modern swordsman, because of the evolved nature of

war (and probably because of luck) enjoys the luxury of learning the martial discipline of swordsmanship and using it as a peaceful means of self-expression and growth. Swordsmanship preserves an honor code which has enriched culture and society because it values the spoken word over the resort to a written contract. If it were not for discipline, no man would be considered to have had the will to suppress his natural inclinations to take easy action which often entails the breaking of one's word. Society, as reflected in its literature, values the man who subordinates his will to the greater good of others. So when a gentleman gives his word, there is a standard which is rarely found in our litigious society.

The suppression of the will, a good working definition of discipline, is a test which separates the dutiful student from the pretender. At the aikido Hombu Dojo in Tokyo, the student, whether Japanese or foreign, continually battles the disinterest of the teachers. The instructions from the secretary who accepts your registration at the front desk is the simple explication that the main dojo is on the third floor and that the change room is next to it. If you were to ask who you should train with, she would probably repeat her earlier statement.

The excellent teacher needs never look for students. If the discipline of his art has not molded his character, which serves as the demonstrative expression of his skill, then he never developed the mastery of his art. A master does not need to demonstrate his mastery, it manifests itself in the very essence of the person: how he carries himself, how he handles the ordinary or stressful situation, how he drinks his tea.

Dave Lowry recounts a story told by his master of a man who came up to the swordmaster seeking instruction in swordsmanship. To test the man, he raised his sword as if he were going to strike him down. Noticing his calm, he told the man that he was already a master. But of what? The man explained that he had no discipline to apply himself to any activity, especially the martial arts. He concluded he would die very quickly and after serious contemplation of his predicament, he came to the realization that he should no longer be afraid to die. The swordmaster looked at the man and said he had nothing to teach him because "to overcome life and death is to know the greatest mastery." It is this imperturbability that manifests itself in the very slightest action. The true swordmaster is complete master of his fear.

Discipline forces a student to learn on his own without the help or the prodding of an instructor. Ultimately, it is the student who is responsible for his own learning. As one of my dearest friends, Greg Angus, a black belt in Shitô ryu karate and partner at Hombu Dojo, "A student has to steal from the instructor what he can." In addition to the formal training in art that makes him also a painter, Greg's statement emphasizes the fact that no one will carry you to the end of your journey. If the artist relies on the assistance of outsiders to make his art, it is, in principle, tainted and corrupt. That is not to say that there cannot be any help from others, but that the ultimate responsibility for artistic expression resides within the student. The mastery of art is never easily obtained. All art is the conjoined expression of an individual's toil, dedication, determination, and resolution.

Struggle and hardship in life is the greatest test of one's character. It separates humans from animals and their animal instincts. Where the man, because of a consciousness, can subordinate his will and sacrifice it for others out of a sense of justice or righteousness is a distinct line separating himself from lesser creatures. If a starving man were to steal a loaf a bread, he can be dismissed for behaving like an animal following his instincts. The true man of personal honor would rather die than descend to the level of an animal. An even greater man would humble himself, suppress his pride, and employ his intellect to ask for the loaf instead of taking it by force of arms.

Despite our aversion to hardship, art improves during economic hardship because there is something over which the artist can express himself. Indeed, the imperative is one of life or death. In the most trying of times, a person feels every emotion to its greatest degree: anger, hate, love, compassion. It is a matter of confronting the struggle and raising one's soul without falter or failure above the pettiness that is so common.

In Kurosawa's *The Seven Samurai*, a band of helpless villagers must obtain the services of samurai to protect them from thieving bandits demanding their harvest of rice at the end of the planting season. The wise man of the village says that in order to find samurai who would work for the meager subsistence which is their harvest, you have to find starving samurai. Powerful and prideful are samurai the villagers say as they contemplate their search for a samurai. Yet they *do* find a samurai who, through the goodness of his heart, is willing to sacrifice his life for villagers who are willing to subsist on millet in order to pay the samurai with three meals of rice a day for their services.

There is a belief in Japan that the spirit is indomitable and permits the body to accomplish unbelievable, mind over matter feats. It is the force of a person's will, his passion to accomplish something that allows the body to surpass its limits. Since the intellect is the safety mechanism which reigns in the physicality of the body, it goes without saying that subordinating the intellect to the will can allow the spirit its full potential.

This appeal to suppress desires of the flesh is considered a healthy expression in the search for enlightenment. The ordinary Japanese engages in ritual acts of purification that seem absurd to citizens of countries in which access to personal and physical pleasure is an inherent right of living within society. Cleaning in Japan is considered an act of personal purification symbolic of the cleaning of the soul. Every year on New Years Day, Japanese do their spring cleaning as a way to wash away the old year and welcome in the new. It is also why students of the martial arts are expected to ritually clean the floor after practice. It is a practice that I continue in my fencing classes at Georgetown University which borrows regular classrooms for practice. The desire after a difficult practice is to simply leave the desks pushed up against the wall of the room. Not only is it proper to return the room to its original state, but it is an act of purification to submit to the humblest of actions after the most empowering of activities.

Ascetics all over the world see perfection of the soul in the perfection of the body. Yoga masters perform incredible feats of their body through extreme belief and practice. The ritual of a repeated mantra and profession of faith helps raise the state of the soul, as does quiet contemplation or prayer. Self-flagellation or the wearing of a sack cloth are Christian expressions of denial of the bodily pleasure of the flesh; meditating in the snow or naked under the frigid flow of a winter waterfall are Asian methods. At Hombu Dojo, windows are opened during daily winter practice. There is no heater and the windows remain open in cold wind and even snow. Though there is a hot water heater, it is never turned on. The building itself is simple, frugal, and unimposing, and yet it attracts the best students of the world for training. It is through the denial of pleasure that there is the possibility of touching the ethereal world. Through ascetic denial, one awaits, but cannot expect, inspiration, epiphany, the touch of God.

This is the reason why the Jedi Code would prohibit Anakin from taking Padmé as a wife. And while there is much evidence in the real world that physical pleasures of the flesh are not incompatible with a religious vocation, there is a strong tradition that a Jedi is already married to the Order in the same way that the priest is married to the Church.

Enduring hardship underscores the fact that no focused work is pointless if it develops the person and allows him or her to change and grow. Dedication develops character, attention to detail, and the refinement of the soul. And despite the ordeal of the struggle, there is often a joy that seems to express itself in the demeanor of the best dojos. Students still enjoy themselves and their practice. No command or order is taken as punitive and expressions of laughter and camaraderie cannot be stifled. It is not the simple satisfaction of accomplishment, but the joy of simply existing in the moment.

For swordsmen, training must be seen as essential, for his life depends on his skills. For the modern swordsman, however, while the imperative of killing is no longer the focus of practice, it does not mean that there should be any less intensity in training. It is the inner joy of tiny achievements through the honing of skills which would enable a modern swordsman to survive an encounter with real swordsmen in battle. The Jedi could just as easily understand this imperative in their daily practice, for it is inherent in the art of the sword.

The joy of students after training certainly reflects the accomplishments of practice, but it is only temporary and brief. So why not revel in it momentarily and then continue with practice? As Eugene Herrigal says *Zen in the Art of Archery*, the archer, after loosing his arrow, "steps quietly into the background." Training begins, finishes, and begins again.

Training

The students's first command is to begin practice with an open mind. He must trust his master without judgment, which truly means a trust in one's self. It is this openness which leads to trust. Trust, in turn, leads to respect, and respect to confidence. Even upon mastering the basics, the student is still charged to develop his own repertoire of techniques. No matter how technically imitative he is of his teacher's technique, the student must master technique in his own fashion. He must make his technique his own.

In the traditional dojo, the beginning student starts training by learning how to serve tea. It teaches servitude. It humbles the most physically powerful person. It forces the strongest ego to obey. It is also a way to test the character of a student who manifests his strengths and weaknesses in his manners at the table; in the way he approaches the table, how he picks up the tea kettle, the manner in which he places down the cups before pouring, and how appropriately in the host's conversation he retrieves their empty cups. Every moment around the master is one of a test, and while most of us fail at some point in our daily activity, the master also recognizes this as part of the process. While the student may feel demeaned by the expectation to serve tea, he may not realize that the sensei is also introducing the potential swordsman to a cultured society. And not only does the master learn about the student, the student is also introduced to his guests by his very presence as a tea server.

During practice, especially in the free flowing practice of aikido which is essentially swordsmanship without the sword, there is a tendency for Western students to intellectualize their way through verbal practice. While there is an internal dialogue in the routine of regular practice, it is not a conversation. A student learns movement not through talking his way through a kata, but by actually doing it.

There are two methods of learning in the martial arts — behavioral and cognitive. The former teaches through experience and practice, training the body and its systems to react and operate efficiently under the challenging circumstances of a fight. The body is trained to perform particular actions in a certain order without hesitation. Reflexes are matured and the stamina and musculature are developed to carry out the movement needed for the execution of technique. Concurrently, the hormonal system is pumping the body with its natural chemicals which heightens awareness and permit rapid and instantaneous execution of the mind's will. Instead of continually asking questions, the student needs to simply practice and forgo their tendency to ask if the particular execution of movement was correct.

Cognitive learning, the other half of mastering a martial system, refers to the brain's retrieval of information from the person's history of learning. Where behavioral learning deals with the physical movement and control of the body, cognitive brain function determines what moves a person does and in what order to perform them. The mind cognitively examines the situation and determines the best attacks, defenses, and counter actions based on its storehouse of information. A harmony between behavioral and cognitive functions of the body lead to an efficient performance of body movement needed for swordwork or any other martial art.

In one practice, Saotome Sensei chided his class for the explanation and conversation in which his students were engaged. He made the analogy that if you wanted to teach someone what sugar tastes like, you don't teach them chemistry. "You shove sugar down their mouth." He continued with a severe affection that we all sounded like babies asking, "Why? Why? Why?"

In the heat of an attack, there is no time for conversation. There is only time for the action of defeating your opponent as efficiently as possible. Once the amygdala has mastered the fight or flight mechanisms, the mind is calm enough to save the body. As opposed to relying on an anticipatory fear and haphazardly adjusting to the situation ("picking up the pieces" as it were), the mind must allow the body to act according to reference experiences that make the individual fearless in face of impending death.

All learning is to be changed by knowledge. And in the situation where an opponent has a weapon design to extinguish a person's life, self-defense training must immediately flow from the mind. Disciplined and repetitive training prepares the body for movement. Free training and competition allows the body use the body's skills to create a strategy which can defeat an opponent who is similarly trying to defeat the martial artist. Yoda's chiding of Luke speaks profoundly to the imperative of allowing a resolution to find itself during combat. "There is no try. There is only do. That is why you fail."

There are two ways of encouraging any enterprise. First to say failure is okay. Let's move on and try again. The second is that there is a goal that needs to be met — success is the only answer and we must find it. To achieve the highest caliber of a person, the second must be the mentality for successful combat. You must survive. But in order to reach this point there must be room for the admission of failure up until the fateful moment of a duel. In the real world of a fight, there is only one mentality — do or do not.

Practice is the place for failure, though practice is a continual striving for perfection. In ordinary drilling, it cannot be any more emphasized that technique needs to be practiced as perfectly as can be mastered. To do otherwise would be to perfect imperfect movement. When a student lunges during drill, he or she must do so with the intention of making it the most perfect lunge possible. There must be perfect form, perfect balance, perfect execution of the different parts of the body. If I, as the instructor, were to let the student do half-lunges, or lunges with a slightly turned ankle, the likelihood of him doing the same during the uncertainty of a real bout is more probable. In the case of the turned ankle, it is more likely that the high energy of a bout will cause the fencer to twist his ankle.

In a metaphorical sense, fencing is likened to the Forms described in Plato's *Republic*. Fencing, like all other activities, seeks to accomplish a goal. In the case of sword fighting, the goal is to strike your opponent with the your weapon. Based on all of the factors of where the sword is, what the opponent is doing, there is an ideal attack which, in the mind, can be executed most directly and efficiently for any given point. What the fencer must do is to execute his attack as closely to the ideal attack as possible. To want to do less would be an unnecessary expenditure of energy. The ideal is perfection, the execution is the attempt at perfection, and the strike on target is the intended goal. Of course, the perfect execution of an act may not be possible in this world, but neither is the goal impossible. A person seeks standards with which he can compare himself, and because the life and death nature of swordsmanship they ought not be anything less than the highest. There may be more than one approach in obtaining a target, but a hit a fraction of an inch away from the intended target is still sufficient to accomplish the fencer's goal. Fencing is the art of the possible but it strives for perfection; and perfection implies the exact control of the weapon, complete grace of movement and action, and the attainment of the goal. This perfection is beauty in the conceptual sense, but also in the physical sense. There is nothing more beautiful than the perfect execution of an attack that even the opponent must appreciate and acknowledge.

In Asian martial arts, instruction is taught through kata,

forms of predetermined and precise movement that contain a series of techniques to be mastered. It is the master who provides this model of perfection for a technique, and it is the student who must discern the essence of the movement in his mind and try to imitate it. He is not imitating the exact movement of the teacher because every movement reflects the circumstances of the teacher in relation to the person with whom he is training. The student is imitating the ideas embodied in the demonstration and then applying it to his own movement.

A story is told of the founder of aikido about a photographer who asked Morihei Ueshiba to repeat a move that he liked so he could photograph it. Ueshiba Sensei tried to recreate the movement but to the consternation of the photographer he could not do it. Finally, Ueshiba told the photographer that technique is free flowing and amorphous, and that whatever technique he saw was a product of the circumstances of that moment. This is what makes the master indispensable to the student, and the very reason why it is important that the newest beginners be exposed to the best instruction, that of the headmaster himself.

At one point in my teaching career I wondered whether I couldn't be accomplishing more by teaching to older students who would be more capable of understanding the intellectual instruction which I like to give. A professor at Howard Law School and friend from my aikido dojo upon learning that I taught 5th grade told me that I can do more for a student at that age than he could for his students in college. He lamented the fact that his graduate students lacked the drive and the intellectual inquisitiveness that were essential in learning. He continued that I would be doing his students and the world a vital service if all I accomplished was to teach my students the importance of an education. Every student in the end is responsible for his education, but excellent teachers are vital to the development of that student.

During a beginner's training, there is the inevitable desire for the student's body to take the path of least resistance, which analogous to the repeated warning from Yoda and Obi-Wan that the path to the Dark Side is easier and more seductive. The student's body only knows one way of moving. With training, his body is being commanded to move itself in new and more demanding ways. In an attempt to practice this new movement, the body resorts to a previous comfort level, which often runs counter to the proper execution of martial techniques the student is learning. The body rebels against the new movement because the relief of pain is a greater imperative during practice than fulfilling the cognitive ideal the mind is trying to achieve: the production of a new musculature and reflexive systems. Compared to a hopelessly reactive defense in the face of danger, the training of a martial system produces efficient and specialized movement.

The ultimate goal is the physical execution of any technique the mind commands the body to perform. Saotome Sensei once compared the execution of technique to the start up system of a car. "Do you want your car to start only 50% of the time?" The threshold of mastery is to be able to do any technique one hundred percent of the time. "How about your heart? Would you be happy if it only worked 99% of the time? You would feel cheated by your car dealership, and you would be dead the first time your heart hit that 1%."

One example from my own experience involved an incident in which someone tried to rob me at night when I was reclined with by back on the ground in a park in Washington, DC looking at the stars. Someone grabbed me from behind, saying he had a knife at my neck, which he said he would use if I didn't give over my wallet. I felt the touch of something against my Adam's apple but knew it wasn't metal so it couldn't have been a knife. Instinctively, I pushed the stick he was holding off to the side away from my neck. Unconsciously, I repositioned my feet into *seiza** and then threw the mugger over my shoulder in a movement called *kokyu ho*. The guy was completely taken by sur-

---

*A formal sitting position with one's feet under one's posterior.

prise. After a quick standoff, I told the guy to head off in one direction, while I went off in the another.

In another instance at a concert, a guy suddenly punched one my friends in the face because we would not sit down. It didn't occur to him that everyone in the stadium was standing up except him. Without a second thought, I jumped over the seats and quickly got the six foot guy in a head lock. With his head in my hands at the level of my stomach, I had one hand on the back of his neck and the other craning his head unnaturally upward. By twisting his head just a few inches I could have killed the man, but something inside of me told me not to hurt the helpless man whose very life I held in my hands. Security and the police arrived. I acquiesced to their authority and released the man. Pulling me to the side, one of the security guards put a flashlight up to my eyes to see if I was drunk or on some kind of drug, which I wasn't.

In both instances, time traveled in slow motion and I acted without any thought, though I was in complete control of my actions. I could feel my heartbeat pumping — the blood, testosterone, and endorphins were racing through my veins. But where training allowed me to move in ways to protect myself, my ability to remain calm under fire allowed me to make decisions that saved not only my life, but also that of my attacker.

The temptation to use violence is a powerful emotion driven by fear and the lack of self-control. The need for me to formally learn some kind of martial art came during an incident in college when two drunks started pushing around and yelling at my friend as we were crossing an overpass walkway. Because I was so angry, my first inclination was to take one of the guys and throw him over the edge of the overpass to the ground some twenty feet below. My emotions told me one thing, but a sense of justice told me that violence, especially the kind that I wanted to inflict, was not appropriate to those circumstances. Somehow I extricated my buddy without incident, but that encounter personally illustrated for me that the desire to take justice into my own hands when the feeling of helplessness overcomes me has monstrous potential. The desire to stand up for yourself or for those closest to you — friends, family, partners — is a powerful urge. Most might think that the ability to use force is justification itself for its exercise. The properly trained martial artist never chooses to settle differences in a fight. He has failed the teachings of his master. The need to use violence is thrust upon a person, it is never chosen. Anakin confronts a similar situation in *Attack of the Clones* when he arrives at a village of Tusken Raiders where his mother has been captured.

After both of my personal incidents, I was overcome by the desire to shout out my victory to the world. At the dojo, I told one of my friends who immediately told Saotome Sensei. Sensei simply looked at me and nodded approval and never mentioned the incident again. The moment paled in comparison, however, when I showed up at the dojo with scratch marks on my face from a partner's finger nails. Sensei, pointing to my face, turned to me and said, "That's real training. Now you'll know that you should keep your hands up to block your face."

While the success of winning a fight can make you feel powerful, the true test of one's skill, however, is how you face failure. Fighting is for self-preservation, never to teach someone a lesson. In a scene in *The Phantom Menace* that was cut from the final movie, Anakin gets in a fight with Greedo, who was a child at the time, accusing Anakin of cheating during the pod race. Qui-Gon ends up pulling Anakin off of Greedo and chides the boy, saying that even if you defeat Greedo once, he's still liable to return to pick another fight. Qui-Gon continues that Anakin cannot use force to make someone come over to his way of thinking. This is a lesson some people never learn in their entire life.

Weapon Training

While empty hands training is the best kind of training for a modern society, weapon training brings an added level of intensity to practice. Since aikido is swordsmanship without the sword, moving from aikido sword to kendo and iaido was an easy transition. Even with wooden practice weapons, any mistakes in movement could mean concussions, broken bones, and even death. With empty hands, a martially trained person can take extreme punishment, but only to a point. Unlike what is seen on TV and the movies where a punch to the face is answered by a counter punch to the face, a real fight must do immediate damage. And unlike the pounding done with boxing gloves, targets in a real fight should be the sensitive areas of the body: the eyes, throat, nose, the ears and side of the head, joints, and the stomach. With weapons there is no room for a mistake.

Weapon training, therefore, begins by teaching students to treat their weapons with respect. In Japan, there is an unwritten rule that no one ever steps over a sword (or any practice weapon) laying on the floor. You walk around it. If a person misplaces a step, he may break the weapon. Moreover, in the case of practice weapons, stepping around the weapon shows respectful treatment for all weapons as well as respect for another person's possessions. Even in my Western fencing classes, I insist that foils, epees, and sabres be treated as if they were true fighting weapons. They should not stepped over, nor should weapons be used to do mundane things like flicking something off the floor or pushing a button or a switch. Not only might an electric weapon get damaged, but it cheapens one's perception of their training weapon. A sword is a weapon, not a tool.

In addition to intensifying practice, there is an undeniable lure of being able to wield a sword, especially among boys and men. In recent interviews with Hayden Christiansen and Samuel Jackson, Christiansen said, "I got to wield a lightsaber." "It was so cool, I can't tell you. It was extemely empowering. It's every boy's dream, really." Jackson says, "I get to do a lot of things with my lightsaber, a lot of good kendo stuff." He continues to say that now that he's acted opposite Yoda, "I can retire now."

The learning of swordwork does not depend on a child-like infatuation with swords, though that may help in motivation. Learning techniques depends on having a proper instructor to teach the fundamentals of swordsmanship. Even in a world where hosts of books on the martial arts are easy to come by, it is important to remember that while they may help in remembering what has already been taught, there is no substitute for an instructor. In even the simplest tasks such as basic posture, it is important that a student is correctly taught by an instructor from the onset.

Learning posture and grip are the starting points for both Western fencing and Japanese kendo and sword, because the way a person holds his weapon determines how he can use his sword. Even the simple act of holding a weapon has dire consequences if done improperly.

One of the biggest problems with *Star Wars* sword fighting is the poor manner in which actors playing Jedi hold their lightsabers, especially in photo stills. Instead of holding their swords with wrists twisted inward, lightsabers are held like baseball bats. Try hold a stick naturally with two hands in front of you. Your fingers would be inward closest to your chest. If you tried to hit your stick against something hard, the pressure of the strike would put pressure on the fingers, the weakest part of the hand. By twisting the wrists inward, the arms and the body are properly placed behind the shaft.

Another area that must be emphasized by an instructor is the importance of the legs in any sword arts, as well as in any martial art. Little credit ever goes to the legs in the minds of the uninitiated fencers who focus on the sword. When non-fencers pick up a foil, they extend their arm from the elbow, thinking it is the push of the arm's muscles which perform the thrusting of the blade. The most elementary lesson an instructor must give a Western-style fencer is to attack with the point *after* the arm has been completely extended and solidly braced. With an extended arm, the legs are only then able to carry the point toward an opponent. This seem completely counter-intuitive to the non-fencer, but students quickly learn that point control comes from the fingers while strength comes from the legs. In kendo, fundamentals of holding a shinai are different. It is the left hand which throws the shinai forward while the right hand guides the blade's direction. And with a live blade, both hands should extend ever so slightly as the legs carry the weight of the body forward.

Without basic footwork, the upper body cannot even think of wielding the sword. Where even a millimeter means the difference between hitting and missing, proper footwork is the key to the proper execution of technique. A fencer cringes more when he sees someone with a broken leg than someone with a broken arm. As is so humorously shown in the Rob Reiner film *The Princess Bride*, a fencer can always switch hands with his sword. He needs two legs to fence.

In both Western and Japanese fencing, there are two ways of using their sword — thrusting and slashing. With its wide sweep, the most natural is the slash. Not only does the body have a natural tendency to throw its weight into the swing, there is less need for precision. And even if the slash is not very effective, any inflicted damage is better than none at all. Point work, on the other hand, requires a lot more precision to hit a more limited target, which is usually more easily covered by armor.

Neither type of attack is actually better, nor exclusive to the other and each has its drawback. The thrust may pierce more easily and is more likely to hit a vital organ, but it is also easy to deflect. A slash is more likely to hit something because there is more of a blade with which to hit, but it is easier to see a slash coming and counter it.

So which does a swordsman use? It depends on the physical properties of the weapon, the style of the fencing school, distance, and training. Obviously a two-handed katana is more suited to a cutting slash, as are Japanese sword schools which emphasize cutting with the edge, while Western fencing emphasizes the point. Thrusts are more effective when the opponent is farther away. Slashing is better at closer distances. But probably the biggest determining factor in whether a thrust or slash will be used is the individual fencer's experience from both training and even in competition or battle.

Proper training in sword and its modern equivalents is learning to hit the opponent without being hit. While that may seem obvious to the non-fencer, beginners immediately feel a hesitancy to hit because 1) they don't think they know how to hit properly (so why even try), and 2) they fear what might happen if after they hit (so why even try). And once the beginner gains the confidence to strike out at their target, they can find they can often hit their target but not without being simultaneously being hit by their opponent.

In both the pointwork of Western fencing and the crossed-blades fencing of Japanese sword (and kendo), the goal is to give so quick and decisive an attack that the opponent is helpless in defending himself. Consequently, early drilling involves teaching the proper attack before allowing the student to engage in free sparing, which allows the beginner to break every rule of fencing they had been learning during drill. While it is not a bad thing for a beginner to engage in friendly sparring, attention must be paid in using basic technique properly in lieu of trying more complicated and fancy techniques.

In kendo, iaido, and classical Japanese sword, *suburi* practice is the staple of learning how to cut correctly. Suburi is the repetition of overhead cuts one after another. The number of cuts might be fifty to warm up or up to two hundred or more for proper practice. It is a kind of training designed to exhaust the mind and body. Because of the physical pain, the mind is convinced that it can no longer continue, but by disciplining one's spirit and will, however, suburi leads to the forced continuation of repeated cuts. At a point the mind begins to relax. When suburi first becomes difficult (after about the first thirty cuts), the mind cannot help but focus on the body's developing pain. Once the brain become exhausted from its concentration, the mind begins to relax. Muscles can no longer maintain their composure and begin to relax. The body gets used to the motions of the hands, arms, and legs. If the swordsman refuses to relax, the pain continues. Finally, the body and mind will realize if the will is forcing the body to continue doing cuts, the body will begin to naturally understand that it is easier and less exhausting to do cuts correctly than to give in to the pain. It is not gaining a second wind, as some might think, but perfecting the most efficient movement of the body, which is discovered not by telling someone to do it, but learning through actually doing it.

Training is fighting the body's tendency to be lazy. Once the fencer resolves to discipline his mind, body, and spirit, then he begins to master technique. It is, therefore, extremely important that fencers avoid dragging their back leg in lunges, relying on the same attack one after another, keeping one's guard in the middle of the body, half lunging, moving their legs first, and neglecting to parry-riposte. Kendo fencers must remember to bring their sword completely above their head, keep their feet parallel, avoid looking at their target, and favoring one side in their defenses. For any style of fencing, the most grievous mistakes is moving the body before an attack with the sword. Not only does this telegraph your intentions, it places the attacker's body closer to the opponent for *him* to attack. Solid attacks over fancy and complicated attacks are more dangerous and threatening. And paramount for the fencer is to attack and never rely on defense.

In today's modern dojos and fencing clubs, because points are simply touches, not penetrations, there is no commanding reason why a student must learn to fence so that they are never hit. But if one's goal is fence properly, then one must learn to fence with the intention of never letting an opponent land a touch. If a student trains with this intention, even in a modern competitive weapon, there is no reason why modern fencers could not compete with swordsmen of past eras.

Had I and the two men opposite me in my two fights been holding sharp swords in our hands, there would have had to be only a single outcome in my mind — survival. With a sword in my hand and standing in the middle of a battlefield, there could be only one outcome — kill or be killed. But in our peace loving societies, the robber or mugger cannot and should not be summarily executed at your own hands if it can be avoided. I am fortunate that I began training in the art of aikido before I began my training in kendo and iaido. From it I learned not only to defend myself, but also to protect the life of the attacker. Had I not learned those two lessons, I might have given fatal injuries to the two assailants who attacked me. In training with a weapon like a sword, the importance of discipline and learning proper control becomes even more importance.

Like Jedi in the *Star Wars* universe, it is patently clear that there are limits in the resort to the use of their lightsabers. Like the modern police officer, abuse of one's privilege of carrying a sidearm does not absolve the officer of responsibility of this actions using his weapons. The ability to use a weapon does not give that person the right to use it whenever he pleases. Quite to the contrary, his recourse to its use should be less likely if his training has taught him that the mind is more powerful than the piece of steal, or the energy of a lightsaber in the case of the Jedi.

The Measurement of Progress

If all master-apprentice relationships were simply contracts between two individuals, there would be no need for the formal ranking system that is present in martial arts. There would be no need of a colored belt system, the awarding of certificates, or the conferring of titles. Yet there is the inevitability to resort to some kind of hierarchy whether it be a formal *dan** system used in Japan, the collegiality of university professors, or the simple deference of disciples to a master.

Teachers are the first to admit that formal testing is an exercise fraught with the potential to mislead the recipients of any award — a trophy, a degree, a badge — that mastery is at hand. Such awards are merely outward symbols meant as a form of recognition of time devoted to a discipline rather than a definitive test of their ability. The fact that a person has a blackbelt is no guarantee that he can do well in a fight, no more than the college degree can guarantee success in life. Yes, these awards may be impressive and they have value to others, but all teachers know that what one does with one's knowledge is infinitely

---

*Degrees in Japanese ranking are called *dan*.

more important than one's ability to pass a test.

Testing, however, can be a useful tool to help instructors learn what a student has mastered in terms of knowledge and technique. In the world of Western fencing, instructors may receive certification after finishing a formal curriculum and then successful completion of a battery of tests at a recognized institution. The World Fencing Championships (the Olympics in Olympic years) are the highest level of ranking for amateur competition. A competitor is given a letter of A, B, C, D, or unrated; an "A" being the highest level. An "A" rating is gained by participating in a tournament in which an individual ranks one of the top fencers in a competition. If a tournament, for example, is composed of A-level fencers, an unrated fencer who wins the competition will receive an "A" rating.

In the modern Japanese martial arts such as judo, karate, kendo, and aikido, ranking is the same for students and instructors.* Most people will recognize the black belt system of modern arts, which actually reflects two levels of training: a novice level called *kyu*, and an advanced level called *dan*. Kyu ranks are usually divided into six levels, sixth kyu being the lowest level. In more traditional dojos, all kyu-level students wear a white belt, though most Japanese dojos use white belts for 6th-4th kyu, a brown belt for 3rd-1st kyu, and then a black belt for dan levels, a 1st dan indicating the beginning level of higher training. The use of colored belts was introduced for the benefit of children who enjoyed the distinction of moving from one color to another. The ranking of one color over another is completely arbitrary according to the martial art or instructor, and in many martial arts, colors are now used for all ranking from children to adults.

Most people assume that the black belt is a high level of achievement, when in reality it means that one has only just begun their serious training. While there are many interpretations about the technical competence of a black belt, I subscribe

---

*Classical martial arts like Yagyu ryu swordsmanship, however, have a certification system of three ranks.

to the theory that a student has not yet mastered the techniques of a black belt level until having obtained the next ranking. In effect, the student who has passed his black belt test is still a white belt who has yet to master expectations of the black belt. A new first-degree black belt must make himself a black belt.

There is no universal level of ability for black belts across the scores of different martial arts, though there is generally a headquarters dojo run by the headmaster of a style to whom all lower ranking students give their nominal fealty and support. In Japan I trained at the Aikido Headquarters Dojo, also called Hombu Dojo, in Tokyo which was run by the 10th-dan headmaster who is the titular head of aikido. Saotome Sensei, my Aikido instructor in Washington, is an 8th-dan who once trained in the same headquarters dojo as a direct student of the founder of aikido Morihei Ueshiba. My kendo dojo, Kyumeikan Dojo, in Tokyo was a personal school established by the father of my kendo sensei, Kubo Sensei, a 7th-dan. His school does not establish a curriculum in the way that Hombu Dojo does, but it does follow standards set by the All-Japan Kendo Federation which awards all formal dan rankings. In both aikido and kendo, individual instructors set the standards for kyu levels and award ranking themselves.

There is generally a formal curricula of skills that are tested for 1st-3rd dans, while 4th dan tests and above are usually awarded by high ranking instructors as an individual contributes to the training and development of the organization. Fourth dan level is generally synonymous with instructor's level when a student would be allowed permission to open up his or her own dojo. He may be called Sensei at that point.

The concept of competition and formal testing is a subject that is quite open to individual interpretation. Some instructors feel competition is vital to a student's performance, others allow it as a bow to modern society's need for formal competitive organization in the form of sports, while the most traditional martial art abstains from competition altogether. For an individual, the importance of competition versus training is not exclusive, though often the lure of amassing trophies and medals is common. Awards are important to many, but such outside trappings are fleeting achievements. Medals commemorate a moment and allow an individual to stand out for all to see, but in the martial arts, practice is the staple of daily existence. Trophies collect dust and may be joyous reminders marking past achievements, but life goes on. It is a temporary thing to be considered the best in the world, but there is the gentle reminder from Obi-Wan in *The Phantom Menace* that "there is always a bigger fish."

Formal testing on the mat, however, is an important rite of passage for students of the martial arts. Testing not only marks achievement by showing one's instructors what a student has learned, but it plays a more important role in that each person testing serves as a model for the lower ranking students who look up to the higher ranking students. It is one thing to see the mastery of the headmaster. It is another to see the skills and technique of individuals who posses skills within a beginner's reach. Ideally, testing is a celebration of the effort individuals have put into their training.

Jedi Training

Unlike the established testing systems of the Terran martial art dojo, the training that has been shown in the *Star Wars* movies to date indicate two methods of training Jedi. These depended, of course, on the circumstances of two time periods: the height of the Republic and the hey day of the Jedi Order, and a post-Jedi period after the extermination and purging of the Jedi Order during the time of the Empire. It has been established that the Jedi training system is similar to the kyu-dan ranking system in that kyu ranks parallel the pre-Padawan status, while dan (black belts) correspond to the Padawan period when a student is attached specifically to a Jedi Knight for the final preparation of his masterly level, that of full knighthood status.

More about the Jedi will be learned in *Attack of the Clones* and *Episode III*; especially in the fact that the greatest strength of an organization like the Jedi is that its openness, its profession to serve the public, and its accountability to the public make it an easy prey to those who would use nefarious means to undermine their position. While their training may prepare the individual Jedi for the hard life of approaching war, even the greatest warriors are not immortal and may fall victim to deceit and a stab in the night.

Luke Skywalker, a child born in the tumult that will be the fall the Republic, went through a very different and personal manner of training. There was no Jedi Temple and whatever training he got was limited and learned under unconventional and difficult circumstances. Obi-Wan in the brief time with Luke worked on some simple training with seeker balls on the *Millennium Falcon*. But by far the most important contribution the elder Obi-Wan gave to Luke was to convince him to begin Jedi training. Sacrificing his own life so that Luke and his companions might live and his subsequent visitation at the beginning of *The Empire Strikes Back* convince Luke to seek out a new instructor; one who trained Obi-Wan when he himself had become a Padawan at the Jedi Temple — Yoda.

Starting with the traditional method of physical conditioning to which any new recruit is familiar, Luke began to feel the pain in his muscles as he strained to physically mold himself into a man who would have to endure unknowable hardships. Raised as a boy in the remote and inhospitable clime of Tatooine, he already has first hand knowledge of an unforgiving world. At his very doorstep came Imperial troops who summarily kill his aunt and uncle, forcing him to leave his home and answer the call to become a Jedi. As in all tragedy, man is confronted by the hideous circumstances that will either render the protagonist something less than a man or it will test his mettle, allowing him to retain his identity as a human being who can and will face challenges even if it means his own destruction.

Yoda already knows the circumstances of Luke's birth, and yet it is not for him to reveal the nightmarish circumstances that revolve around the fact that Luke's own father is responsible for the destruction of the great Jedi Order. Yoda must prepare Luke

for his future encounters not by indoctrinating him into a
political mold, but by teaching him respect, courage, justice, and
loyalty. When Luke finally learns his family secret, it is no longer
in Yoda's hands to command Luke to a particular course of
action. Yoda may attempt to convince Luke of one plan or another, but when it comes to training swordsmen, the inherent
reality is that they will one day have the power and the will to
discover a destiny of their own. The neophyte fencing teacher
will soon discover their students' independence. The master's
only charge is proper training, not the living out of their apprentice's life. It is hoped, however, that a student's instruction will
be enough to allow the apprentice to make the proper decisions
based on firm concepts of justice, honor, and a deep trust in
peace.

After all of Luke's physical training, Yoda tells Luke of a cave
powerful in the Force. Luke feels drawn to the it and approaches.
Luke asks what's inside. Yoda replies, "Only what you take with
you." Admonishing Luke not to take his weapons, Luke hooks
his utility belt with lightsaber and blaster to his waist as he turns
away from his master to enter his first test.

The event of the cave needs little elaboration. Luke encounters Vader, strikes him down, and then sees his own face in
Vader's mask. Though it was Vader's specter who approached
Luke with an ignited lightsaber, it is Luke who, out of fear, immediately strikes out at Vader. We, the audience, like the master
of a young swordsman, know that the events of the cave were
portents of a life that is yet to come. Luke, as he learns the power
of Jedi training, may yet become like Vader. Lucas' message,
however, is that all swordsmen have the potential to become
evil, and more frightening still is that every person, no matter
how innocent and caring as a child, also bears a similar possibility.

The cave sequence is not a realistic test, but a cinematograph-
ic exposition that allows the movie goer to leave the world of
reality for that of the mind. In this case, action speaks louder
than conversation, the simple premonition of the final confron-

tation between Luke and Lord Vader. This certainly is not a standard test that the Jedi Temple would be able to recreate in some kind of spiritual holographic room that can read the mind's greatest fears and then test the individual's mettle.

A cave strong in the Force is a literary device easily used in books and film to get the audience to go through an experience without the possibility of personally failing ourselves. For humans, as it will be later for Luke, our trial comes not from presuppositions and "what if" scenarios. It comes from actual tests in life which in turn become tests of our humanity. It manifests itself in our greatest life decisions and in our daily life; from the decision to commit to a marriage, to join the military, or to become a nurse; as well as during a simple stroll down a street when a beggar holds out his cup. These are the true tests that determine who we are or what we are to become.

Fortunately, the audience can live the swordsman's life through proxy in *Star Wars* without having to bear the burden of real suffering. In *The Empire Strikes Back*, Luke is still brash and impetuous. He leaves his training and his masters now become fearful that Luke, too, will fall prey to the Dark Side like his father. The rich symbolism of this film shows Luke's arrogance and his fear, his impending doom, and that of the universe. When he confronts Vader, he loses, as should any swordsman who breaks away from his training before he is ready. But Luke is not without choices. Upon hearing that Vader is really his father, Luke resists the temptation to join his father and sends himself off the edge of the precipice at the end of the metal gantry when the final acts of their lightsaber fight take place. Luke's survival is a literary device, an exposition on Luke's shattered ego, his humiliation, and his humbling. Without resorting to tragedy, Lucas in Greek god fashion preserves his actor for another encounter.

Luke has a second chance to face Vader in *Return of the Jedi*. At the beginning of the movie, Luke enters in the priest-like colors of black. He is reserved, more mature and confronts Jabba fearlessly. He does not leave his actions to extemporaneous action. Luke has a plan and uses his intelligence as well as his martial skills to extricate himself and his friends from the clutches of Jabba the Hutt.

His first venture is a success; Han is safe, the notorious gangster is dead, and their attention can now turn to the defeat of the Emperor. Luke returns to Yoda to complete his training, but Yoda is at the twilight of his life. Even if Yoda could continue to train Luke, his ultimate test will not depend on the perfection of technique so much as it is to be mindful of the learning he has already received. In his final confrontation with Vader at the end of the movie, Luke faces his greatest fear — confronting his father — and again rejects the Emperor's temptation to rule the universe by taking Vader's place.

Luke refuses. By shutting down his lightsaber, Luke takes the high moral road of the Light Side and is willing to sacrifice himself. The reality, however, presents a moral dilemma which may, in itself, be untenable. By sacrificing himself, he has at least denied his use to the minions of Evil. His sacrifice at the hands of Vader and the Emperor is the greatest good Luke can do, but is it the greatest good he could do for the universe? If Luke will not attack Vader and the Emperor, they *will* continue their reign of terror and evil in the universe. Luke will have failed to achieve the goal of destroying the leadership that commands the Empire, the very objective of the Rebel fleet attacking the second Death Star. This is the moral question that moral individuals must answer.

But Vader draws Luke closer to the Dark Side when he discovers the existence of Luke's sister Leia, which drives Luke into a rage. The possibility of loosing Leia to Vader fuels Luke's anger. He ignites his lightsaber and attacks Vader in a powerful demonstration of brute force. Vader cannot take the onslaught manifested in Luke's love for his sister, and the Dark Lord is beaten down by the young Jedi's raw determination. But at the very moment he can defeat Vader, Luke realizes that though he has the power to strike down Vader, wisdom stay his hand. Consciously, though with reluctance, Luke gives up the lightsaber, denying the Emperor both his abilities and his weapon. In the epic tradition, Luke's faith in his father and his friends allows him to conquer the Emperor when Vader turns from the Dark Side. Repeating the cinematic phrase from *The Empire Strikes Back* when Luke throws himself off of the gantry on Bespin, the Emperor is thrown into the pit by Vader, as if Satan had been cast back into Hell.

Unlike the ad hoc preparation Luke goes through in the Original Trilogy, *The Phantom Menace* illustrates a more reflective and prayer-like kind of preparation learned in the more formal training of the Jedi Temple. In the moments before the final battle between Darth Maul and Qui-Gon Jinn, Qui-Gon drops down to his knees and meditatively prepares for their imminent confrontation. That powerful moment captured the mental and even sacred preparation a swordsman goes through when confronting the possibility of his own destruction. Like soldiers before a battle, mass is said and clerics seek to give solace to human beings confronting the impending moment of their death. The swordsman's momentary reflection is not defeatist — it is preparation for the inevitable reality of combat.

The Technology of the Lightsaber

Those last moments when Luke gives up his lightsaber illustrate the fleeting nature of a sword for the swordsman. By definition, a swordsman is defined by his ability to use the sword, but it is not the lightsaber that makes Luke, Obi-Wan, and Qui-Gon Jedi no more than a painter is defined by his ability to use a brush. Both the Jedi and the painter are artists which simply use one tool as a means of expressing their creative energies. Where Jedi in their heyday served the Jedi Order by assisting the Galactic Senate on missions of peace, arbitration, and negotiation, the painter, as well as all other artists including Lucas the filmmaker, serves humanity by helping men and women understand something about themselves.

A major difference between the art of the swordsman and that of the painter is that only one has the potential to physically destroy society and all of its creativity. This is the swordsman's paradox. He is both an instrument of creativity and destruction.

An interesting conundrum for the *Star Wars* universe is the extent to which lightsaber technology is used in general society. No one gave Obi-Wan a second glance when he brandished his lightsaber in the Cantina, cutting off one of its patron's arms. Is lightsaber technology so common in the universe? Or perhaps the lightsaber, being an outdated technology, was no less common than if Obi-Wan had pulled out a knife instead. An Expanded Universe novel mentions that the technology of the lightsaber was so secret that Jedi were not permitted to reveal details about the lightsaber's workings.

But would not such a fantastic technology benefit the world in many other applications: carving stone, shaping metal, felling trees, and many others? It is hard to believe that no one for thousands of years has developed technologies that employ the focused and controlled energy of light. But that is what has happened in most Expanded Universe writing, which lacks the firm understanding about the education of swordsmen. Instead they've perpetuated the romantic notions of the sword, which have, in the real world, dire consequences that accompany the deification of the sword.

There should be a healthy balance between respect for the weapon as an instrument of destruction and a fanaticism for it. The samurai lived and died by the sword, but that was only one aspect of the unique role they had in society. Samurai, Jedi, and all swordsmen are also humans endowed with gifts to do good and the potential to do evil. The sword may represent ideals, but swords are not in of themselves those very ideals. For the swordsman, the blade is simply a particularly shaped piece of metal. In this sense, the sword is a simply a tool. For the Jedi Knight or the swordsman, their greatest tool is not his weapon, but his mind.

The lure of power has the potential to make the brotherhood of the sword into a cult of the sword. The method of training a swordsman, similarly, must contain a mode of questioning the master without exalting him to the status of a god. History gives many examples where citizens have followed charismatic individuals for the wrong reasons. When such leaders can coopt the general feeling of the population, the whole society can be made into a veritable military camp in which freedom and creativity are stifled when opposed to the regime in authority. And when individuals take so myopic a view of the world that everyone else's views and life styles are simply wrong, this fanaticism goes underground into terrorist cells. *Episodes II* and *III* will elaborate on the hidden agenda to circumvent power for one's personal use — that of the Emperor. It is no different than what past megalomaniacs and dictators have wanted — absolute and complete security in their position gained by the means of authoritarian rule. Steps in that direction include political bullying, black mail, and the threat of retribution, whether political or physical.

In face of the impending threat to order in society, the Jedi must remain calm. In *Attack of the Clones*, the Jedi, with their outdated lightsabers, will see technology augment to the point where their feeble weapons will no longer be any match for the new armies being clandestinely formed and constructed. Where the battle droids in *The Phantom Menace* were no match for the Jedi and his skills, *Attack of the Clones* will lead to a universe on the brink of complete turmoil. The limited number of Jedi will not be enough to repel the numbers of battle droids, super battle droids, and Geonosian warriors. And somehow the Jedi will be discredited in the same way that the Templar Order was in the past. How will the Jedi respond to the new threats to peace and order? Their struggle is the search for order at the edge of a blade of steel and their own humanity.

The pursuit of any martial skill requires a deep understanding of an individual's motivation. Is it a lust for the power to rule others? Is it to avenge a past wrong? These are the same questions that concern Yoda and the Jedi Council when they consider the appropriateness of training the gifted Anakin Skywalker.

Just before I left for Japan in 1991 to begin teaching, I was counseled in a short letter from a friend, Fr. Bob Brown, to "come back from Japan with knowledge and wisdom, rather than with military weapons." Friends, in their love, become reminders of the lessons swordsmen learn from their masters. The goal of all martial arts is not the reliance on power but the wise and judicious use of it. Training is meant to teach humility, humbleness in the use of your skills, and the reigning in of one's temptation for power. Wisdom means nothing without the discipline to know when to draw the sword or to stay its use. This is the greatest repayment a student can give to his master.

The danger of the master-apprentice system is the implicit reliance on obedience which is meant to instill discipline and to prepare the mind for learning. Students are expected to implicitly imitate the technique that is put before them even though their own intellect is telling them that there is probably a better and easier way to accomplish the same act without the punishment of hard and severe training. Though this may seem to go against common sense when one understands the apprentice system, it would be unnatural for a student not to question his instructors. Despite the fact that swordsmen have been training in swordsmanship for hundreds of years, each new novice will exhibit the unwillingness to accept that the instruction they are receiving is already the easiest road to the mastery of technique.

Westerners are well versed in the tradition of doubt. It is the impetus for revolution, creativity, and re-birth. From the earliest days, parents and teachers attempt to imbue in their children and students a sense of identity and individualism while at the same time demanding that they conform to the norms of behavior to which parents and teachers where themselves subject. But the flippant disregard for a master's instructions is a perversion of the apprentice system. Where the master swordsman may not be competent in arts of chemistry or medicine, he is a master of his own art, and it is not for students to question the master's motivation or his intentions. His intentions are already higher than the beginning student can even imagine.

A master through the voice of his command is really asking

for the student to trust in his wisdom. Often, however, in the student's desire for autonomy, independence, and recognition, he prematurely questions the authority of the master and his harsh demands. It was out of kindness that Kubo Sensei pushed me harder than I could ever push myself. If I asked permission to do one drill of kakari-geiko, he would ask, "Why not two?" and then drill me three times. The symbolism of karaki-geiko is symbolic of the nature of the master-apprentice system in swordsmanship. In drilling of all sword styles, it is the master who offers up his body to be struck so that his student may learn. The last action in kakari-geiko is the student striking his sensei on the top of the head. And in Western drills, it is the master who allows his student the practice of hitting the master who is wearing a thick protective jacket. It is proper etiquette for the student to thank the instructor for a lesson; in Japan they bow solemnly.

Western students are always tempted to give up one teacher in favor of the search for the perfect teacher. The freedom and ease of registering at the front door leaves a modern student with the impression that he is also free to leave as he or she wishes. It is for precisely this reason that new students do not receive the attention of the master. It is the student who must demonstrate his dedication, not the master's. And yet this is precisely what happens to Anakin in *Attack of the Clones*. He begins the road to the Dark Side by questioning the role of the instructor and chooses himself to find a way of his own free of the constraints of a master's training.

Yoda in later years reveals himself to Luke in stages. First, as a quizzical and diminutive creature, then as a host in his own home, and finally as the great instructor which in fairy tale fashion can literally commune with the dead. The fear of a student's departure is reason for a master's hesitancy in taking on a student. Any yet the instructor must not give in to *his* fear. He too must trust in the student as he will do of the master.

The master must in due course diminish the student's ego, a self-effacement which will become a strength when ability begins to match the most advance techniques of the style. If he learns that raw power only bows to raw power, the swordsman's soul is put in jeopardy. The tradition of imparting knowledge from a master to an apprentice is the best assurance that the lust for power, for which the Force is a metaphor, does not take hold in the student's education.

The transformation of Anakin into Vader is a device of storytelling to make clear in concise terms what takes years for a student of the sword to learn. *Star Wars* in its epic brevity teaches the greatest lessons a swordsman will ever, or, if fortune wills it, never have to face in his lifetime.

For the Master, the satisfaction that a student is learning the wisdom of swordsmanship is compelling and profound. The learning that teachers give their students lasts for a lifetime. From the simplest act of learning how to tie one's shoes, to matching letters with sounds, to the invention of a new technology which will revolutionize the world, the gift of learning infinitely changes the individual's life. But teachers and masters are but helpers in the process. As someone once put it, teachers are simply students with a longer history of learning. Teachers are only made great by the students who, in their actions, become great people in their own right.

Within the master-apprentice system is a system in which a good teacher asks the hardest question their students can handle. The great teacher, a master, however, gets students to ask the hardest questions of themselves. Within what has been shown in the four latest movies, there is no indication that Darth Vader has had his own apprentice. Expanded Universe comics and books have proffered the possibility that Vader has had numerous students, but Lucas has yet to weigh in on this fact.

In *The Empire Strikes Back*, Vader tries to make his own son as an apprentice, but he fails. Instead, Luke returns to Vader's childhood and adult master for instruction and training. Through discovery on his own and the guidance of his master, Luke breaks the cycle of evil that the existence of the Sith implies. The Sith is representative of the breakdown of our own goodness, our recourse to the easy path of action instead of the difficulty of acting out of justice, goodness, and what is right.

Star Wars is a cautionary tale and warns of the potential in each of us. Whether as modern Jedi or the common man or woman, we, as individuals, are defined by our actions, which, in turn, define our being, our character, and our honor. We must always be vigilant. Through the apprentice's trust in his master, the wisdom of the sword will be learned, benefitting the individual and the society in which he lives. A point when the master and apprentice will part will come naturally. Duty will call one or the other away to the duty of a profession or to teach a new set of students. Hopefully the ability of the student will exceed that of the teacher.

The greatest teachers have the ability to inspire a good person into becoming great. By the same token, the greatest teachers are also those who are most inspired by their students. Teachers, by their very nature, fight against the indifference and pessimism of society, and if they simply challenge their student to look to the horizon, they might actually get the student to begin a journey of a lifetime. Swordmasters have the unique charge at their command, but it is up to their students to discover on their own that the power of the sword is not in its use but in its abandonment. The swordsman's journey is complete when he realizes that he is a swordsman when he can toss aside his sword as Luke did his lightsaber. It is at that point that Luke became a Jedi.

7

The Sword Fight in *Star Wars*

When George Lucas released *Star Wars* in 1977, he had no idea that the Jedi Knight would have such a profound impact on the lives of millions of people around the world. Because so many identified with the virtues of the Jedi fighting for justice and peace in the universe, it was inconceivable that years later thousands of Commonwealth citizens would list "Jedi Knight" as their official religious creed. I now goes without saying that the Jedi would not have made such an impact on our collective psyches were it not for the fact that the sword fight is the perfect visual medium to portray humanity's struggle between good and evil, a story with which every person in the world can identify. The struggle of the Jedi, as it is for the swordsman, however, is one not only of having the ability to use a lightsaber or a sword, but knowing when and where to use it. As Obi-Wan Kenobi says to Luke in *A New Hope*, "You must do what you feel is right, of course." Understanding what is right, however, is a long and difficult journey for the swordsman, *Star Wars* being the ultimate swordsman's adventure tale.

We all have popular concepts of sword fighting from the movies that have influenced George Lucas — *Zorro, Robin Hood, Prince Valentine, The Three Musketeers*. It is the world of gentlemen, soldiers, and warriors, though Lucas outdid them all in his creation of the Jedi. He took the swashbuckling choreography and stunt work of his predecessors to create a universe of swordsmen unlike any other. Most influential on Jedi lightsaber fighting was the samurai of Akira Kurosawa and the tales of

Japanese warriors torn between their commitment to duty and the obligations of society and the world around them.

Unlike the real world of the fencer, however, silver screen is not about technique. It's about entertainment. It is but imitation fighting that creates the illusion of real swordsmanship which is contrived and predefined in terms of its dialogue, the deliberate cadence and tempo of the fights, and every feint, thrust, and ripostes, which were designed down to the exact second to create an emotional effect that glues the movie goer to his seat.

As the story of *Star Wars* saw its first expression in the artwork of Ralph McQuarrie, years of sword fighting cinematic experiences inspired Lucas' final concepts of the Jedi. He wanted a tribute to the sword flicks of his childhood, but he also wanted something even more epic and grandiose. Key to his story telling, however, were not swordsmen, but actors who had to appear as if they were the best swordsmen in the universe. Especially with a masked character like Darth Vader, the emotion of anger and rage and sentimentality had to be conveyed in both subtle and dramatic movements of the body. Every step, every line of dialogue, every close-up on Vader's mask had to convey the intensity of the sword fighter.

With *A New Hope*, Lucas established the rules of his universe. He made only minor changes during the many steps in the creation of his saga, but on the whole, Lucas remains consistent with his own universe and that of the real universe which makes his fictitious sword fighting even more realistic. The two major deviations concerning the lightsaber involve the blood shown on the floor in the Cantina scene in *A New Hope* (the lightsaber cauterizes flesh in other instances) and the lack of more realistic lightsaber fighting when Luke frees Han and Leia from Jabba the Hutt's barge. In *The Phantom Menace*, Lucas expands speculation about the lightsaber, confirming it is does in fact cut through virtually any metal, even the thickest metal that protects the bridge of the Neimoidian Control Ship.

Creating the conceptional background for the lightsaber and realistically portraying that weapon in front of cameras presented a plethora of practical problems. Because the weight of a steel sword has a tremendous impact on the use of a Terran sword, there was a problem of how to a lightsaber fight would appear. Mostly because of technical factors, the lightsaber fight of *A New Hope* was straight forward. Held with two hands, the swordsmen would exchange slashes and thrusts. They couldn't be any more complicated because the filming requirements expected to capture the shimmering effect of the lightsaber through the use of metal coated dowels turned by a rotating motor hidden in the lightsaber casing. Unsure that the special effects department would be able to enhance the blade's light effects, the movements of the two actors lacked much latitude in movement so that the delicate spinning blade would not be damaged during the fight.

In theory, the real power of a light energy blade depended on its ability to "push" the light edge of the lightsaber into a target. Whereas a Terran sword relies on a combination of gravity and the physics of a slicing blade, the lightsaber is made up of weightless energy. Certainly the balance of a lightsaber would be different than that of a steel sword. To add to the realism, there had to be degrees of penetration such that the lightsaber would more easily cut through living tissue than it would wood, plastic, or steel. It would take little effort with a lightsaber to cut through flesh, though, as shown in Luke's strike to Vader's shoulder in *The Empire Strikes Back*, there is real resistance to the lightsaber's blade, which, more or less, proves that the blade's "grabbing" into a substance gives the Jedi kinesthetic feedback into the penetration of an object or a "feel" for the way another Jedi handles his own lightsaber. Overall, Jedi lightsaber fighting follows Terran properties of fencing. The viewer can imagine that the stronger and tougher the target, the slower the lightsaber will be to penetrate. Without this realism, the audience would be less likely to believe in the power of the blade.

The Phantom Menace introduces a slightly different kind of lightsaber fighting, though it is virtually indistinguishable from earlier swordfighting from the Original Trilogy. Whereas the lightsaber was always a prop in which a slender colored tube represented the light blade of the lightsaber, with the many computer generated image (CGI) creatures, in particular the battle droids, the prop the Jedi used was simply the lightsaber handle with a small flourescent blade extension of about a foot in length. From this, computer graphics specialists could digitally insert the blade and artificially create the cutting penetration of slicing into metal robot warriors. Actors were literally cutting through air as they imagined the enemies that they were fighting.

What makes lightsaber fighting so vastly different from any other type of fighting is the speed and rapid succession of one attack into another. Any metal sword (or even a resin or plastic prop) has a particular weight and balance that affects the manner in which the sword prop is used. The light blades of many swashbuckling movies allowed a style of fencing which did not correspond to actual sword fighting had they been using real sabres. The use of metal props (especially of the Chinese broad sword genre) creates a styles that is much heavier than one would hope for an action film. Their answer, as is the case of most martial arts films, is to increase the speed of the film so that movement appears faster than it actually was during live filming.

The Phantom Menace did not have to speed up the film in order to make the duel between Qui-Gon and Obi-Wan, and Darth Maul look any faster. Most of the speed comes from the physical weight of the lightsaber props, which were balanced aluminum rods painted in flourescent colors. Earlier versions of fiberglass was tried, but when the blades shattered from heavy practice, shards of dangerously sharp shrapnel exploded from breaks in the blade. Even the final aluminum lightsabers that were used had to be coated with plastic coating to prevent bits of metal shrapnel from showing up on film.

The other factor contributing to the speed of the lightsaber fighting was due to the physical abilities of the actors and their stunt doubles. Ewan McGregor has demonstrated himself to be quite adept in wielding his lightsaber. Often, still photographs also show his hands in the proper position for holding his lightsaber (wrists twisted in with fingers aligned one on top of the other). Some stills show McGregor in unbalanced position, either up on his toes (which no fencer in any style does) or with his lightsaber directly in front of his eyes, obscuring his vision. Liam Neeson has a basic simple stance, characteristically holding his lightsaber in the baseball fashion. Ray Park is most impressive in both his footwork as well as his manipulation in both the single and double-bladed lightsaber. From his years of training and competition, it is evident that experience and practical necessities of wielding the staff and broad sword have informed his Sith style of fighting.

Apart from the telekinetic ability of tossing objects with their mind, there is very little emphasis on the Force in the swordfighting. While dialogue portrays a Force as the source of the Jedi's lightsaber abilities, the practical fact is that all of the lightsaber fighting and stunts were the result of technical sword fighting skill or acrobatics. And contrary to what many think, Han's use of the lightsaber to open the belly of the Tauntaun in *The Empire Strikes Back* speaks definitively that someone without control of the Force can easily ignite and use a lightsaber.

In the real world, the concept of ki (qi or chi in Chinese, pranja in Sanskrit) is fundamental to many Asian martial arts. Ki is the energy that flows through the body, giving vital energy to a human's physiological function. While Western scientists have not been able to prove the existence of ki, they do admit, in their complete reliance on the tangible and reproducible qualities of scientific knowledge, that there are currents of energy that transmit signals through the body's nervous system. Oriental doctors and even Western homeopathic and holistic doctors have believed and have studied ki energy of the human body. Without ki, there could be no life. While millions do believe in ki, as do many practitioners of Oriental martial arts, many of the technical abilities can be explained in terms of human physiology and physics.

The true Force in *Star Wars* is ILM's special effects and the angles of the director's cameras, which create the illusion of a reality influenced and penetrated by some "mystical energy field" that controls one's destiny. Created to convey a mystical sense of a Jedi's existence, the Force is a loose and general construct that allows movie goers to interpret the meaning and significance of the Force according to their own interpretation. Even in *Star Wars*, the Force has only limited power. Most of a Jedi's skills, especially those with his lightsaber, come from practice and discipline. As has already been stated, it is not the lightsaber that makes the Jedi, but in the way that he uses it.

Star Wars Swordmasters

Key to the success of the *Star Wars* sword fight are the two swordmasters who are charged with making the director's vision for the sword fight into reality. Starting out in a typical and mundane fashion, the swordmaster goes through an interview process like any actor or technician. Their resumés are submitted and their experiences are examined to glean whether or not a person can handle the job for which they are interviewing. Sword fights in past movies are examined to see if the technical requirements can be met by the swordmaster. Once that is done, early in production a sample fight is created and filmed to show what the sword fight scene might look like as it would appear within the context of the episode at hand. If approved, the swordmaster could then begin training the actors for their roles to make their performances look believable and realistic.

In the case of *Star Wars: A New Hope*, Lucas expressed the desire for a sword fighting that was reminiscent of the samurai style. It would be exotic to Western audiences which were accustomed to the sabre fight from swashbuckling, and it captured the essence of Japanese samurai films. For *The Phantom Menace*, a time during what Lucas calls the Prime of the Jedi, Lucas looked for a fencing style that was more dynamic and energetic. Lucas describes the sword fighting in the Original Trilogy as combat between an old man (Obi-Wan), a cyborg half-human (Darth Vader), and a young boy (Luke). The Prequel Trilogy style was to be martial arts between trained lightsaber adversaries.

It is not clear why Lucas went with a new swordmaster in *The Phantom Menace*, but it is possible that in the world of Hollywood where networking is everything, the new producer, Rick McCallum, simply called on talents of a person with whom he was familiar, which meant Nick Gillard instead of Peter Diamond, who did the sword fighting choreography in the Original Trilogy. Both are talented fight choreographers. They simply have different styles of interpreting Lucas' vision.

Action movies these days require at a minimum the skills of a stunt coordinator who is in charge of any scene that requires the doubling of an actor because of safety concerns. Whether it is jumping from a wall, scaling a dangerous height, or taking a fall, it is up to the stunt coordinator to solve the problems necessary to substitute a double for the actor. Even minor injuries like a broken arm can delay shooting for weeks. In a movie like the *Star Wars* films, the stunt coordinator is also required to be a swordmaster and action sequence choreographer.

When the actor feels he or she can do a stunt or sword work him or herself, the stunt coordinator/swordmaster must teach choreography of the fight scene to the actors and/or his doubles. Actors do not learn a style of fighting, which takes years, even a lifetime to accomplish, but a series of moves that will have, if executed properly, the appearance of being real. In Peter Diamond's words, he teaches his actors in "parrot fashion." The new Anakin, Hayden Christiansen, says, "If you ask me to pick up a lightsaber and do some tricks, I can. But put someone in front of me and say, 'Fight'? Unless I've been told where to step and swing, I can't."

The stunt coordinator/swordmaster of the Original Trilogy, Peter Diamond, has an illustrious career in the film industry. A graduate of the Royal Academy of Dramatic Arts, Diamond has extensive training at the foremost acting school in the world. Knowing the requirements of the performing arts in both the acting and technical aspects of film have served him immeasurably in the films that include *Raiders of the Lost Ark*, *Highlander*,

The Master of Ballantrae, and *The Princess Bride*, which has the most memorable, if not the best, Western sword fight choreography in modern movie history.

Diamond's talents as a trained actor and a technician allow him to communicate directly in the language of actors as well as that of directors. He has personally directed second camera footage and entire episodes of the TV version of *Highlander* and in the Original Trilogy, he has played the roles of the Tusken Raider who attacked Luke, the stormtrooper who fell to his death in Luke/Leia cable swing scene, a scout trooper thrown off of one of the speeder bikes, and a detention center guard.

An extremely amiable personality who treats actors, directors, technicians, and extras in the same respectful way, Peter Diamond has made a profound impact on the sword fight in *Star Wars*. Concerned about continuity in the saga, he hoped he would have been asked to choreograph the fight scenes in the Prequel Trilogy, but without bitterness or a bad word about Lucas and the entire crew with whom he worked, he continues on in his personal projects with an eye to maintaining the highest level of professionalism. When asked about the sword fighting in *Episode I*, he admits that he was surprised by the change in sword fighting style, but adds that it is Lucas' vision that has to prevail.

The Phantom Menace fight choreography was done by Nick Gillard who helped create some of the most memorable scenes in the entire movie. Gillard left military school at the age of sixteen and began working for the Moscow State Circus. Eventually he became a world-class horse-trick rider before making the jump into film. Known for world records in power boat jumping and full fire burning (holding one's breath while on fire), Gillard is a jovial just-one-of-the-guys kind of fellow. He likes to laugh and was even caught on film engaging George Lucas himself in friendly mock fisticuffs. Prior to *Episode I*, Gillard worked on *The Thief of Bagdad*, his first movie, *Indiana Jones and the Last Crusade*, *Aliens*, *Interview with the Vampire*, *The Three Musketeers*, to just name a few. He even worked on the original *Star Wars* and expressed his desire to improve on the sword fight scenes in the earlier films.

Because of the increasing demands on the actors for the later sword fight scenes, both Diamond and Gillard engaged the help of expert swordsmen. In *The Empire Strikes Back*, Diamond had the help of Bob Anderson, with whom he had done extensive work on the past projects. As Anderson and Diamond say about each other, "The sword fight is only as good as the swordsmen." And to have a good fight, you had to have a good partner. Anderson, an Olympic competitor and national fencing coach in Britain and Canada, brought a wealth of experience to the role of Vader in the scenes with Mark Hamill. Reassured by Anderson's expertise, Hamill was able to qualitatively improve his performance as a sword fighter in *The Empire Strikes Back* and *Return of the Jedi*.

Gillard brought in Ray Park with his experience in wu shu, a general term for Chinese martial arts. Hailing from Wales, Ray Park competed in national and international competitions and broke into the movie business in *Mortal Kombat: Annihilation*. In addition to his impeccable handling of weapons, Park brings his background as a gymnast to his work in *The Phantom Menace*. Without his professional expertise, Ewan McGregor and Liam Neeson would never have look as good as they did.

Professionals

The focus on actors remains, however, the most important aspect of the sword fighting characters in the *Star Wars* films. Where a stuntman or double must act to imitate the actor and his movements in order to tell the story, the gift of truly telling the story rests with the professional actors who breathe life into the dialogue found in the script.

Principal and the most respected of all *Star Wars* actors, even more than Peter Cushing, was Alec Guinness who passed away in 2000. Not only did his appearance fit the part of the wise, elderly master, but his mere presence on screen was enough to convince everyone that there were such a thing as Jedi Knights.

Exaggerated gossip and stories portray Guinness as bitter about his role repeating incomprehensible "mumbo-jumbo," but he admitted in an interview soon after the release of the first movie that he was attracted to his role as the Master Jedi by the competence of George Lucas and his vision for the film. While members of both the cast and crew were rolling their eyes at what everyone expected to be another sci-fi bomb like *Silent Running*, Guinness stood steadfastly beside Lucas telling others that he had complete trust in Lucas' abilities.

For sword fight enthusiasts and martial artists of the Asian tradition, Guinness uttered some of the most profound lines in the entire saga. With the pauses and the tempo of "It is an energy field created by all living things. It surrounds us and penetrates us. It binds the galaxy together," Guinness gave life to the mystical words that seem to succinctly express the Asian concept of ki. That the Force gave the Jedi power was confirmation to Eastern ears what Asians had felt about the body's life giving energy.

In the same way that Guinness was able to convince the audience of the mysteriousness of the Force, he was also able to demonstrate the power of the Jedi Knights. Swordplay was considered a skill for actors of his generation, and as a two-handed swordsman, he pays homage to the samurai that Lucas so admired. It was Guinness who was able to set the example for Mark Hamill. Not only was Luke able to convince us of the naiveté of a farm boy on Tatooine, he was able to create a character with whom children, men, and women alike could identify. As Luke looked out over the desert toward the twin suns setting at the horizon, it is hard for the audience not to feel a sense of longing in Luke's desire to find adventure somewhere beyond the Tatooine home he has known. Not only does his performance in *The Empire Strikes Back* convince us of his burning desire to be treated with respect equal to his worth as an individual, but also of the fear of confronting the terror of growing up in a hostile world. This coming of age film set the stage for Hamill to return in the subsequent film as a Jedi who enters into the full rites of the Jedi Order. Not only does he reinvent himself, but he also reinvents the order of the universe in which good triumphs over evil. Though many cynically see Hamill's failure to achieve the cinematic accomplishments of Harrison Ford, the impact his role has had on the lives of youngsters all over the world is hardly insignificant. Hamill, in his role as Luke Skywalker, inspired generations to reach out for the stars. And unlike the world of the difficult times of the sixties and seventies, the message was positive and good.

Considering the fact that Dave Prowse played one of the most memorable villains in film, it is unfortunate that he has received more derision for his contribution than any other actor associated with *Star Wars*. Early stories about Prowse expressed grumbling about being denied full recognition for his role. In Lucas' initial reluctance to unveil the magic of the movie, the actors behind the masks were kept out of the media eye for fear of dispelling the illusion of alien creatures from the *Star Wars* universe.

Eventually all the characters were unmasked for the public, but still residual bad blood continued to hound Prowse's relationship with Lucasfilm, starting with the fact that he was not allowed to wear the Darth Vader costume in public and then unmask himself. Another controversy involved the fact that Prowse's voice was replaced by another actor James Earl Jones because of concern that there were no black actors in the film. The biggest problems, however, occurred when a reporter revealed spoiler information in an interview with Prowse that Vader was going to die in *Return of the Jedi*. Because filming was not yet complete, Prowse was ostracized during the rest of the shoot.

In the final tally, Prowse played all of Vader in *A New Hope*, and most of *The Empire Strikes Back,* and some of *Return of the Jedi.* The sword fighting in both *The Empire Strikes Back* and *Return of the Jedi* was done by Bob Anderson. Memorable scenes in which Prowse played Vader include him in the meditation chamber in *The Empire Strikes Back* and throwing the Emperor, a double for Ian McDiarmid, into the tower shaft. Prowse never did get to meet the director of *Return of the Jedi* Richard Marquand, and his experience on the set remains one of the most difficult times of his life.

The role of Darth Vader as a foil for the Rebel heroes played well in *A New Hope*, but no one was ready for the importance of Vader in the continuing saga. Vader was not just the evil bad guy, he was an integral part of a longer story whose complete telling will not be done until the release of *Episode III* in 2005. Contrary to what common sense might tell us, Anakin did not start out as the incorrigible problem child. Instead, he was an ordinary kid, albeit with an amazing pedigree, who was as kind and as innocent as the neighborhood kid around the block. He is not one of the terrorizing bullies we encountered on the playground, but the nice, carefree child who is tempted by the lure of power.

The much expected *The Phantom Menace* in 1999 heralded a new age of sword fighting. More expository than revelatory, *Episode I* was anticipated with unprecedented world-wide expectation. Before *The Empire Strikes Back* no franchise had been as successfully hyped as the *Star Wars* saga. *The Phantom Menace* was no different, and despite its lackluster reception, anticipation for *Attack of the Clones* will receive no less the attention than *Harry Potter and the Sorcerer's Stone* and *Lord of the Rings* received in the winter holiday leading up to the May 2002 release of *Episode II*.

Much of the success of *The Phantom Menace* was due to the introduction of the new Jedi, Qui-Gon Jinn and a younger Obi-Wan Kenobi, and their nemesis Darth Maul. Senior among them was Liam Neeson who is a veteran Scotsman in such films as *Rob Roy* and *Schindler's List*. Known more for his roles as a lead romance, Neeson brings a new dimension to the master-apprentice relationship.

Soon after the announcement of the new cast, Neeson expressed his love with his simple association with the *Star Wars*. Mark Hamill had a similar experience on *A New Hope*, being infatuated with an adventure story that took place out in space. Harrison Ford in his many interviews associated with the *Indiana Jones* films expressed that same boy's desire to play the iconographic movie hero. Admired in particular for his work in Spielberg's black and white masterpiece, Liam as savior to Jewish laborers was a hard earned experience for his role as Jedi Master. Neeson loves having a lightsaber in hand, and when asked why he decided to take the role, Neeson admits that he's always had a spot in his heart for the *Star Wars* saga.

His experience of sword fighting in *Rob Roy* also provided additional preparation for his role in *The Phantom Menace*. Playing the heroic Scotsman, Neeson wielded the broad sword with realistic alacrity. While the steel is vastly different from the shell of a prop which is the lightsaber in *Episodes I* and *II*, simply knowing the expectations of a sword fight and how to take direction from Lucas and Gillard proved immeasurable. Apart from his baseball grip of the lightsaber as he takes a stance opposite Darth Maul, Neeson is a passionate example of the cool and experienced swordmaster.

Neeson is at the perfect age for the real swordsman at his peak. Well beyond the energetic and often reckless drive of a young swordsman, Neeson captures a moment in life when wisdom and the body's health and fullness are at their peak. While not those at the physical peak of male development, the acquired and practiced skills of a swordsman reaches an apex at a much later age than in most modern sports. The philosopher Socrates is believed to have participated on the battlefield combat into his early forties.

While he effectively fought off questions about the fate of Qui-Gon in *The Phantom Menace*, there has always been speculation that Neeson might return in spectral form in later films as Alec Guinness did in the Original Trilogy. The whole polemic revolves around the question of whether Qui-Gon was able to master the "trick" of retaining a physical, though ghostly form as Obi-Wan had when they vanished just before their death. Neither Vader nor Qui-Gon had vanished before their death, though that did not stop Lucas from placing Sebastian Shaw in the penultimate scene with Yoda and Obi-Wan. The fairy tale message in *Return of the Jedi* was, of course, that even a bad heart turned good in the final moments merits an eternal existence.

At Qui-Gon's side is newcomer to the blockbuster Hollywood release Ewan McGregor. Known for his rambunctiousness in *Train Spotting*, McGregor and his vivacious personality brought a youthful excitement to the cast. Though quite demure in his interpretation of Obi-Wan ("You were right about one thing. The negotiations were short."), McGregor was adopted by the paparazzi as bad boy fanboy. Quick to express his doubts about the title for *Attack of the Clones*, his free wheeling enthusiasm is quite evident in his terse but respectful judgements. He likes to cuss in his interviews, and because he still remains a darling in the eyes of the public, he receives little, if any flack from his caddishness.

As a swordsman, McGregor quickly garnered a reputation for having a knack with the mock lightsabers used in training. Footage from *The Phantom Menace* DVD certainly conveys the vigor of his fencing style. No holds barred, Ewan revels in the excitement of the sword fight. Speed, dexterity, accuracy are all words to describe his ability to learn the lightsaber choreography. Like Neeson, McGregor fell in love with *Star Wars* as a kid, and tells the story of the day the prop department came up to him with a wooden box filled with lightsaber handles. He weighed each one in his hand and waved them around to find the one with the best feel. As recently as January 2002, Ewan was quoted as having said handling a lightsaber is "a more gentlemanly way to fight a war."

Surprisingly, Ewan's soft spoken questioning of his master is a complete opposite of his real personality. The most emotional moment in the entire film is his declaration that no one on Amidala's ship should communicate with Naboo for fear of giving away their position on Tatooine. McGregor plays Obi-Wan as the submissive and dutiful apprentice more in the fashion of the conservative Jedi Council than to his own master. In early screenplays and in the novel, there are more instances where the importance of Obi-Wan's assistant status was emphasized. One scene, in particular, stands out in which Qui-Gon chides Obi-Wan for dropping his lightsaber in the water and temporarily shorting it out. Another memorable scene occurs when Obi-Wan expresses his dissatisfaction that he is easily replaceable by a 10-year-old boy. Obi-Wan does not discover some key clue that leads to the unknotting of the Sith mystery (Wesley Crusher Syndrome). Instead, he is the attentive student who watches his master's every move and obeys unquestioningly. His love for his master is finally expressed at the moment of Qui-Gon's death at the hands of Darth Maul. McGregor first gives his primordial cry of anguish, and then in a tearful moment, he holds his master in his arms just before he dies. The master's last words are not a fond farewell, but an exhortation to take his place and become the master to the boy whom Qui-Gon sees as the Chosen One.

The fact that Qui-Gon had already declared before the Jedi Council that Obi-Wan was ready to pass the Trials is the first allusion to the eventual passing of the mantle from a master to apprentice. Obi-Wan's commitment to training Anakin was clearly expressed in his stubborn declaration that he *will* train the boy with or without the approval of the Jedi Council. A foregone conclusion even in the eyes of Yoda and the Council, Obi-Wan is then promoted to Knighthood without having formally passed the Trials. McGregor's portrayal of the defiant knight in the closing scenes of the movie is just the tip of the iceberg in his development into manhood, as he becomes master to a spry teenager at the precipice of his destiny. The relationship between the two will reach a strain that prepares the audience for Anakin's eventual embrace of the Dark Side.

With the same youthfulness, actor Ray Park brings his expertise as a wu shu martial artist to the screen. Though early training in wu shu involves unarmed fighting, advanced techniques involve the extended use of bladed weapons, including the Chinese broad sword and spear. From work with these weapons and his experience in gymnastics, Park raises the quality of Jedi sword fight to the level more commonly found in Chinese martial arts films. From his experience with the long staff in *Mortal Kombat: Annihilation*, Park mesmerizes us with the twirling skill of Darth Maul's double-bladed lightsaber. *The Phantom Menace* benefits from the infusion of Chinese martial arts which are more fluid and acrobatic than the grounded feet style of Japanese martial arts. Even in karate, which stresses high kicks, Japanese martial arts by comparison to Chinese, Korean, and Indian martial arts have broad stances that lower the center of the body for a solid foundation. Most would be familiar with Ray Park's wu shu from the fighting style found in *Crouching Tiger, Hidden Dragon*, less the fantastic flying through the air.

Where Ray Park's physical stature is diminished by the towering frame of Liam Neeson, he makes up for sheer size by enthralling the audience with an energy that surpasses previous *Star Wars* episodes. Starting with the devilish make-up, the horned Maul immediately evokes fear in the viewer. Park with his quiet and soft-spoken personality mentions the revulsion cast and crew gave him when he looked up during breaks in filming. He'd be sitting in a chair letting the time pass away when an aide might come up to ask him a question. When Park looked up to answer, the person would usually turn their head to avoid looking into his red contact covered eyes. The designs of the shapes and colors combined with his ten horns gave Maul the feral quality that evokes fear in civilized beings.

Despite the meager list of Darth Maul lines in the movie, Park enhances the evil of his character with a body language that epitomizes the dangerous nature of Darth Maul; his jagged teeth, threatening scowls, and the pacing back and forth behind the energy screen and above the pit staring down at Qui-Gon and Obi-Wan. Maul is evil incarnate, a minion of hell sent by his master to execute the first stage in a plan that will finally rid the universe of the Sith's archrivals the Jedi.

Even though the novelization of *The Phantom Menace* explains how the Sith were fallen Jedi planning over thousands of years to destroy the Jedi, the audience knows virtually nothing of Maul or his master Darth Sidious. Yet, as all things in *Star Wars*,

Maul's appearance by design was made to evoke primal urges of repulsion — blackened eyes and mouth, horns, and blood red skin. Maul is a creature from our worse nightmare, transcending culture and language as a minion of evil. In his flowing black robes, the creature of death faces an unexpected, but predictable end when he is cut in half by Qui-Gon's lightsaber.

The sword fights would not have come to their full fruition without the help of the crew and designers who created the world in which the Jedi fought. Of course Lucas is ultimately responsible for the sword fighting, but credit also goes to the stunt and sword fight doubles which make the Jedi into something more than the Terran sword master. Bob Anderson filled the shoes of Darth Vader, Andreas Petrides and Rob Inch doubled as Obi-Wan and Liam Neeson, respectively. One cannot forget the artistry of Ralph McQuarrie, who first designed the initial images of Darth Vader and Luke Skywalker, and Design Director Doug Chiang who took the first steps in creating the new images for the Jedi in their prime, as well as the Sith lords. Story board artist Benton Jew committed the action sequences to life by visualizing the dynamic motion of the sword fight on a still, non-moving sheet of paper. And lastly the prop makers who created the balanced weapons from the creative designs of the art department. For *The Phantom Menace*, over three hundred lightsabers were made, as many as twenty destroyed during daily practice.

Without the skills and effort of the many people associated with the fight scenes, *Star Wars* would have been less the richer. From the first inklings of designing characters and choreographing the fights to the final enactment of their movement in front of the camera and in the editing room, the sword fight would not have had the dramatic effect it does in the *Star Wars* film. Sword fighting would have simply been another action sequence among a host of many.

The Phantom Menace — Opening Act in the Prime of the Jedi
    The latest installment of *Star Wars* gives us the most dynamic

lightsaber fighting yet. First on the droid control ship, then on Tatooine, and finally on Naboo where the two Jedi heroes Obi-Wan (the Younger) and Qui-Gon confront Darth Maul. During the time of the Jedi Knights, Qui-Gon and his apprentice Obi-Wan use their skills to uncover and defeat the Sith Order which was supposedly destroyed over a thousand years ago. Caught unaware, the Jedi are unprepared to fight a sinister force which threatens to foment galactic disorder that could lead to the end of the Galactic Republic itself. Caught in a middle of a grand and unfolding scheme, the Jedi must demonstrate their prowess with only lightsabers against the battle droids, droidekas, and a light-saber trained opponent.

Upon his return to the *Star Wars* universe, Lucas was imme-diately motivated to create a more energetic style of sword fight-ing that would step beyond the fights of the previous three films. With Jedi trained in the full arts of the Jedi Temple, Qui-Gon and his apprentice Obi-Wan have undergone rigorous training. Their skills are tested when they are attacked by battle droids and shield protected Droidekas. Battle droids are no problem, being completely defenseless against their lightsabers which turn laser bolts back on the droids who shot at them, but Qui-Gon and Obi-Wan are tested to the limits when the destroyer droids threaten to overcome even their abilities. They escape and smuggle them-selves down to the surface of the planet where the Federation army is massing its troops for an invasion of Queen Amidala's planet.

The Jedi succeed in escaping from the landing ships and arrive at the Gungan city Otoh Gunga with the help of a comical sidekick Jar Jar Binks. In their bongo submarine, they arrive at the capital city of Theed and rescue Queen Amidala as she's being escorted to her ship by Federation droids. Employing their lightsabers with efficient ease, the Jedi are forced to rely on a de-ception to save the boy Anakin who is discovered to have even higher midi-chlorian[*] counts higher than that of even Yoda, the

---

[*] The microscopic creatures that create the Force.

head of the Jedi Council. Just as they escape the planet after winning Anakin's freedom in a pod race, Anakin and Obi-Wan are attacked by an unknown lightsaber wielding assailant. Reporting to the Jedi Council, the first stirrings of an invisible threat to the Republic is unveiled.

On Coruscant, the capital planet of the universe, Naboo representative Palpatine is elected to replace the High Chancellor. Unknown to even the Jedi is a carefully crafted plan to wrest control of the universe under the rule of a new Emperor. At the Jedi Temple, Qui-Gon brings Anakin directly to the Jedi Council asking that Anakin be trained in the Jedi arts. Qui-Gon's request being refused, he must settle with the simple supervision of the child. At Queen Amidala's request to return to Naboo, Qui-Gon and Obi-Wan are assigned to protect the Queen from the threats of the Sith.

Being an opening act, *The Phantom Menace* is a primarily exposition for the characters who will play the most crucial roles for later films, *Episode II* and *III*. Queen Amidala, Anakin's future wife, the two Jedi, and the newest Jedi, Anakin, are introduced for the first time. In the climax of *The Phantom Menace*, the three scenes of a space battle, a Gungan ground battle, and the lightsaber battles take place concurrently. Not only must the Anakin prove himself to be the Chosen One capable of unknown potentiality, Qui-Gon and Obi-Wan must show their ability to stop the first wave of a Sith attack.

As the Naboo enter the Theed Palace in an attempt to capture the Trade Federation Viceroy, they encounter Darth Maul who is ready to deal a death blow to the Jedi Knights who stand in the way of foiling Darth Sidious' plan to destroy the Jedi Order and take over the universe. Taking off their robes, the Jedi and Sith ignite their lightsabers and participate in an impressive display of sword fighting. In the Sith Lord's possession is an unusual double-bladed lightsaber which permits its user to almost simultaneously fight opponents attacking from opposite sides.

At first the Jedi seem to hold their own against the Sith Lord, but they are quickly pushed to the edge of their limits as the

Maul proves skilled and determined to overcome the Jedi. Having undergone years of training, Maul finally has the opportunity to openly strike out against the hated Jedi Knights. As they fight into the Theed generator room, Maul engages in a series of tactical retreats to gain better position against the pressing Jedi Knights. Using flying leaps and effective kicks, Maul fights competently but to no obvious victory in face of two determined Jedi adversaries. Maul is being doubly taxed without being able to effectively destroy one Jedi before then going after the other. Numbers will eventually overcome any swordsman, which is the reason why Jedi and Sith alike use their power of telekinesis to assist them in their fight.

When the two are separated, Darth Maul finally gets his opportunity to take out each of the Jedi one by one. Separated by an energy shield, Maul fights against Qui-Gon Jinn engaging in a fierce fight which eventually leads to the death of the Jedi Knight. Obi-Wan watches helplessly but then rushes to attack the Sith Lord who has defeated and killed his master.

Obi-Wan and Maul engage in quick attacks and defenses with Obi-Wan gaining the upper edge when he cuts Maul's double-edged lightsaber in half. Now armed with a single blade, Maul engages in an effective attack and parry strategy which allows him to regain his advantage. Maul uses a Force Push to throw Kenobi over the edge of a deep pit. Hanging for dear life, Obi-Wan watches as the evil Maul gloats over the taste of his first victory over the Jedi Knights. But Obi-Wan, upon seeing the body of his slain master, musters the power to throw himself up from the pit and over Maul. Simultaneously reaching out for his master's lightsaber, he cuts Darth Maul in half, sending his cloven body into a shaft foreshadowing the one into which the Emperor will ultimately fall.

Even at the worst moment, Obi-Wan finds the energy to avenge the death of his master. Anger, hate, rage, like it did for Luke in *Return of the Jedi*, fill Obi-Wan with the energy to overcome his dire circumstances and best the Sith Lord only because Maul does not immediately destroy his cornered prey. It is a lesson, that has only begun to be fully exploited in future episodes. Obi-Wan's later death reflects the anger Anakin will have earlier exhibited against his own master in *Episode III*. As is explained to Anakin on Coruscant, fear of death leads to anger, anger leads to hate, hate leads to suffering, which in the ends leads to the Dark Side of the Force.

Speed and technique seem to be the focus of the sword fights in *The Phantom Menace*, as is a reliance on the gratuitous destruction of worthless battle droids who are defenseless against the Jedi. Qui-Gon provides us with a new perspective on Jedi training as he perishes in a state of grace. As he awaits his confrontation with Maul, he prepares himself for the inevitable. He is ready to win or die, and he must move toward his destiny without anger or hate; just a concern to protect Anakin from the threat of the Sith.

And what about the Darth Sidious? Is the death of Darth Maul a setback for the Sith? The Jedi Council is still not certain whether the master or apprentice has been destroyed. Soon the greater threat of an unknown menace, a phantom menace, will reveal itself openly. Until then, Darth Sidious is still an agent of doom in the universe. One of the greatest Jedi has been lost in the opening round as the Jedi and the Galactic Republic is on the eve of the Clone Wars, the cataclysmic struggle which will elevate the Sith to the highest position in the universe.

Star Wars: A New Hope — Testament to Mastery

The episodic subtitle *A New Hope* suggests the fundamental plotline for the first movie of the Original Trilogy, providing the subtext for every line of dialogue and action sequence. It also acts as a starting point of each sword fight. Implicit in the title is a back story of stellar proportions. Hope — a small, lackluster word — is the answer to the despair a person finds in life. Especially for those in their most desperate need — the impoverished, the oppressed, the neglected, the ostracized, the forgotten — hope is the single pinprick of light in their lives. Their plight is a struggle for mere existence, and yet deep within a person's heart is the yearning for an act of goodness that may alleviate them of the lot under which they have suffered. Like Anakin and his mother on Tatooine, the downtrodden are slaves to their circumstances being unable to escape until something or someone like a Luke Skywalker will come along and release them.

When audiences saw *Star Wars* for the first time, the tiny rebel blockade runner being pursued by the massive star destroyer instantly explains the plight the forces of freedom are up against. But it is also the opening act of rebellion against a seemingly all-powerful Empire. In the fourth act, Luke is not the Chosen One, but a New Hope; one who will answer the call of those in the universe who need a chance to escape oppression. *A New Hope* by its very nature also implies the means to awakening the eyes of the chosen redeemer through the sacrifice of one person for another, Obi-Wan's sacrifice for Luke in *Episode IV* being a recurring motif for Qui-Gon's sacrifice for Anakin.

In *A New Hope*, the elder Obi-Wan and Darth Vader meet in a duel after an obvious but unexplained history. One is the former master of the other, and both know that the outcome of their duel must end with the destruction of one or the other. It is a showdown in its classic sense, but because of its pivotal role in a greater context, Obi-Wan knows that it is inevitable that his doom is sealed, as Darth Vader has already discerned the threat from Luke and R2-D2, who carried the plans of the Death Star in his memory banks.

Obi-Wan could not have escaped, and had to play the rearguard for an escaping army that is so celebrated in the stories of Roland, Paladins of the French King, or the tale of the Spartans who held back a massive Persian army. These tales never disparaged the quality of the main body of the army, but illustrate that even the greatest commanders may find themselves in a defensive withdrawal. The *Song of Roland* is paean to the greatest knights of the realm who sacrificed themselves for the greater good of the many. So too does Obi-Wan follow in a grander and more glorious tale. Obi-Wan, like the Paladins and Spartans, had to act as the rearward defense which prevented a phalanx of stormtroopers from entering the docking bay in which the *Millennium Falcon* was parked.

Alec Guinness's climactic in *A New Hope* remains to all Japanese swordsmen the greatest testament to their culture and style of swordsmanship. This duel certainly follows in the rich Hollywood tradition of the fencing duel interspersed with dialogue, but when both Obi-Wan and Darth Vader grip their lightsabers with two hands, there could be no other style of fencing than that of the Japanese samurai.

In the Obi-Wan/Vader duel there are no flashy tricks. Even Obi-Wan's only "twirl" slash amounts to a very small departure from traditional kenjutsu and kendo. Attacks are made to the head or leg. One will attack first in a series of two or three attacks, alternating between the higher and lower targets. And then the other would respond in a similar way. Head-head. Head-head-leg. Leg-head-head. Vader uses simple thrusts which Obi-Wan must deflect with circular parries. Accompanying Vader's small steps forward, Obi-Wan must respond in kind by stepping back an equal amount of steps to retain the proper fencing distance. A thrust forward without a step back places the one man's blade closer to his target while the other's weapon is still being used defensively. It is the perfect opportunity to attack, but also easily foiled by the simple act of maintaining distance.

In the last scene just before Obi-Wan raises his lightsaber in a transcendent salute, Vader slashes forward and moves deeply into Obi-Wan's space, forcing him to step to the side and then back in the place where Vader originally stood. In order for Obi-Wan to avoid turning his back to his opponent, the exchange of positions becomes a common tactical move during a traditional kendo competition in which *kendoka* (a person who does kendo) circles around in the arena of the bout.

The stances of the two men are those of Japanese fencing called *chudan no kamae* (swords held in front with the blade at the midline of the body), its point at eye level. The kendoka must look into the opponent's eyes, where, like the Western saying that the eyes are the windows into a person's soul, the swordsman can see the intention and determination of his opponent. When the opponent blinks an eye or averts his gaze, that is the moment to attack. Poor and novice fencers make the unconscious betrayal of their attack by moving their eyes to the area they are attacking. The expert need not see where he will attack, he only need know it.

Footwork is the key to proper upper body movement. Without it, the use of the sword will lack balance and the power of the lower body. Though the feet are hidden behind the folds of their robes, the experienced fencer must discern their opponent's footwork from the movement of his upper body. A tilt forward, a small step to the side, the slight displacement in one direction. Though they may have lacked the power and speed of a strong swordsman, both Guinness and Prowse demonstrate a strong centered feeling in their footwork throughout their duel.

Were Obi-Wan and Vader holding real swords, their cuts would have had to have started from positions closer to the head. Obi-Wan would have had to raise his sword completely over his head, while Vader, because of his helmet, would have had to have lifted his lightsaber to the left or right side of his face. In *The Seven Samurai*, there is a scene where the youngest samurai lifts a stick over his head in a position called *jodan no kamae* waiting for an "invited" samurai to walk through the door.* More power is given to the cut, the higher the sword is held.

The short movement of the blade during the *Episode IV* duel is similar to the quick attacks from kendo that come from flicking the wrists. This attack is only to be used against an opponent's wrists where tendons and ligaments are easy to cut. Such feeble attacks are so often made to the opponent's head during kendo bouts that it appears to spectators that this attack is a proper

---

*The story of peasants looking for warriors to protect their village, the young samurai's attack was a test for potential samurai who might help them defend the village.

attack to the head. During *kakari-geiko* (attacking drills), a proper sensei requires that the student always raises his weapon completely over his or her head before making attack to the upper body.

This kendo style of lightsaber fighting, with its short slashing movement, is easily excused by the fact that the lightsaber requires less momentum to penetrate the skin and bones of an unarmored opponent. On the other hand, perhaps Luke might have been able to penetrate Vader's armor in *The Empire Strikes Back* if he had had more momentum in his cut to Vader's shoulder.

On the whole, the sheer simplicity of the sword fight in *A New Hope* conveys a critical element of the story line — the sword may be the tool of the Jedi, but even in death Obi-Wan, the symbol of good in the universe, will become more powerful than the agent of darkness. For the swordsman, the lack of dynamic movement actuality illustrates their mastery of swordsmanship. No more energy than that of a single attack needs to be expended. With a single attack, the dispatch of an opponent is accomplished with minimal effort.

Very few people in the world will ever have the opportunity to watch headmasters of separate dojos engage in friendly competition, but in my time at Kyumeikan Dojo, I had several opportunities to watch Kubo Sensei engage in friendly competitions with his childhood peers who had become Sensei in their own right. Because the focus of training revolves around the progress of students, the match between masters of comparable quality is rare. In addition, because of Kubo Sensei's relationship with the All-Japan Kendo Federation, I have personally had several opportunities to spar with its president. It is extremely humbling to be bested by a man in his seventies who expends such little energy to get such perfect hits.

Between fencers of this caliber, there is only the slightest movement before an attack is made. Unlike junior fencers prodding and experimenting to discover their opponent's weakness, the master needs only find the opportunity to attack. Instead of a badgering movement to test an opponent, there is only the explosion of the attack. No effort is wasted. Only the simple execution of extraordinary power and precision without distraction. The power and skill is so awesome that only a swordsman will fully appreciate the mastery of a teacher who tames the most limber and lightning speed of a kendoka in the vigor of his youth. It is not the crudeness of the muscles that allows the master to effortlessly trounce the cream of the student cadre, it is timing and the simple execution of the most basic of techniques.

If *A New Hope* is a lesson to any swordsman, it is that the most skillful swordsmen are not they who can execute the most complex series of feints and attacks, but they who can execute the most basic attacks with impeccable timing. Technically, Dave Prowse and Alec Guinness will not be a model for real swordsmanship, but they do serve as exemplars of the ideal fencing style which is effective and dangerous, not ostentatious and effete.

Even Lucas himself misses the elementary sophistication of the sword fight when he says that we have only seen an old man and a half-human cyborg fighting with lightsabers. Peter Diamond gave Lucas the best example of true swordsmanship, which lacks the display of the sword fight in every other swashbuckling movie. In the life or death struggle of a fight, a victor is determined in minimal, not excessive movement. The greatest swordsman, in effect, need never resort to extravagant fencing because he can accomplish in a couple of simple steps what a lesser swordsman can only do after extreme physical exercise. The expert seems profoundly enigmatic to even the most experienced but naive fencers because there is never enough opportunity to see the master execute a complicated series of movement. The truly experienced fencer will observe that the most sophisticated technique is the basic technique that was taught to the student on the first day of practice.

When the casual observer looks at the sword fight in *A New Hope* with the desire to be impressed with complicated action, he will walk away let down for not seeing the spectacle of the match. The mastery in technique is not in what one sees, but in what one does not see, which is the perfection of the most basic of moves. Mastery is so obvious that we are blind to its simplicity. No instructor can simply tell a student that mastery is accomplished by learning fundamentals. The student naturally desires to graduate to the complexity of advance techniques. Successful swordsmanship, however, is not accomplished in complexity, but in simplicity, which is the very essence of the sword fight in *A New Hope*.

The duel between Obi-Wan and Vader accomplish the several goals necessary in the script: establish the two men as Jedi Knights of an as-yet-to-be-explained order of warrior-monks, establish that one is the former master of the other, and pay homage to the ultimate personal sacrifice which assures that a greater good can be accomplished. In Obi-Wan's death, the forces of goodness gain the final convert to their side. Luke understands that greatness is not found only in victory, but in disciplined sacrifice as well. From the moment Luke sees the fall of his mentor, he finally makes the commitment to repay the honor Obi-Wan has bestowed upon him when he was accepted by Obi-Wan as a student. There is no greater duty for the apprentice swordsman than to learn the wisdom that will allow him or her to become the great swordsman his master had always seen in his apprentice.

The Empire Strikes Back — Struggle Against the Leviathan

Without question, the rite of passage of *Episode V* dominates the thematic tenor of the entire movie. It is a coming of age film for an individual whose very development and maturation is critical to the survival of the Rebellion and the destruction of the Empire which has reduced entire galaxies to its control. Dave Prowse calls *The Empire Strikes Back* a "thinking man's film," while the most devoted fans (and its harshest critics) agree it is the most dramatic and poignant of the four episodes made thus far. Not only does the middle act provide the most important development of the story, it provides the swordsman a chance to learn how the struggle in training is the only road to mastering the art of the fence. There is no trick anyone can teach a novice. He must discover on his own that it is futile to desire mastery in swordsmanship. There is only training.

From the opening scenes of the movie, there is the ominous threat of the Empire amassing its forces just over the horizon. Invasion is imminent and it quickly becomes evident after the invasion has started that the Rebel Alliance is now a fugitive force on the run. By destroying an AT-AT walker with the assistance of his lightsaber, Luke does what he can to minimize the damage the Empire can do to the Rebellion, but upon his own escape, he knows he must follow Obi-Wan's command to seek out his own teacher Yoda. Departing from the original plan to rendezvous with the remnants of the Rebel headquarters, Luke sets his destinations for Dagobah.

From the first instant he crashes on the planet, Luke's every move is now a test for a Jedi Master who has trained the greatest lightsaber swordsmen of the universe. Lurking in the undergrowth and watching from afar, Yoda observes the angry and impatient aspiring Jedi establish himself on the planet. Whining and endlessly fretting, Luke does not realize that his attitude is the greatest indication of his preparedness to begin his Jedi studies.

Appearing first as an insignificant denizen of the jungle forest, Yoda comically makes his appearance before Luke as a crazed and silly alien of insignificant bearing. "Wars not make one great," Yoda declares to Luke's desire to find a Jedi warrior. It is not long before Yoda reveals himself to be the master that Luke is looking for. Not only has Luke failed to recognized his new teacher, he demonstrates with every child-like excuse that he is still a babe in the woods. The use of the lightsaber against an AT-AT walker hatch is hardly proof that he knows how to use the Jedi weapon. None-the-less, Yoda takes Luke as a student and begins his Jedi training through the physical and mental conditioning of a full routine of anaerobic exercises as well as the honing of his telekinetic abilities.

Luke faces his first challenges when he enters the cave where he encounters a spectral Vader. Taking his weapons despite being commanded not to, Luke ignites his lightsaber and prepares to fight the Sith Lord who has killed his first mentor. Taking a classical kendo stance, there are simple attacks to the leg, the head, and then to Luke's side. In a moment of delay, Luke lashes out and decapitates his enemy. Vader's helmet falls to the ground and rolls to his feet. The mask's face explodes and Luke sees his own face; a premonition of things to come: Luke's potential to become the Sith Lord himself, as well as a thematic indication that Luke is of the same bloodline as Darth Vader.

Luke continues his training traipsing through the jungle with Yoda clinging to his back. He learns that the Dark Side is not more powerful than the Light Side, but easier, quicker, and more seductive. Early scripts had Luke practicing lightsaber deflection with seeker balls, but control of his telekinetic powers remain the essence of his mental training. Early in the movie in the Wampa cave, Luke enjoys his first steps in his mastery of telekinesis by summoning his lightsaber through emptying his mind not by concentration, but by allowing his mind to become calm. On Dagobah, Luke must now use the Force to help him perform incredible acrobatic feats: to levitate objects, to unify his body with his spirit so that the Force becomes more connected to his will and intention. The Force controls the Jedi's actions, but it also obeys his command. Enigmatic to the beginner, the martial artist eventually learns that the best technique is that which is instinctive and in harmony with the mind and body rather that the kind which responds cognitively and more slowly to the mind.

Luke's new heightened abilities in the Force also allow him to begin to see visions of his friends Han and Leia whose very lives seem threatened unless Luke does something to save them. Foolishly, and arrogantly, he leaves his training without regard for himself and the fact that the torture of Han is a set-up for a trap to bring Luke as a trophy to the Emperor. Though he promises he will return to his training, both Obi-Wan and Yoda fear that all the effort they have expended on Luke will be lost because again Luke demonstrates a defiant restlessness which brings him closer to the brink of oblivion.

Luke soon arrives at Bespin and quickly finds himself in the presence of Darth Vader, who hopes to easily trap his son frozen in a protective slab of carbonite metal. As in the cave, Luke is the first to ignite his lightsaber and takes a confident stance against the former Jedi who killed his mentor Obi-Wan Kenobi. The lightsaber clash begins and it becomes evident early on that Darth Vader is the master of the two men. Luke attacks violently only to be quickly blocked by Vader wielding his lightsaber with a single hand. Starting out in *chudan no kamae* of Japanese swordsmanship, Luke's attacks are made in vain against the Leviathan Vader.

Vader attempts to end the duel quickly but is thwarted by Luke's ability to propel himself out of the carbonite freezing chamber. Luke regains some momentum and pushes Vader into a defensive posture, eventually knocking him down to a lower level of the smoke-filled room. Carefully, he descends to the next level and is confronted by Vader who lowers his lightsaber point and employs the Force to throw debris at Luke who is powerless to fend off Vader's debilitating challenges. Luke is pulled out of the room when a metal casing smashes through an observation window. Clinging for dear life, Luke recovers his senses and re-enters the observation room only to be violently attacked by an increasingly enraged Vader. He charges powerfully at Luke with his lightsaber and pushes him out onto a gantry where Luke fights for his very life.

With only one unsuccessful strike at Vader's neck, Luke is finally defeated when Vader cuts off Luke's hand at the wrist, sending his lightsaber falling down into the deep abyss of an interior reactor shaft of Cloud City. Vader offers him a place at his side, but Luke responds in the realization that his greatest duty now is to deny the Emperor the possibility of subverting his abilities to evil. Luke plunges himself over the edge in the sacrificing manner that Obi-Wan confronted Vader on the Death Star. Of course, Luke survives the ordeal, alive with the knowledge that his own father is responsible for the destruction of the Jedi

Order.

Again, the script of the sword fight serves to carry out the plot of the movie. Luke takes his first steps in training to master his Jedi skills, and because he rushes out to use them before he has truly mastered them, Luke faces his utter defeat at the hands of his own father. Within the context of training in swordsmanship, Luke learns firsthand how knowledge of basic skills without the wisdom to use them well is as effective as not have any skills in the first place. Like the young fencer who sees an old man standing in front of him with a sword, he rushes headstrong to his own defeat.

From the opening exchange, Vader uses the extremely difficult technique of catching and holding Luke's lightsaber immobile with his own lightsaber. With superior strength and leverage, Vader is able to quickly throw Luke back to the ground. Unscathed, Vader presses his fight, evening disarming Luke with a circular flourish of his blade. Luke's lightsaber flies from his hand in a turning motion forces Luke to retreat to a position where he can use the Force to summon his lightsaber.

After escaping from the freezing chamber, Luke is able to regain the initiative by surprising Vader with the simple gymnastic ability to escape the carbonite freezing process. With smoke in his eyes, Vader's own arrogance is revealed in his contempt for a young boy. While the best swordsman are technically superior to the less experienced, the uncertainty of swordsmanship is the creativity of the novice who is put in position of recovering or dying. Vader succumbs to his own anger at not being able to more quickly defeat Luke. Uncontrollable emotion swells in Vader. As was the case with Obi-Wan in *Episode I*, anger allows Vader to once again dominate Luke. With punishing fury, Vader makes Luke retreat to a position where there is no hope. In one last attempt, Luke attacks Vader but is defeated by a simple circular control of the blade called a *prise de fer* which pushes Luke's blade out of the way so Vader can cut to Luke's wrist.

The sword fight in *The Empire Strikes Back* best illustrates the spirit of the drama that is the sword fight duel. The sword fight in *Episode V* is the visual poetry of film. With the mesmerizing reds, blues, and whites of the freezing chamber, Vader and Luke become alluring silhouettes commanding the shimmering blades of their lightsabers. From the flowing twirl of Luke as he engages Vader's red lightsaber with his own green one, the colorful play of light frames the struggle of an aspiring swordsman against that of a master in his own right.

The self-assured confidence of Luke early in the fight is later replaced by the terror of defeat at Vader's hands. Visually preparing for the climactic scenes in *Return of the Jedi*, Vader seeing Luke hanging off the edge of the metal gantry leads to a renewed spirit against the aspirant Jedi. But Vader, himself, succumbs to the arrogance that Luke is still a youth engaged in child's play. He gives in to anger, and as the Emperor has shown him since his early days under his tutelage, anger can and does lead to power. Vader's determination fueled by his embarrassment to be temporarily bested by Luke leads to his eventual domination of his opponent. It is this back and forth edge which paints in both the color of the frame and the choreography of the fight the unseen struggle between swordsmen in a real fight. And where time in the mind of the swordsman takes place in units of milliseconds, the sword fight in Empire creates the image visually on the silver screen for the audience to recognize and understand.

During the filming of *Return of the Jedi*, Richard Marquand was reported to have criticized the sword fighting in *The Empire Strikes Back* because it showed Vader fighting with a single hand. Peter Diamond responds, however, that the use of one hand and then the change over to the traditional style of using two hands was deliberate from the very beginning. Diamond brought in a trusted collaborator Bob Anderson who had vast knowledge and experience in sabre fighting in competition and in film to dramatize the subtleties of the one-handed sword.

The Empire Strikes Back certainly achieves the goals needed to prepare the world for the third and final stage of the Original Trilogy, the very climax of Lucas' *Star Wars* epic. Foreshadowed first by Luke's failure at the cave, Vader demonstrates that he is a more powerful force to be reckoned with than Luke could have ever imagined. Not only is Vader a superior swordsman, but he is also kith and kin, his own father whom he has never known. The mood is set to lure Luke under the sword of Damocles, and we, as an audience, are visually enticed and enthralled by the light play of lightsabers in the swirling world of smoke and the cavernous interior of Cloud City. Luke's rite of passage is his survival, as is that of the Rebellion which is fleeing the might of the Empire.

Luke learns to understand first hand that Vader is the embodiment of evil of the universe. He is tempted by Vader to embrace the Dark Side and take the mantle of an easy knighthood at the hands of his father. Luke is a powerful swordsman, but still yet in need of supervised training. So great is his potential that the Emperor has foreseen Luke's threat to his order. Vader, seeking to increasing his own position by taking the Emperor's place, thinks he can corrupt his own son into following the path to the Dark Side. His hopes are set back when Luke, recognizing right from wrong, good from evil, denies Vader and the Emperor the means to even greater power in the universe. As long as Luke lives, the threat to the Galactic Empire still remains effective, though it hangs delicately on a thread.

The lesson for the swordsman is made clear by the easy fall of inexperience and an inflated view of one's ability to the demonstrable experience of a Sith Lord. No matter one's skill and enthusiasm, without the tools of mastered technique *and* the wisdom in its use, one's potentiality remains simply that — potentiality. When Luke is ready to return to his master to complete his training, Luke will again have the opportunity to redeem his first attempt. Until then, the potential Jedi Knight must simply focus on the daily drama of basic training and practice.

Return of the Jedi — Epic Battle

Since Lucas announced that he would not be making movies after *Episode VI*, *Return of the Jedi* has become the battle royale in which the two part arc of two trilogies culminates in the lightsaber battle at the end of the movie. The highest form of human drama, this last episode is the struggle between good and evil. It is a conflict between son and father observed under the malefi- cent eyes of Satan incarnate. The sword fight is the cinemato- grapher's perfect subject to showcase the fight between good and evil with which the human race must wrestle. Lucas' screenplay becomes a story not of mythology, but of epic which addresses the struggles of man pitted against man. *Star Wars* is not only about his own nature to do violence, but it is also about the struggle of Man against technology, devices of his own creation which may in the end lead to his own destruction.

Luke and Vader confront each other in *Return of the Jedi*, but the younger is now more mature after the chastening experience on Bespin. At the beginning of the movie, Luke demonstrates the ability to think like a Jedi instead of relying on impulses to dictate his actions. Even before he enters Jabba the Hutt's palace, Luke has already devised a two-part plan that will save himself as well as his closest friends.

Instead of an outright assault, Luke enters the palace in a face-to-face confrontation with Jabba. Leia has fallen into the Hutt's clutches, and by a freak accident he, too, becomes prisoner of the Tatooine gangster. Not to be caught completely off guard, Luke has hidden his lightsaber within Artoo who shoots it out to Luke at the critical moment just before his execution.

Armed with his Jedi weapon, Luke begins his assault on the gangster's minions. He attacks them immediately and directly, cutting down attackers with a single stroke of his lightsaber. He thwart's Boba Fett's blaster fire and the extending rope that wraps around him. In accordance with a makeshift plan that seems hopeless until the last moment, Luke rescues Han and frees his friends while ridding the universe of the notorious Jabba the Hutt.

Now free, Luke return to Yoda to complete the training he promised he would finish. Expecting to continue the physical practice of rigorous exercise and the honing of his Force powers, he meets Yoda just as he enters his death bed ready to pass into the next life. He questions Yoda about the true identity of his father. Yoda confirms every fear Luke has contemplated since his encounter with Vader in Cloud City; Luke is indignant that he has been lied to about the identity of his father and bitter about his realization that both Obi-Wan and Yoda had always intended for him to battle and kill his father. In spectral form, Obi-Wan visits Luke and explains the true but simple facts relating to the way each person perceives the world. When Vader turned to the Dark Side, "He ceased to be Anakin and became Darth Vader."

There is no more training that will prepare Luke more for his meeting with Darth Vader. He has an inkling that there is still good within Vader. Obi-Wan and Yoda do not see the merit in his Luke's perception of the reality, and with Luke's refusal to destroy his own father, the two Jedi Masters are resigned to accept that the Emperor has already won. But uncertain is the future, as Yoda so tersely puts it. In *The Empire Strikes Back*, Yoda alluded to the fact that there was another who could save them from the Emperor. The existence of Luke's sister Leia is finally divulged as Luke and Obi-Wan talk. With the possibility that Luke may perish or be turned to the Dark Side, there still exists the possibility that Leia may still be able to defeat the Emperor.

In the middle act of the movie, the heroes of the saga descend on Endor to destroy the shield that protect the Death Star II. Vader is on the star destroyer as the Rebel lambda-class shuttle passes through the security zone surrounding the planet. Luke then realizes that Vader is aware of his presence and that he has jeopardized their mission. Before Vader can act, Luke hands himself over to Vader (and the Emperor), again in hopes of sacrificing himself for the sake of his friends. He speaks with his father and attempts to draw the goodness out of Vader who, while acknowledging the potential of the boy Jedi, hands Luke over to his master for his summary disposal. Where Vader failed in pulling Luke to the Dark Side, it is now the Emperor's turn.

The climactic end is a balancing act between the three battles: on Endor, out in space above the planet, and on the new Death Star. In the Emperor's throne room, Vader and Luke first engage in a battle of emotions as each of the Dark Lords tries to tempt Luke into joining their cause. Luke fights off his desire to strike out at the two Sith, as the Rebel cause seems doomed from the very outset. At each step in the Rebel's plans, the Emperor had foreseen its planning and had taken countermeasures to bring the Rebellion and Luke onto his own doorstep so he could personally crush the Alliance once and for all. At last Luke succumbs and draws his lightsaber frustrated by his inability to further help the plight of his friends. He ignites his lightsaber and slashes out at the Emperor only to be stopped by his father who has ignited his own lightsaber.

As the battles on the surface of Endor and the space above it turn ill for the side of Light, Luke is now embroiled in a battle against the very man who had taken his own hand in their last encounter. Luke is a changed swordsman. He is controlled, calm, and in command of his emotions. His motivation to save his friends is clear and his battle, if it is to end with his death, may in the very least give his companions the opportunity to do what he could not do himself — destroy the second Death Star.

Luke fights well and dominates his father who seems helpless to stop his son's advances. "Obi-Wan has taught you well," Vader says after being knocked down by Luke, who, in response, shuts off his own lightsaber when he realizes that his hate for Vader and the Emperor are what is allowing him to defeat Vader. Luke feels the goodness within his father and challenges Vader to search deep inside of him for an answer. Vader responds by attacking, forcing Luke to retreat by leaping up toward a walkway high above them. Throwing his lightsaber, Vader causes Luke to fall into the lower level of the throne room. Outside of the Death Star, the battle goes against the Rebellion and Luke is left hanging, hoping yet that his friends will be able to succeed.

Back in the Emperor's high tower chambers, Vader begins his search for Luke in the darkness of the lower level. He reads Luke's mind and finally realizes that Luke has a sister who Vader might yet be able to turn to the Dark Side. Enraged at the thought of losing his sister to the Emperor, Luke screams out and attacks Vader with a ferocity Vader has never before seen. Driving him back, Luke lashes out in a punishing fury until he cuts Vader's own hand from his own arm, as had befallen Luke in *The Empire Strikes Back*. Upon realizing that the tide has turned back in his own favor, Luke now comes to understand that in order to become powerful, he has become what he most despises in his father. In order to defeat his father, he has become like his father. The symbolism of Luke's prosthetic hand echoes in his mind as an epiphany reveals that the power to do evil is within his own actions.

The drama of the climax has been masterfully played out in Lucas' script and receives its final performance in the editing room. He creates a pinnacle to the trilogy in which light and darkness are pitted against each other in a sword fight to end all sword fights. At last the final irony of Luke's training reveals itself — you cannot use evil to destroy evil. It only supplants one evil for another.

In the final moments of the lightsaber scene, Luke makes the greatest statement any swordsman can ever make. He tosses aside his lightsaber. Power does not reside in his weapon, but within own heart where the goodness of his being is best expressed in his love for his family — Leia — and his friends, Han and Chewbacca, as well as the entire Rebel Alliance. By willing to sacrifice his own life in order to save others as Obi-Wan had done for him, Luke makes a discovery that some swordsmen never learn. At that very moment when he dispenses with his lightsaber, Luke becomes what he has always aspired to achieve. Never would he have guessed that it had nothing to do with his lightsaber, but with what becomes of his heart. Without his lightsaber, Luke becomes a Jedi Master.

Conclusion

Long before the world sees the final installments of the *Star Wars* universe, it becomes clear that the swordsman's tale in a universe in a galaxy far, far away... is an epic story of man. While

myths explain the pseudo-religious origins of a universe controlled by the externalities of the gods and the omnipresence of unbridled nature, Lucas' story of swordsmen tells of the conflict of
humanity as it continually weighs the needs of a peaceful society
and the need for protectors capable of violence against those
who would subvert the desire for order, personal growth, and
spiritual development.

Lucas' epic is the story of our own development in a universe
where the human being is the measure of all things. Instead of
being the subject of the unpredictable whims of the gods, man
raises his quest for inner peace to mythic proportions. *Star Wars*
is the story of good versus evil, but not of the world around us,
but of the greedy and selfish desires within us. The conflict is
between the quests for spirituality, self-fulfillment, wholeness,
contentment, and the threats of fear, desperation, domination,
and extinction.

Society seeks stability and equilibrium for the possibility of
growth and development. Threatening this peace is the chaos of
disorder and the need to protect ourselves from inner and outer
destruction. Therein is the call of the Jedi in Lucas' fictitious
universe — the need for peace and the need for the tools of
violence to safeguard the peace. The Jedi must know the desires
of the heart, but they also subordinate personal desires for the
greater good of others. They also know the risk of using the skills
of violence for abuse or oppression. This must never come to
pass. Ultimately, the swordsman's reliance on the sword, as is
the Jedi's reliance on the lightsaber, is a state of being that may
be necessary to assure the obtainment of peace and justice.

The swordsman's life in the heat of battle is grievously short,
but it also serves as an imperative to live one's life as fully as
possible. When called upon to protect and serve others, the
sword may be used as a tool to further that greater end, but
when the very evil nature of which men and women are capable
confronts our very soul, Luke gives swordsmen around the
world the highest example of a good life. If it were possible to
defeat evil by resorting to violence, evil would never be truly

defeated, but simply supplanted. When Luke throws down his sword, a modality for life dependent on goodness of the heart and a purity of purpose becomes the ultimate goal for what was once an outdated and violent tool. Through effort, discipline, and the influence of an experienced master, swordsmanship becomes a means for inner peace, inner spirituality, and represents a positive and hopeful belief in our humanity. This is the goal of the Jedi Knights and their fabled shimmering sword.

Afterword

Every year in Tokyo at the Budokan, an All-Japan Martial Arts Demonstration is held in which representatives from the four modern Japanese martial arts give a demonstration on the main floor of the arena. Aikidoka (of which, I was one) roll around calmly. Judoka sport their aggressive and sharp throws. Karateka fill the room with their harsh shouts and quick punches. Kendo, too, makes its appearance. In the grand finale, ordinary practitioners of each art come out to take a section of the entire floor. One by one, each is introduced and students begin training on the floor simultaneously with the others in a spirit of cultural unity. Last to be announced is the most traditional of the arts — kendo. When the kendoka begin their practice, the room becomes dominated by a sound of martial screams called *kiai* made when any strike is made. Under the huge dome of the famous training arena, I have never encountered a din that would better approximate what it must have been like to have been on a battlefield between swordsmen.

How apropos that I would know what it would have been like to have been in the Geonosian arena when the Jedi made their stand in *Attack of the Clones*. From my walk around the stadium in Zagreb to the Budokan in Tokyo, there is nothing like the spectacle of the swordsman who takes his walk out under the auspices of the spectacle of the parade. That was how swordsmen were meant to walk; with their sword at their side, moving proudly with a distinguished air and a calm demeanor. A Jedi would walk in this manner.

With one final installment in the entire saga yet to be completed, a swordsman's dream is still possible. *Episode I* gave us an all computer generated image (CGI) battle between Gungans and battle droids. *Episode II* showed us Jedi Knights against more CGI creatures. (Who can forget Yoda wielding a lightsaber?) But the ultimate battle would include Jedi Knights fighting against lightsaber carrying Sith Knights.

Despite the continual assertions by the Jedi Council that there were only two Sith Lords, there is nothing that would bar Lucas from breaking with this rule. The Jedi Council only believes there to be two Sith Lords, but nothing prohibits the Sith Lords from having their own network of servants: support staff, technicians, acolytes, apprentices. With a Sith Lord as powerful as Count Dooku, there is no reason why an elite group of lightsaber swordsmen could not begin teaching an army in the very arts that the Jedi have mastered over millennia. Take DNA from a dead Jedi (or a living Jedi) and produce the elite Mandalorian Troopers the Expanded Universe has been alluding to for decades. Then give them lightsabers.

If I had any wishes for the final installment, it would include some or all of the following:

- Real swordsmen (kendoka or fencers) would play Jedi

- There would be lightsaber v. lightsaber armed adversaries

- Artists would stop drawing the baseball grip of the lightsaber

- There should be an emphasis of swordfighting technique on lightsaber swordplay

- The climactic fight between Obi-Wan and Anakin would resemble the duel of *Return of the Jedi*

- The Jedi are realistically portrayed as having to chose between fighting and dying with dignity or living and suffering complete public humiliation, and not simply being executed capriciously by stormtroopers

- Jedi are shown wearing battle armor and carrying blaster rifles along with lightsabers

- More secrets of the Sith are revealed

- *Episode III* would be 3 hours long

Glossary

aiki-jujitsu

Japanese martial art that focuses on joint-lock techniques to defeat an opponent. Important influence on aikido.

aikidoka

A person who does aikido.

bokken

A wooden practice sword in Japanese swordsmanship and kendo.

bushido

"Way of the warrior." The martial ethics that samurai follow.

chudan no kamae

Japanese fencing stance with the point toward the middle part of the opponent's body.

daimyo

Japanese feudal lord.

daisho

The long and short sword worn by samurai.

divsirme

Quadrennial tribute of Christian boys to Ottoman Janissary.

dô

Attack to the middle of the body. The breastplate worn in kendo.

dojo

Japanese word for training hall.

double-bladed lightsaber
> Lightsaber with a light blade emitting from two opposite ends of a grip. Darth Maul's lightsaber.

epee
> A Western fencing weapon with a large bell guard. Points are scored by touching any part of the body.

foil
> A Western fencing weapon with a small bell guard. Points are scored by touching the torso of the opponent.

furusiyya
> The horse riding fighting skills of the Steppe nomads of the Black Sea area.

gedan no kamae
> Japanese fencing stance with the point toward the lower part of the opponent's body.

iaido
> The art of sword drawing. Techniques meant to cut an opponent upon drawing the sword.

infighting
> Fighting within close quarters among swordsmen in which the arm cannot be extended.

Janissary
> Slave warrior of the Ottoman Turks.

jodan no kamae
> Japanese fencing stance with the point pointed above the head.

jodo
Short staff fighting.

jujitsu
A modern, usually competitive form of aiki-jujitsu.

kata
Japanese for a series of pre-determined movement to teach, remember, and practice martial techniques.

katana
Japanese long sword with a single sharpened edge carried with its blade upward in the belt.

kendo
Competitive form of Japanese fencing.

kendoka
A person who does kendo.

kenjustu
The techniques of the Japanese sword designed for injuring or killing an opponent.

ki

The energy which gives a person life. Control of ki also gives power to a martial artist.

kote
Attack to the wrists. The gloves worn in kendo.

lightsaber
A light sword in *Star Wars* that can cut through virtually any substance.

long sword
> A sword with two cutting edges.

Mameluke
> Muslim warrior fighting for Egypt, originally coming from the Afghanistan Steppes.

men
> Attack to the head. The protective mask worn in kendo.

midi-chlorians
> Living forms which permit the manipulation of the Force in *Star Wars*. It gives the Jedi his powers.

naginata
> Japanese halberd.

Padawan
> A student apprentice of a Jedi Knight.

rapier
> A long sword with a slender blade. It can cut with its sharp edge or pierce with its point.

riposte
> An attack after parrying (defending) an opponent's attack.

ryu
> A style of Japanese fencing.

sabre
> A single edge curved sword.

salle (*salle d'escrime*)
> A training hall for Western fencers.

samurai

> The military class of Japan.

shinai

> A competition sword in kendo made up of four bamboo slats.

shogun

> A Japanese military dictator.

sohei

> Japanese warrior-monks.

suburi

> Sword cutting practice by swinging the bokken repeatedly to develop proper basic technique

tachi

> Japanese long sword with a sharpened edge carried in a scabbard at the waist with the blade hanging downward.

wakizashi

> Japanese short sword.

Select Bibliography

Anderson, Kevin J. *The Illustrated Star Wars Universe*. NY: Bantam Books, 1995.

Black, Jeremy. *Cambridge Illustrated Atlas of Warfare: Renaissance to Revolution*. Cambridge, UK: Cambridge University Press, 1996.

Bottomley, I. & A.P. Hopson. *Arms and Armor of the Samurai*. NY: Crescent Books, 1988.

Bouzereau, Laurent & Jody Duncan. *Star Wars: The Making of Episode I The Phantom Menace*. NY: Ballantine Publishing, 1999.

Bouzereau, Laurent. *Star Wars: The Annotated Screenplays*. NY: Ballantine Publishing, 1997.

Bresman, Jonathan. *The Art of Star Wars: Episode I The Phantom Menace*. NY: Ballantine Books, 1999.

Brooks, Terry. *Star Wars: Episode I The Phantom Menace*. NY: Ballantine Publishing, 1999.

Bryant, Anthony J. & Angus McBride. *Elite Series: The Samurai 200-1500 AD*. London: Osprey, 1991.

Campbell, Joseph. *The Power of Myth with Bill Moyers*. NY: Doubleday, 1998.

Cavelos, Jeanne. *The Science of Star Wars*. NY: St. Martin's Press, 1999.

Cinefex 78. July 1999.

Coe, Michael D. et al. *Swords and Hilt Weapons*. NY: Weidenfeld & Nicolson, 1989.

Collier's Encyclopedia. Vol. 2. Crowell Collier and MacMillian, Inc., 1967. Armor, pp. 667-677.

Edge, David & John Miles Paddock. *Arms & Armor of the Medieval*

Knight. Crescent Books, 1988.

Glut, Donald F. *Star Wars: The Empire Strikes Back Illustrated Edition.* NY: Ballantine Books, 1980.

Hanson, Victor Davis. *The Western Way of War.* NY: Oxford University Press, 1989. (Highly recommended.)

Harris, Victor & Nobuo Ogasawara. *Swords of the Samurai.* London: British Museum Publications, 1990.

Henderson, Mary. *Star Wars: The Magic of Myth.* NY: Bantam Books, 1997.

Herrigel, Eugene. *Zen in the Art of Archery.* NY: Pantheon Books, 1953.

Jenkins, Garry. *Empire Building: The Remarkable, Real-Life Story of Star Wars (Revised and Updated).* Secaucus, NJ: Citadel Press Book, 1999.

Kahn, James. *Star Wars: Return of the Jedi The Illustrated Edition.* NY: Ballantine Books, 1983.

Kammer, Reinhard. *The Way of the Sword: The Tengu-Geijitsu-Ron of Chozan Shissai.* Boston: Arkana, 1978.

Kaplan, Robert D. *Warrior Politics.* NY: Random House, 2002.

Keegan, John. *A History of Warfare.* NY: Vintage Books, 1993.

Keegan, John. *The Illustrated Face of Battle.* NY: Viking, 1989.

Kershner, Irvin, dir. *Star Wars: The Empire Strikes Back, Episode VI, Special Edition,* Twentieth Century Fox, 1980. Videocassette.

Leibovitz, Anne. "The Force is Back." *Vanity Fair.* February 1999: pp. 118-29.

Lucas, George, dir. *Star Wars: A New Hope, Episode IV, Special Edition,*

Twentieth Century Fox, 1977. Videocassette.

Lucas, George, dir. *Star Wars: The Phantom Menace, Episode I,* Twentieth Century Fox, 1999. DVD.

Lucas, George. *Star Wars: Episode I The Phantom Menace Illustrated Screenplay.* NY: Ballantine Publishing, 1999.

Lucas, George. *Star Wars: From the Adventures of Luke Skywalker.* NY: Ballantine, 1976.

Lowry, Dave. *Autumn Lightning.* Boston: Shambhala, 1985. (Highly recommended.)

Luceno, James. *Star Wars: Cloak of Deception.* NY: Ballantine Books, 2001.

Lund, Kristin. *Star Wars: Episode I The Complete Guide to the Incredible Locations from The Phantom Menace.* NY: DK Publishing, 2000.

Marquand, Richard, dir. *Return of the Jedi, Episode VI, Special Edition.* Twentieth Century Fox, 1983. Videocassette.

Moyers, Bill. "Interview: George Lucas." *Time* 26 April 1999: pp. 90-94.

Parisi, Paula. "Grand Illusion: The Master of Myth Rewrites History." *Wired.* May 1999: 137- 39.

Parker, Geoffrey. *The Military Revolution, 2nd Edition.* London: Cambridge University Press, 1996.

Pollock, Dale. *Skywalking: The Life and Films of George Lucas.* NY: Harmony Books, 1983.

Ratti, Oscar & Adele Westbrook. *Secrets of the Samurai.* Rutland, Vermont: Charles E. Tuttle Company, Inc., 1991.

Reid, Howard. *The Way of the Warrior.* London: Century Publishing Co., Ltd., 1983.

Reynolds, David West. *Star Wars: Episode I The Phantom Menace Incredible Cross-sections*. NY: DK Publishing, 1999.

Reynolds, David West. *Star Wars: Episode I The Visual Dictionary*. NY: DK Publishing, 1999.

Reynolds, David West. *Star Wars: Incredible Cross-sections*. NY: DK Publishing, 1998.

Reynolds, David West. *Star Wars: The Visual Dictionary*. NY: DK Publishing, 1998.

Richie, Donald. *The Films of Akira Kurosawa*. Berekely: University of California Press, 1984.

Robinson, B.W. *The Arts of the Japanese Sword*. London: Faber and Faber, 1961.

Sansom, G.B. *The Western World and Japan*. Rutland, Vermont: Charles E. Tuttle Company, Inc., 1990. (Highly recommended.)

Sato, Hiroaki. *The Sword and the Mind*. New York: The Overlook Press, 1988.

Smith, Bill. *Star Wars: The Essential Guide to Weapons and Technology*. NY: Ballantine, 1997.

Thompson, Anne. "George Lucas." *Premiere* May 1999: pp. 68-77.

Turnbull, Dr. Stephen. *Samurai Warfare*. London: Arms and Armor Books, 1997.

Vale, Malcolm. *War and Chivalry*. Athens: University of Georgia Press, 1981.

Watson, Jude. *Star Wars: Jedi Quest*. NY: Scholastic, Inc., 2001.

Windham, Ryder. *Star Wars: Episode I The Phantom Menace Scrapbook*. NY: Random House Printing, 1999.

Internet

Bernard Lewis. *Race and Slavery in the Middle East*. Oxford University Press, 1994. www.fordham.edu/halsall/med/lewis1.html.

Divsirme. *Encyclopaedia of the Orient*. www.i-cias.com/e.o/devsirme.htm.

The Military Orders: Introduction. *ORB Encyclopedia: Online Essays*. www.org.rhodes.edu/encyclop/religion/monastic/milintro.html.

The Near East: Janissaries. www.tughranet.f2s.om/janisary.htm

The Official Dave Prowse Website. www.daveprowse.com.

Personal Sources

"Jedi Style: Swordfighting in Star Wars and The Phantom Menace." 1 April 1999. http://echostation.com/features/jedistyle.htm

Life By the Sword. Nick Jamilla. Introduction to Christian Ethics. Prof. J. Donahue. 15 December 1988.

"On Becoming a Jedi: The Relationship between Master and Apprentice." 21 May 1999. http://echostation.com/features /apprentice.htm.

"On Mastering Fencing." N.P. Jamilla. *USFA Magazine*, Oct/Nov/ Dec 1991. March 30, 1999. http://www.uncg.edu/student.groups/ fencing/AmericanFencing/arcticles/42_1_22 .html

"A New Style? Cultural Influences on Jedi Style Sword Fighting." 11 June 2000. http://echostation.com/features/ep2sword.htm

Notes on kendo book. Includes personal thoughts of Kubo Sensei, 1991-95. 100 pages.

Personal Aikido Journal. 1991-95. 600 pages.

Index

About the Author

Nick Jamilla [Ha meal ya] is a novelist and teacher at the Sheridan School in Washington, D.C. Author of 3 novels — *Grey Eminence, Bridge Builders,* and *The Montani Chronicles,* graduate of Georgetown University where he studied International Relations, competitor in the 1987 World Fencing Championships and World University Games, Jamilla holds blackbelts in aikido, kendo and jodo. He worked at the Supreme Court for two years, lived in Paris for one, and Japan for four. When not attending aikido classes at the U.S. Naval Academy, he teaches fencing at his alma mater.